Issues in American Economic History

Issues in American Economic History

Roger LeRoy Miller
Institute for University Studies,
Arlington, Texas

Robert L. Sexton
Pepperdine University

SOUTH-WESTERN

™

THOMSON LEARNING

THOMSON

SOUTH-WESTERN

Issues in American Economic History

Roger LeRoy Miller and Robert L. Sexton

VP/Editorial Director:
Jack W. Calhoun

VP/Editor-in-Chief:
Mike Roche

Publisher:
Mike Mercier

Acquisitions Editor:
Peter Adams

Developmental Editor:
Andy McGuire

Marketing Manager:
Lisa Lysne

Production Editor:
Stephanie Blydenburgh

Manufacturing Coordinator:
Diane Lohman

Production House:
OffCenter Concept House

Printer:
Malloy Litho
Ann Arbor, MI

Internal Designer:
Sheryl Nelson

Cover Designer:
Mike Stratton

To our family and friends

Without theory, history becomes undisciplined and disorganized, shaping its material by whim, or purely by rheotric. Without history, theory loses any grounding in the actual course of human events.

William N. Parker
Economic Historian
Economic History and the Modern Economy (1986)

Contents

Preface vii

PART ONE INTRODUCTION 1

Chapter 1 Introduction 3

Chapter 2 Economic Growth in the Global Economy 11

Chapter 3 Economic Systems Before the Opening of the New World 25

PART TWO THE COLONIAL ERA 45

Biographies

A Pioneering Effort in Early Agriculture: Eliza Lucas (1723–1793) 47

A Man of Common Sense: Benjamin Franklin (1706–1790) 48

Chapter 4 The Age of Exploration and Spanish Colonization 51

Chapter 5 Opening Up North America 63

PART THREE THE RISE OF A NATIONAL ECONOMY 89

Biographies

The Man Who Faced the Jacksonians: Nicholas Biddle (1786–1884) 91

The Man Who Made Cotton King: Eli Whitney (1765–1825) 92

Chapter 6 From Unification to Secession: Nonagricultural Development 95

Chapter 7 Agriculture, Cotton, and National Growth 115

Chapter 8 Secession, War and Economic Change 131

PART FOUR NEW STRIDES TOWARD ECONOMIC PROGRESS, 1865–1919 145

Biographies

The Ruthless Businessman Par Excellence: Jay Gould (1836–1892) 147

The Great Steel Maker: Andrew Carnegie (1835–1919) 149

Chapter 9 Peace and Renewed Progress 151

Chapter 10 Increasing the Tempo of Economic Life 169

Chapter 11 The Great War 179

PART FIVE ECONOMIC LIFE IN MODERN AMERICA, 1920–1990   **191**

Biographies

The Industrial Unionist: John L. Lewis (1880–1969) 193

The Miracle Man of Wartime Merchant Shipbuilding
Henry J. Kaiser (1882–1967)   195

Chapter 12   The Roaring Twenties and the Depressed
Thirties   199

Chapter 13   Facing Another World War   215

Chapter 14   Issues in the Postwar Decades   225

Index   245

Preface

Economics is more alive today than ever before. We are all faced with continuing economic crises, problems, and proposals for solutions. We are bombarded with economic statements through all the media—-newspapers, TV, radio, magazines, books—from economists, cabinet members and advisors, Congress, and labor leaders. Now more than ever before, students can appreciate the importance of having at least a minimum, fundamental understanding of the economic world in which we live. The question remains, then, how best to teach this basic understanding.

Numerous instructors desire to impart to students not only some sense of the current economic issues but also a sense of history, of a continuity of economic problems and solutions throughout the history of the world and, more specifically, of the United States. This book is meant to satisfy the need for a historical development of basic economic principles.

The book begins with a general introduction to economics and history. After a chapter on medieval societies and population problems, the development of the American economy is studied.

Economic jargon has been kept to a minimum. Economic terms that it was deemed necessary to include occur the first time in bold type, which means that the student will find a further definition at the end of the chapter. Because another helpful pedagogical device is repetition of economic concepts in different contexts, references to the laws of demand and supply and references to such issues as the government's budget constraint recur throughout the text.

This book is not intended to be all-encompassing, either historically or theoretically; its goal is to get students interested in economics so that they can be better informed citizens. The historical issues approach should be useful and effective either as an accompaniment to a regular principles course or, more generally, as a main text for a one-term introduction to economic thinking from a historical point of view. Also, with appropriate additions during class discussions and lectures, and perhaps accompanying historical materials, this text is suitable for a nonrigorous introduction to American economic history—"nonrigorous" because not all of the institutional or historical facts have been included that a more rigorous upper division course would require. Instructors of social science survey courses should find this book especially appealing for the weeks spent on economics.

Above all, we want to thank our students who have used the book in draft form and made comments and suggestions to improve it. Student response to this text has been extremely encouraging. It is our sincere hope that you will share this enthusiasm; we look forward to your comments on this book and encourage you to send them to us.

Roger Leroy Miller
Robert L. Sexton

Part One

Introduction

One Introduction

ECONOMICS AND HISTORY

Archaeologists tell us that, sometime during the Ice Age, hunters of mammoths in the great Russian steppes began to trade ivory for Mediterranean shells. We have been exchanging one thing for another ever since. Of course, the methods of exchange have grown much more sophisticated. Today we use currency, checks, credit cards, and other mediums of exchange instead of shells, and the direct **barter** of earlier time has given way to a host of other activities, some of them not obviously related to exchange at all. These range from the foreign exchange market and the New York Stock Exchange to such matters as labor-management relations, government regulations, and welfare. But dig deep enough into these and other economic issues and, at the core you will find exchange.

The reason people have sought to exchange things with other people from the beginning of history, is to make themselves better off. And the reason they have wanted to make themselves better off is because they haven't had all of the goods and services they would like. And why is that? Because we live in a world of scarcity, always have, and always will.

This book studies the fundamentals of exchange (that is, economics) by examining aspects of the American economy and its evolution from colonial times to the present. Do present day economic theories help us understand this history? What do early America's problems and the solutions adopted teach us about contemporary economic concepts?

WHY ECONOMICS?

Whether we recognize it or not, every one of us applies economic principles in our daily lives—whenever we shop, figure a budget, or even sign up for a college course. A great share of everyone's time is taken up with economic concerns. Will going to college pay off better than going straight to work? What kind of job is best? How do we live within a limited income? We may not be conscious of it, but each of these types of questions and many, many more call for economic analysis.

When understood and properly applied, economic principles are keys to interpreting not only a wide array of present-day concerns, but historical events as well. To evaluate governmental policies or political party platforms, or to decide how to vote in elections, we can learn how economic principles have operated in the past and study how the same principles can be expected to operate under today's conditions. Once basic economic concepts have been firmly grasped, many issues, in history and politics, as well as everyday life, will prove less confusing than they once seemed.

In virtually any area you care to mention, an understanding of economics can go a long way in explaining how and why humans behaved as they did in the past, how they behave today, and how they may be expected to behave tomorrow.

IS ECONOMICS A SCIENCE?

Two categories of science exist: natural sciences and the social sciences. Natural sciences deal with natural order. Chemistry, physics, and even astronomy are concerned with laws embodied in nature. Social sciences, in contrast, deal with the social interaction of people constrained by the laws of nature. Since most social behavior deals with complex interactions that cannot be examined in repeatable experiments, say under a microscope, some have argued that the social sciences are less exact than the natural sciences. This is true in some ways, but it is the common scientific approach to problems, not the precision of exact answers, that establishes both as sciences.

All scientists begin by looking at what happens in the real world—they make empirical observations. Then, by a process of logical deduction, they formulate theories based on those observations, making simplifying assumptions in order to better focus on the central aspects involved. Finally, they test the validity of the theories derived by comparing their implications with the evidence.

It is at this point that the difference arises. In the natural sciences, experiments are designed to isolate a particular interaction controlling all the other conditions. Social scientists, in contrast, have little such opportunity. People can seldom be subjected to controlled experimentation. Therefore, to test theories and to make predictions, social scientists must generally be content to examine what is happening now and what has happened in the past without the luxury of being able to hold everything else constant.

The sciences are more like different breeds of cats or dogs than like entirely different species. Even though the different disciplines often take unique approaches, they all conform to a common logical structure and conceptual orientation.

THE NEED TO SIMPLIFY

Like all organized bodies of knowledge, economics and history must be selective. The human mind simply cannot absorb the complexity of an entire economic system or the entire course of history. That is why we have chosen to examine basic economic concepts in the context of the history of a specific area during a specific period—the United States from colonial times to the present. Economics helps us to understand the history; history helps us validate the usefulness of economic concepts.

But simplification must go further. All scientific investigations rest on some body of assumptions. For instance, sociologists often assume certain behavioral patterns or characteristics of groups, and political scientists use assumptions to explain why a nation acted as it did toward an enemy or an ally.

Economic theories, too, rest on assumptions and simplifying givens: *Given* that this assumption is true, then *this* sequence of events will occur. In this book, as we study historical issues in the U.S. economy, we will put to use a whole array of assumptions. Perhaps the most important of all is one that, although still debated by some, is the basis of most of today's accepted economic theory (You, too, may initially balk at accepting it as a basic fact of human behavior). Throughout this book we assume that *all people continually seek their own betterment:* They prefer control over more resources to less and will respond to opportunities for gain. This self-interest premise underlies most of the explanations and predictions that can be drawn from theory.

If you question this premise, and therefore the implications derived from it, you should still be willing, as a scientist, to put them to the test. See whether they work. If, based on this assumption and the others that comprise a theory, you can predict how people will react to a certain change in their environment, and if they actually do react that way, you can say that the evidence is consistent with the theory. If your prediction fails, you must then ask yourself why. Should some other set of assumptions be put in its place?

The statement that self-betterment is a universal incentive may oversimplify the matter. It is not the only thing people care about. But simplification of some sort is necessary in reaching any hypothesis. If the facts and motivations in a particular situation are so complex that they can refer only to that specific situation, no general conclusions can ever be drawn that can be reliably extended to what may happen in similar but slightly different cases. This is one reason why each science tends to draw boundaries around what issues it concerns itself with. Sociologists frequently downplay the political aspects of the problems they consider. Psychologists often leave economic factors out of their analysis. This doesn't mean the other considerations are irrelevant. It simply means that we must set some limits to what we view.

However, more and more researchers are engaging in what are called *interdisciplinary* approaches. They seek to cooperate with scientists in other fields in order to draw wider and more useful conclusions. In this book, we undertake an interdisciplinary approach and consider economics as related to historical facts and events. Occasionally, we shall also assume the perspective of some other social scientist, but economics and history are our main tools and focus. As a student, you should always feel free to add other dimensions—to ask, "What would political science say about this? Or sociology?" The further question should then be asked: Does such an addition change in any way the capability of the economic analysis presented here to predict what would happen in the situation described?

LOOKING BACK TO SEE THE FUTURE

Many people have a tendency to view the past as essentially tranquil unlike the always turbulent present. This is a serious mistake and will inevitably lead to a distorted view of both the present and the future. Take, for example, the history of price controls: Anything more than a cursory examination reveals that almost all past attempts failed to achieve their stated goals. After having looked at such a history of failure, how much confidence should be placed on current attempts at controlling prices to achieve similar ends? So, just as a doctor would examine a patient's medical history before prescribing medication or performing surgery, policymakers should look at the historical record of related policies before advancing "reforms."

The past is *not* just the historians' sandbox; it is also an important "laboratory" where economists can test their theories. After all, economists and historians are both striving to meet the same objective. That is, trying to construct plausible "stories" about past situations to make some sense of the present or future. And we learn about the present by observing how current patterns resemble and differ from the past. Consider an example of how a careful reading of history might change one's analysis of a current situation. Some people today contend that the United States should go back to the "Good Old Days," for then we were happier and less alienated from our environment. One version of this fable holds that during its early years, this nation was composed of content yeoman farmers who helped each other build homes and barns and shared equitably in the economic pie. And those same people contend that, today, there is an extremely unequal distribution of **income** and **wealth** in comparison. To be sure, to deny the inequality in income that exists today would be denying the truth. However, we must put our views about the current situation in line with what actually existed in the past. It is only then that we can make informed judgments to determine whether we are better or worse off in some subjective sense.

Going back to any year before the Civil War, we discover substantial inequalities. In 1770s, almost one-fourth of the working population were either indentured servants or slaves. At the top of the wealth distribution were merchants and large landholders and at the bottom laborers and seamen. Statistics show that in 1860, on the eve of the Civil War, the top 1 percent of families held 24 percent of the total wealth in the United States and the top 10 percent held roughly 75 percent of the wealth in this country. This may be surprising to many, but there was an even greater amount of wealth inequality in the mid-nineteenth century than today. In the 1990s, the top 10 percent of the population owned approximately 65 percent of all the wealth. While admittedly, the mid-nineteenth century was a period of great wealth inequality, the point here is to demonstrate that wealth inequalities have been with this country since the 1600s when immigrants came to this country with different resources, different skills, and under different circumstances.

Having seen that wealth inequalities have always been with us, how about urban problems? Some think that urban problems like congestion, crime, pollution, and poverty are twentieth century phenomena. However, this too reflects an ignorance of the past. Colonial cities were confronted with an entire array of problems. One serious problem was congestion, as coaches, wagons, and men riding horses competed with pedestrians on the narrow and busy streets of colonial cities. Law enforcement was minimal, with common thieves, pickpockets, and prostitutes roaming the cities with little fear of being caught. Even if arrested, urban jails were reputedly so poorly constructed that many prisoners were not detained for long.

Other problems that often plagued the early colonial cities included short supplies of firewood (the main energy source for heating and cooking) and a lack of clean water. Also, pigs and dogs would prowl through the streets rummaging through garbage and destroying vegetable gardens. Most structures were built with wood since it was the least expensive building material to the colonists; hence, there was a constant problem with fires. And not all fires were accidental. The arsonist, unfortunately, had his place in urban colonial history. Again, so much for the "Good Old Days."

What about pollution a hundred years ago? At the turn of the twentieth century, horses and carriages were still the predominant form of urban transportation in New York City. Consequently, the city was often "knee high" in a mixture of mud and horse manure during inclement weather. Even during favorable weather conditions, it was too costly to rid the streets of this waste. Not only was there a problem of manure disposal but horses that died "on the job" had to be disposed of as well. Ironically, automobiles, now a major source of pollution, were hailed as the solution to the pollution problem.

INCOME UNCERTAINTY

Something else that wasn't so good in the past was the extreme variability in income that was suffered by farmers. For many generations, farmers made up a very large segment of our economy. And farmers, after all, were at the mercy of pestilence, droughts, bumper crops in other countries whose farmers competed in the world market, floods, hailstorms, frosts, and every other conceivable natural calamity, which would cause their income to be great in one year and small in the next. Today, less than 5 percent of our population is engaged in agricultural pursuits. Compare this with over 90 percent back at the start of this nation. Even if we didn't have any special programs—which we do—to help out farmers, a much smaller proportion of our population is now subject to such variability in income.

Moreover, today income uncertainty is significantly reduced by numerous government programs. We have government relief at federal, state, and local levels. And we have government unemployment insurance. There are numerous salary continuation plans that guarantee steady incomes even when the wage earner is unable to work because of some disaster.

AND LIFE ITSELF

Not only has income become more certain for the vast majority of Americans today, but today life itself has become a more certain prospect. This increased certainty about life has been an improvement for most members of our society. At the turn of this century, the expected lifetime was perhaps 47 years. By the middle of the century, this number had jumped to almost 71. It has now risen to 76 years. Certainly not all Americans participate to the same extent in improved health conditions, but even those who participate least still lead healthier lives than most of our forefathers. The above sketch of the "Good Old Days" certainly wasn't intended to sidestep a discussion of today's real problems, for America is certainly not without its problems. Even though we are in most ways better off economically than in the past, this improvement in economic well-being has not been bought without costs. With it has come a plethora of sociological and psychological problems, all related to our industrialized way of life.

DEFINITIONS OF NEW TERMS

BARTER In a barter system, goods and services are exchanged for other goods and services without using the intermediary good called money.

WEALTH Wealth is a stock of scarce things that people value, such as land, houses, clothes, and cars. It is also possible to include one's income earning capacity as part of wealth.

INCOME The flow of money earnings or payments to people in a given time period (usually taken to be a year) is called income.

Two Economic Growth in the Global Economy

W hat are the determinants of long-run economic change in our ability to produce goods and services? What are some of the consequences of rapid economic change? Why are some nations rich while others are poor? Does growth in output improve our economic welfare? These are a few questions that we need to explore before we turn our attention on American economic history.

The Rule of 70

If Nation A and Nation B start off with the same size population and the same level of real GDP but grow at only slightly different rates over a long period of time, will it make much of a difference? Yes. In the first year or two the differences will be small but even over a decade the differences will be large, and huge after 50 to 100 years. And the final impact will be a much higher standard of living in the nation with the greater economic growth, *ceteris paribus*. **Economic growth** is usually measured by the annual percent change in real output of goods and services per capita (real GDP per capita).

A simple formula, called the Rule of 70, shows how long it will take a nation to double its output at various growth rates. If you take a nation's growth rate and divide it into 70, you will have the approximate time it will take to double the income level. For example, if a nation grows at 3.5 percent per year, then the economy will double every 20 years (70/3.5). However, if an economy only grows at 2 percent per year, then the economy will double every 35 years (70/2). And at a 1 percent annual growth rate, it will take 70 years to double income (70/1). So even a small change in the growth rate of a nation will have a large impact over a lengthy period.

In Exhibit 2.1, we see the growth rates in real per capita GDP for selected industrial countries. Because of differences in growth rates, some countries will become richer than others over time. With relatively slower economic growth, today's richest countries will not be the richest for very long. And with even slight improvements in economic growth, today's poorest countries will not remain poor for very long.

Because of past economic growth the "richest" or "most-developed" countries today have many times the market output of the "poorest" or

Exhibit 2.1

Growth in Real per Capita GDP, Selected Industrial Countries

| | Ten-Year Averages | |
	1982–1991	1992–2001
United States	2.3%	2.1%
Japan	3.5	0.9
Germany	2.4	1.4
France	2.0	1.7
Italy	2.1	1.8
United Kingdom	2.4	2.5
Canada	1.1	2.1

Source: International Monetary Fund, *World Economic Outlook,* September 2000. Printed by permission from International Monetary Fund, http://www.imf.org.

"least-developed" countries. Put differently, the most-developed countries produce and market more output in a day than the least-developed countries do in a year. The international differences in income, output, and wealth are indeed striking and have caused a great deal of friction between developed and less-developed countries. The United States and the nations of the European Union have had sizeable increases in real output over the past two centuries, but even in 1800 most of these nations were better off in terms of market output than such contemporary impoverished countries as Ethiopia, India, or Nepal.

Productivity: The Key to a Higher Standard of Living

Will the standard of living in the United States rise, level off, or even decline over time? The answer depends on productivity growth. Productivity is the amount of goods and services a worker can produce per hour. Productivity is especially important because it determines a country's standard of living. For example, slow growth of capital investment can lead to lower labor productivity and, consequently, lower wages. On the other hand, increases in productivity and higher wages can occur as a result of carefully crafted economic policies, such as tax policies that stimulate investment or programs that encourage research and development. But why are some countries so much better than others at producing goods and services? We will see the answer in the next section, as we examine the determinants of **productivity**—quantity and quality of labor resources, physical capital, and technological advances.

Determinants of Economic Growth

FACTORS THAT CONTRIBUTE TO ECONOMIC GROWTH

Many separate explanations of the process of economic growth have been proposed. Which is correct? None of them, by themselves, can completely explain economic growth. However, each of the explanations may be part of a more complicated reality. Economic growth is a complex process involving many important factors, no one of which completely dominates. We can list at least several factors that nearly everyone would agree have contributed to economic growth in some or all countries.

1. The quantity and quality of labor resources (labor and human capital)

2. Increase in the use of inputs provided by the land (natural resources)

3. Physical capital inputs (machines, tools, buildings, inventories)

4. Technological knowledge (new ways of combining given quantities of labor, natural resources, and capital inputs) allowing greater output than previously possible

LABOR

We know that labor is needed in all forms of productive activity. But other things being equal, an increase in the quantity of labor inputs does not necessarily increase output per capita. For example, if the increase in the quantity of labor input is due to an increase in population, per capita growth might not occur because the increase in output could be offset by the increase in population. However, if a greater proportion of the population works (that is, the labor force participation rate rises) or if workers put in longer hours, output per capita will increase—assuming that the additional work activity adds something to output.

Qualitative improvements in workers (learning new skills, for example) can also enhance output. Indeed, it has become popular to view labor skills as **human capital** that can he augmented or improved by education and on-the-job training. Human capital has to be produced

Institutional Economics

Douglass C North, an economic historian, was the recipient of the Nobel Prize in Economics in 1993. One of North's contributions is his analysis of the linkage between institutional changes and economic growth. According to North, "the sources of sustained economic growth and the determinants of income distribution are to be found in the institutional structure of a society. Economic historians can no longer write good economic history without explicitly taking into account the institutional structure of the system, both economic and political. We can't avoid the political aspect because decisions made outsider the marketplace have had, and will continue to have, a fundamental influence upon growth and welfare."

Institutions matter because they affect the choices open to people, shape incentives and are an important determinant of human action. The institutional structure of a society (or the "rules of the game," as Mr. North calls it) includes formal rules (such as constitutions, property rights, laws of contract), informal constraints (conventions, customs, codes of conduct), and the means of enforcing both formal and informal standards of behavior (courts, social ostracism, personal beliefs). As in sports, the way the game is played and its outcome depends on the nature

like physical capital with teachers, schoolrooms, libraries, computer labs, and time devoted to studying.

NATURAL RESOURCES

The abundance of natural resources, like fertile soils, and other raw materials, like timber and oil, can enhance output. Many scholars have cited the abundance of natural resources in the United States as one reason for its historical success. Canada and Australia are endowed with a large natural resource base and high per capita incomes. Resources, however, are not the whole story, as is clear with reference to Japan or Hong Kong, both of which have had tremendous success with relatively few natural resources. Similarly, Brazil has a large and varied natural resource base yet its income per capita is relatively low compared to many developed countries. It appears that a natural resource base can affect the initial development process but sustained growth is influenced by other factors. However, most economists would agree that a limited resource base does pose an important obstacle to economic growth.

of the rules, the character of the players and the fairness (impartiality) of the referee. Moreover, the choice of the rules and the enforcement mechanisms will be affected by prevailing ideology and culture.

According to North, rules must be credible if they are to be effective. That is, they must be enforced. Private enforcement is possible, but as economic life because more complex, political institutions become the major instrument for defining and enforcing property rights. The history of economic performance cannot be separated from the history of political performance. The New Institutional Economics studies both.

North has shown is that those countries that (1) adopt a rule of law, one which limits the power of government over economic life and protects the rights of persons and property and (2) maintain open markets and freedom of contract are more likely to achieve long-run economic prosperity than those who do not.

According to North, economic change is "path dependent": The future depends on the past and present choices. History is not predetermined or based on some grand design; it is the sum of human actions. How we act will depend on the rules we inherit and formulate, as well as on our cultural and moral heritage. But ultimately, it is individuals who must choose.

Source: See Douglass C. North, *Growth and Welfare in the American Past,* Second edition, (Prentice Hall: Englewood Cliffs, NJ, 1974) and James Dorn, "North Wins Nobel for New Institutional Economics," *The Margin* (Spring 1994), 56.

PHYSICAL CAPITAL

Even in primitive economies, workers usually have some rudimentary tools to further their productive activity. Take the farmer who needs to dig a ditch to improve drainage in his fields. If he used just his bare hands, it might take a lifetime to complete the job. If he used a shovel, he could dig the ditch in hours or days. But with a big earth-moving machine, he could do it in minutes. There is nearly universal agreement that capital formation has played a significant role in the economic development of nations.

TECHNOLOGICAL ADVANCES

Technological advances stem from human ingenuity and creativity in developing new ways of combining the factors of production to enhance the amount of output from a given quantity of resources. The process of technological advance involves invention and **innovation**. Innovation is the adoption of the product or process. For example, in the United States, the invention and innovation of the cotton gin, the Bessemer steel-making process, and the railroad were important stimuli to economic growth. New technology, however, must be introduced into productive use by managers or entrepreneurs who must weigh the perceived estimates of benefits of the new technology against estimates of costs. Thus, the entrepreneur is an important economic factor in the growth process.

Technological advance permits us to economize on one or more inputs used in the production process. It can permit savings of labor, such as when a new machine does the work of many workers. When this happens, technology is said to be embodied in capital and to be labor saving. Technology, however, can also be land (natural resource) saving or even capital saving. For example, nuclear fission has permitted us to build power plants that economize on the use of coal, a natural resource. The reduction in transportation time that accompanied the invention of the railroad allowed businesses to reduce the capital they needed in the form of inventories. Because goods could be obtained more quickly, businesses could reduce the stock kept on their shelves.

Raising the Level of Economic Growth

THE IMPACT OF ECONOMIC GROWTH

Economic growth means more than an increase in the real income (output) of the population. A number of other important changes accompany changes in output. Some have even claimed that economic growth stimulates political freedom or democracy, but the correlation here is far from conclusive. While there are rich democratic societies and poor authoritarian ones, the opposite also holds. That is, some features of democracy, such as majority voting and special interest groups, may actually be growth retarding. For example, if the majority decides to vote in large land reforms and wealth transfers, this will lead to higher taxes and market distortions that will reduce incentives for work, investment, and ultimately economic growth. However, there are a number of policies that a nation can pursue to increase economic growth

SAVING RATES, INVESTMENT, CAPITAL STOCK, AND ECONOMIC GROWTH

One of the most important determinants of economic growth is the saving rate. In order to consume more in the future, we must save more now. Generally speaking, higher levels of saving will lead to higher rates of investment and capital formation and, therefore, to greater economic growth. Individuals can either consume or save their income. If individuals choose to consume all of their income, there will be nothing left

Exhibit 2.2

Savings Rates and GDP Growth during High-Growth Periods in Selected Economies

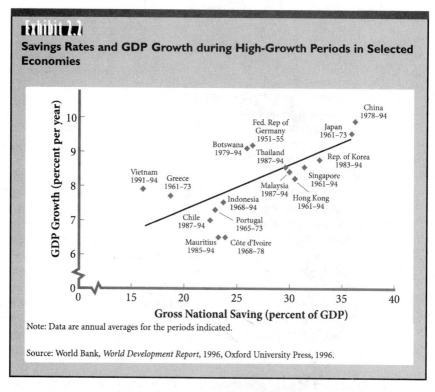

Note: Data are annual averages for the periods indicated.

Source: World Bank, *World Development Report*, 1996, Oxford University Press, 1996.

for saving, which businesses could use for investment purposes to build new plants or replace wornout or obsolete equipment. With little investment in capital stock, there will be little economic growth. Capital can also increase as a result of capital injections from abroad (foreign direct investments), but the role of national saving rates in economic growth is of particular importance.

Exhibit 2.2 clearly shows that around the world sustained rapid economic growth is associated with high rates of saving and investment. However, investment alone does not guarantee economic growth. Economic growth hinges on the quality and the type of investment as well as on investments in human capital and improvements in technology.

RESEARCH AND DEVELOPMENT

Some scholars believe that the importance of research and development (R&D) is understated. The concept of R&D is broad indeed—it can include new products, management improvements, production innovations, or simply learning-by-doing. However, it is clear that investing in R&D and rewarding innovators with patents have paid big dividends in the past 50 to 60 years. Some would argue that even larger rewards for research and development would spur even more rapid economic growth. In addition, an important link exists between research and development and capital investment. As already noted, when capital depreciates over time, it is replaced with new equipment that embodies the latest technology. Consequently, R&D may work hand-in-hand with investment to improve growth and productivity.

THE PROTECTION OF PROPERTY RIGHTS IMPACTS ECONOMIC GROWTH

Economic growth rates tend to be higher in countries where the government enforces property rights. Property rights give owners the legal right to keep or sell their property—land, labor, or capital. Without property rights, life would be a huge "free-for-all," where people could take whatever they wanted; in this scenario, protection for property, such as alarm systems and private security services, would have to be purchased.

In most developed countries, property rights are effectively protected by the government. However, in developing countries, this is not usually the case. And if the government is not enforcing these rights, the private sector must respond in costly ways that stifle economic growth. For example, an unreliable judiciary system means that entrepreneurs are often forced to rely on informal agreements that are difficult to enforce. As a result, they may have to pay bribes to get things done, and even then, they may not get the promised services. Individuals will have to buy private security or pay "organized crime" for protection against crime and corruption. In addition, landowners and business owners might be fearful of coups or takeovers from a new government, which might confiscate their property altogether. In short, if government is not adequately protecting property rights, the incentive to invest will be hindered, and political instability, corruption, and lower rates of economic growth will be likely.

FREE TRADE AND ECONOMIC GROWTH

Allowing free trade can also lead to greater output because of the principle of comparative advantage. Essentially, the principle of comparative advantage suggests that if two nations or individuals with different resource endowments and production capabilities specialize in producing a smaller number of goods and services and engage in trade, both parties will benefit. Total output will rise. This will be discussed in greater detail in the chapter on international trade.

EDUCATION

Education, investment in human capital, may be just as important as improvements in physical capital. At any given time, an individual has a choice between current work and investment activities like education that can increase future earning power. People accept reductions in current income to devote current effort to education and training. In turn, a certain return on the investment is expected, for in later years they will earn a higher wage rate (the amount of the increase depending on the nature of the education and training as well as individual natural ability). For example, in the United States, a person with a college education can be expected to earn almost twice as much per year as a high school graduate.

One argument for government subsidizing education is that this investment can increase the skill level of the population and raise the standard of living. However, even if the individual does not benefit financially from increased education, society may benefit culturally and in other respects from having its members highly educated. For example, more education may lead to lower crime rates, new ideas that may benefit the society at large, and more informed voters.

With economic growth, illiteracy rates falls and formal education grows. Exhibit 2.3 shows the adult literacy rates for selected countries.

EXHIBIT 2.3

Literacy and Economic Development

Country	Output per Capita	Adult Literacy Rates
United States	$30,200	97%
Japan	24,500	99
Italy	21,500	97
Brazil	6,300	81
India	1,600	52
Haiti	1,070	53
Ethiopia	530	28

Note: The literacy rates are based on the ability to read and write at an elementary school level.
Source: *Times Almanac, 2000*. Copyright © Time, Inc. All rights reserved.

The correlation between per capita output and the proportion of the population that is able to read or write is striking. Improvements in literacy stimulate economic growth by reducing barriers to the flow of information; when information costs are high, out of ignorance many resources flow to or remain in uses that are rather unproductive. Moreover, education imparts skills that are directly useful in raising labor productivity, whether it is mathematics taught to a sales clerk, engineering techniques taught to a college graduate, or just good ideas that facilitate production and design.

However, in developing, poor countries, the higher opportunity costs of education present an obstacle. Children in developing countries are an important part of the labor force starting at a young age. But children who are attending school cannot help in the field—planting, harvesting, fence building, and many other tasks that are so important in the rural areas of developing countries. A child's labor contribution to the family is far less important in a developed country. Thus the higher opportunity cost of an education in developing countries is one of the reasons that school enrollments are lower.

Education may also be a consequence of economic growth, because as incomes rise, people tend to increase education consumption. People increasingly look to education for more than the acquisition of immediately applicable skills. Education becomes a consumption good as well as a means of investing in human capital.

Issue: Economic Freedom and Economic Growth[*]

WHAT IS ECONOMIC FREEDOM?

The key ingredients of economic freedom are personal choice, voluntary exchange, freedom to compete, and the protection of person and property. Institutions and policies are consistent with economic freedom when they provide an infrastructure for voluntary exchange, and protect individuals and their property from aggressors seeking to use violence, coercion, and fraud to seize things that do not belong to them. Legal and monetary arrangements are particularly important: governments promote economic freedom when they provide a legal structure and law-enforcement system that protects the property rights of owners and enforces contracts in an even-handed manner. They also enhance economic

[*]Source: James Gwartney and Robert Lawson, "Economic Freedom of the Word: 2002 Annual Report," http://www.freetheworld.com.

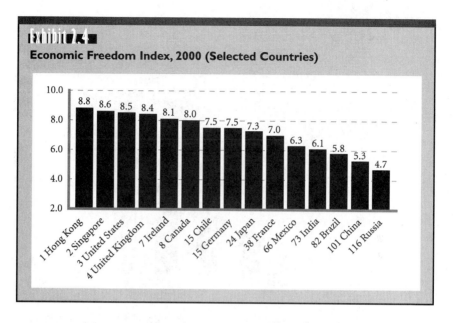

Exhibit 2.4

Economic Freedom Index, 2000 (Selected Countries)

freedom when they facilitate access to sound money. In some cases, the government itself may provide a currency of stable value. In other instances, it may simply remove obstacles that retard the use of sound money that is provided by others, including private organizations and other governments.

However, economic freedom also requires governments to refrain from many activities. They must refrain from actions that interfere with personal choice, voluntary exchange, and the freedom to enter end compete in labor and product markets. Economic freedom is reduced when taxes, government expenditures, and regulations are substituted for personal choice, voluntary exchange, and market coordination. Restrictions that limit entry into occupations and business activities also retard economic freedom.

Exhibit 2.4 displays a sample of selected countries and their Economic Freedom Index.

CORRELATIONS BETWEEN ECONOMIC FREEDOM AND OTHER INDICATORS

The EFW index is very useful as a correlate with other *desiderata* such as income per person, economic growth, income distribution and so on. The following bar charts (Exhibits 2.5 through 2.8) illustrate some of these basic relationships.

Many critics of economic freedom focus on the supposed inability of the free market to create a "just"distribution of income or in caring for the poor. Exhibits 2.7 and 2.8 present the evidence on the validity of these arguments. First, the distribution of income is no more unequal in countries with market oriented economies

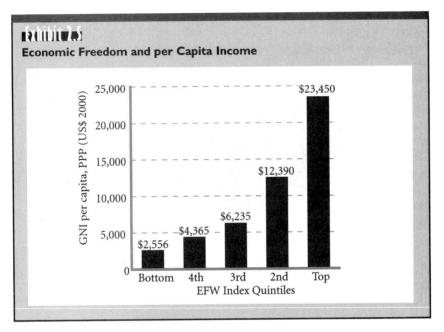

Exhibit 2.5

Economic Freedom and per Capita Income

GNI per capita, PPP (US$ 2000)

- Bottom: $2,556
- 4th: $4,365
- 3rd: $6,235
- 2nd: $12,390
- Top: $23,450

EFW Index Quintiles

than in those that are economically repressive. The bottom tenth of the income distribution receives essentially the same share—between 2.06 percent and 2.90 percent—of total income in all the quintiles. Moreover, it bears

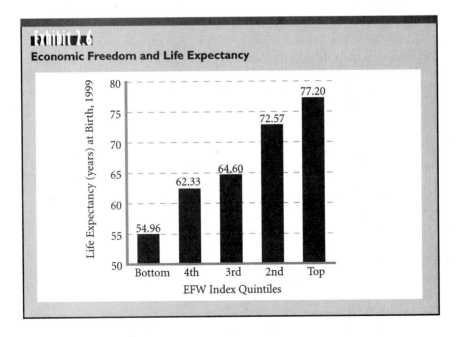

Exhibit 2.6

Economic Freedom and Life Expectancy

Life Expectancy (years) at Birth, 1999

- Bottom: 54.96
- 4th: 62.33
- 3rd: 64.60
- 2nd: 72.57
- Top: 77.20

EFW Index Quintiles

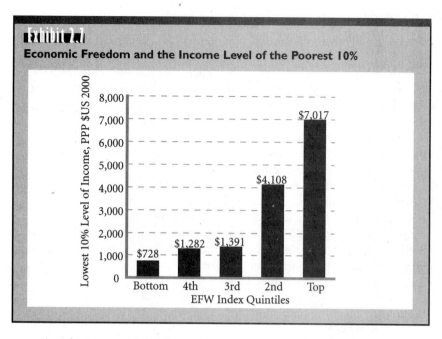

Exhibit 2.7

Economic Freedom and the Income Level of the Poorest 10%

Chart: Lowest 10% Level of Income, PPP $US 2000 vs. EFW Index Quintiles

- Bottom: $728
- 4th: $1,282
- 3rd: $1,391
- 2nd: $4,108
- Top: $7,017

repeating that economically free societies are more productive and that this added productivity translates into higher incomes for everyone. The final bar chart shows the average level of income of the poorest tenth in society. Clearly freer markets lead to a more

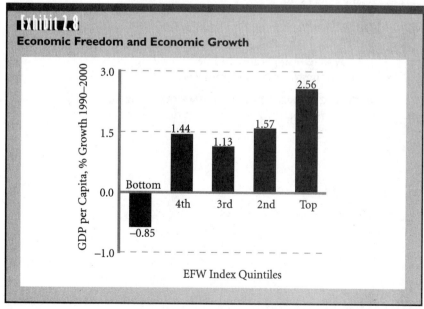

Exhibit 2.8

Economic Freedom and Economic Growth

Chart: GDP per Capita, % Growth 1990–2000 vs. EFW Index Quintiles

- Bottom: −0.85
- 4th: 1.44
- 3rd: 1.13
- 2nd: 1.57
- Top: 2.56

productive economy, which increases incomes for all economic classes.

CONCLUDING THOUGHTS

The degree of economic freedom present is influenced by numerous factors. No single statistic will be able to capture all of these factors or to represent their interrelations fully. According to Gwartney and Lawson, the index presented here captures most of the important elements and provides a reasonably good measure of differences among countries in economic freedom. However, something as complex as economic freedom is difficult to measure with precision. Thus, *small differences* between countries should not be taken very seriously.

As this work goes forward, it should open doors for fruitful research in several areas. Certainly, it should be of value to those seeking to pinpoint the strengths and weaknesses of institutions and policies. It should also be useful to those seeking to enhance our knowledge of economic development and the process of economic growth. Researchers analyzing the interrelations among economic freedom, civil liberties, and democratic decision-making should also find these data of value.

KEY TERMS

ECONOMIC GROWTH an upward trend in the real per capita output of goods and services

PRODUCTIVITY the amount of goods and services a worker can produce per hour

HUMAN CAPITAL the accumulation of investments in education and on-the-job training

INNOVATION applications of new knowledge that create new products or improve existing products

RESEARCH AND DEVELOPMENT (R&D) activities undertaken to create new product and processes that will lead to technological progress

Three

Economic Systems Before the Opening of the New World

E conomics concerns itself with exchange and choice. Examples of early exchanges date as far back as the Ice Age. Archaeologists contend that even as early as the Bronze Age, the universal phenomenon of the traveling salesman can be found. However, although some of the basic precepts of an exchange economy were evident from the beginning of social interaction, some important distinctions must be made, for we now live in a (modified) market economy. We use the market to solve many of our basic economic problems: who gets what, where, when, and how much? But, if we could go back (given more time and space) to study, for example, the economic organization of antiquity in Rome, Greece, and Egypt, we would find systems of massive slavery, long periods of technological stagnation, and the use of custom to guide the vast majority of economic activities that the ancients engaged in. Instead, however, let's start with the fall of the western part of the Roman Empire in A.D. 476. We will briefly trace the development of economic society to the opening of the New World.

AFTER THE FALL OF ROME

When Rome fell, the Huns and the German tribes started to invade everything in sight. For the next thousand years, the mislabeled Dark Ages were cast upon European society. Throughout this period, Europe depended on a **premarket economy,** otherwise known as a **traditional system.** The period, also called the Middle Ages or the Medieval Period, was one of extensive political fragmentation; this had important consequences for the economic organization of society, for, as we shall see, it takes a certain amount of consistent legal, political, and, more broadly speaking, **institutional arrangements** to be conducive to what we know today as a market-oriented economic system.

THE DARK AGES WEREN'T REALLY DARK

While certain historians have classified the Middle Ages as a period when there was essentially no change in the structure of society, we shall see that this was not indeed the case. During this time, there were periods of expansion and contraction—things were happening which were prerequisites to modern European and American societies of today. In fact, when we consider how long it took the Greeks and the Romans to develop their civilizations, the Middle Ages don't look so dark or so lacking in progress.

Just look at the technical innovations that occurred in Europe during this period. By A.D. 1100, the Moors had developed a paper-making industry. A mere hundred years later, the Italians had sophisticated silk-throwing machines. By 1250, Milanese craftsmen had started making plate armor. During the same year in France and the Low Countries, the great age of stained glass had started, the results of which can be seen in churches and cathedrals throughout Europe. By the thirteenth century, broad-beamed fishing and transport boats had been built for northern trade. By the middle of the fourteenth century, the cast-iron cannon had developed in Germany, as had the cast-iron furnace. And, of course, in the year 1440, Gutenberg began using movable type in his printing press. And during the same period, in the agricultural sector, things were not stagnating either. The process of selective breeding of animals was spreading throughout Europe.

THE RENAISSANCE

The Dark Ages were certainly not utterly dark, and by the fourteenth and fifteenth centuries the Renaissance had started. This was a period when kings, queens, and nobles increased support of the arts. The University of Paris had already been founded in the twelfth century, and Kings College—the beginning of Cambridge University—was started in the early 1400s.

Now, it is true that change was relatively slow. In terms of the economic well-being of the population, there was probably on average no real change during much of this period, which is why it is sometimes called an age of stagnation. One of the best-known and most conspicuous institutions of this period, and basic to the organization of society, was the manor, a topic to which we now turn.

LIFE ON THE MANOR

After the fall of Rome, continuous invasions brought the European countryside into chaos. Out of this chaos emerged a system of a large number of visually self-sufficient microcosmic societies, each formed around a manor. At the same time, there was not a complete collapse of all social institutions. In particular, there was a continuity of religious beliefs. They ended up providing the fundamental warrant for the feudal system, with its divinely instituted hierarchy of statuses and functions.

This was the era of feudalism. The manor, or farm estate, was ruled by a lord. In the feudal system, the lord was essentially responsible for whatever happened on his estate: He straightened out marital quarrels or arguments between anybody living within the estate's boundary, and he provided "police" protection. He was, indeed, the lord and master over all of his serfs.

WHY BECOME A SERF?

The institution of serfdom arose out of the colonies of Rome. It developed fairly gradually, but became a ubiquitous feature of the feudal medieval society. Serfs were the lowest on the totem pole, which looked like the following:

Dei

The Pope

The Big Lords

The Little Lords

The Serfs or Villeins (villager)

Put yourself in the place of a European peasant in the tenth century A.D. Roaming the countryside were hoards of Huns and Germanic tribes, periodically raiding villages and anything else they could get their hands on. Your life wasn't worth much those days because it could not be easily protected if you were alone in the world, or even with a few of your friends. It was an era when might made right. As you're walking along in your travels, you've avoided all encounters with marauding Huns, and you come across a large estate where you seek refuge. The owner of the estate, the lord, offers you a deal. In exchange for a certain part of your labor services—that is, a certain part of your working week—he will provide you with protection and justice. This exchange is how serfs originally became serfs. And, of course, once the system was well established, it was pretty hard for the son of a serf to be anything else but a serf. This arrangement lasted for a number of centuries until some external forces caused it to decline. But more on that later.

TYPES OF EXCHANGE

What's important to note in this discussion is that originally the arrangement between serf and master was, implicitly at least, a voluntary exchange. The serf exchanged labor services and perhaps a few "goods," like so many pieces of firewood per year, for the protection of the manorial master. Eventually, of course, the system grew to resemble a slave/master relationship. Serfs could not marry—could hardly do anything—without the express consent of the manorial lord. And, in fact, it was usually the lord who decided on the type of crops that should be tilled and the type of labor that serfs were to engage in.

THE MANOR'S ECONOMIC ACTIVITY

You have to remember that well over 90 percent of the working population during medieval times was engaged in agriculture. The manor was the basic unit of organization for providing the agricultural products necessary for survival. In fact, during much of this time, agricultural productivity was close to the subsistence level; that is, barely providing enough for the subsistence needs of the population. There was little surplus in many of the centuries during the Middle Ages.

The key to understanding the manorial life was that it was one of near *self-sufficiency*. The manorial was often a small village in the midst of either a forest or some cleared land. The field crops were typically planted in narrow strips. It was a very primitive method, one that did not lend itself to increasingly efficient use of the land. Fertilizer was seldom used, and it wasn't until the development of the soft horse collar that horses could be effectively employed in plowing fields.

POSITIVE ASPECTS OF THE MANOR

Although, as we said, the manorial organization of agriculture prevented any attempt at increasing yields on crop lands, it did provide the basis of cooperation. We find the use of the gang plow, for example, and the rotation of crops and crop land on certain manors. In other words, the manor allowed for the sharing of equipment and labor. Moreover, this type of agricultural organization did provide a floor against famine. In fact, that is another reason why free men would choose to become serfs—because, in addition to police protection, manorial lords provided food during periods of agricultural shortages.

ISOLATION OF THE MANOR

We find ourselves, then, during this period of the early Middle Ages, with a feudal society characterized by manors that were more or less isolated and spread across a sparsely populated area of Western Europe. Although nominally ruled by lords and Church people higher up on the hierarchy of feudal society, manors were really self-sufficient. They maintained extremely loose ties with any central political authority. It would be wrong, however, to say that in this period the manorial system was universal, for, at the same time that feudalism was going strong in the west, there were some flourishing cities in the south, such as Venice, Pisa, and Florence, which, as we shall soon discuss, were chiefly commercial cities, and, in the west and the north, cities were developing that were much more self-sufficient.

THE RISE OF MEDIEVAL CITIES

Villages in England were almost totally self-sufficient except for a few items, such as salt, iron for plows, and millstones. They developed as walled fortifications for the lords of manors to inhabit, initially inhabited also by his attendants and by a fighting garrison. In times of danger, the population under the lord would also come behind the walls of the city. Eventually, those living in these fortifications wanted to have certain manufactured products, so business as we know it started to become noticeable. Merchants, craftsmen, and artisans moved to these towns in response to increased demand for their products. Notice here that a rise in the relative rate of return induced movement of labor, or human resources, to these areas. So, even in the medieval society, which was based largely on custom and which was thought of as a nonmarket-oriented organization, simple economic rules and principles still held.

As more and more people came to the city in search of economic gain and security, these cities became more and more crowded. We have evidence that as early as the tenth century, Cologne and Verdun extended their city walls. In the eleventh, so did Geneva, Rouen, Antwerp, and others. Then, in the twelfth and thirteenth centuries, there was a veritable deluge of city wall extensions; city populations were expanding by leaps and bounds. Cologne more than doubled from the eleventh to the thirteenth century, as did Strasbourge. (These population trends were later to be reversed, of course, in the fourteenth century when the Black Death hit.)

We find that during this time, as merchants, craftsmen, and artisans gathered inside city walls, the forerunners of modern-day business and labor organizations developed. One of the most prevalent was the medieval guild.

COMBINATIONS IN RESTRAINT OF TRADE

Guilds developed among craftsmen probably around the start of the 1200s. They were generally found in middle-sized towns of about 25,000 people. Here some division of labor or specialization prevailed. Italy had the strongest guilds until the cities became dominated by merchants or oligarchies. In France, guilds had to pay dues to feudal powers in order to exist. In England, they became so obvious and seemingly influential that political powers tried to prohibit them because they seemed inimical to the royal interests.

Craft guilds were a special type of exclusive association of producers. Typically, a guild was run by a master or several masters. These were usually craftsmen who did their work in their own houses and sometimes in special shops. These so-called guild masters voluntarily agreed to set up a system of rules which would govern the conduct of each other and, more importantly, the conduct of anyone attempting to enter that particular craft in that particular town. Herein lies the restrictive nature of guilds and why we titled this section "Combinations in Restraint of Trade." To prevent entry into the particular calling that the guild masters were making money at, they required a long apprenticeship for anyone who wanted to become a journeyman (master craftsman). The apprenticeship was ostensibly designed to ensure the adequate training of journeymen, but, as an aside, it also prevented "too" rapid an entry into the profession itself, hence maintaining the incomes of the guild masters at levels that they thought appropriate to their station in life.

There were many types of guilds: the glovers' guild, the hatters' guild, the scribners' guild, and so on. Guilds also were designed to control the social conduct of their members. Members could be fined for improper behavior and for not contributing enough to charitable organizations. Basically, however, we can view the guilds as economic units that were used to establish monopoly positions for the guild masters and those who were lucky enough to enter the guild later on.

We can define a **monopoly** as an organization that has control over the selling of something. (The term actually means, in Greek, single seller.) The guild masters were essentially establishing themselves as the single seller of a particular type of service and its product, such as hats. They attempted to prevent entry by specifying criteria for apprenticeships and by changing the length of the apprenticeships.

They attempted to prevent competition *within* their guild by specifying how many threads per inch had to be in a piece of cloth, how the cloth had to be shrunk, how much buttons had to weigh, and what type of production techniques could be used. In fact, in certain places it was necessary for craftsmen to keep their windows open so that passersby could easily see if they were cheating on the guild's production-technique restrictions. Ostensibly, these monitoring techniques were used to establish "standards" and to protect the guild's "good name."

USING THE LAW OF DEMAND

The restriction on the number of guild members can be easily understood by using the simple law of demand. There is an inverse relationship between the price of a product, say, hats, and the quantity demanded. In other words, if members of the hatters' guild produced more hats, the only way they could get rid of them was by, in effect, lowering the price. Looked at another way, if the guild members produced very few hats, they could effectively charge a higher price per hat and sell all of this smaller quantity supplied. If the guild master were to let in lots more hat makers, all of the hat makers would have to accept a lower price if everybody was to get rid of their hats. By restricting the number of producers of hats, the guild masters and members made sure that what they received for their hats provided them with a steady, relatively higher income. Of course, there were problems of monitoring all the members of the guild. What if some of them started to make more hats than they were allowed or started to offer a different style of hat? These hatters might start taking away business from other people. Consequently, it is not hard to figure out why there were so many restrictions on guild members.

AND MERCHANTS TOO

Merchants also started to band together in what were called merchants' guilds. These organizations were not, however, the same as craft guilds. Merchant associations, which were known in Italy and England during the twelfth century, were interested mainly in self-regulation of trade and, of course, in peripheral social interactions among the members. They often found themselves in competition with craft guilds. In fact, in London in 1200, one succeeded in persuading the King that the weavers' craft guild should be abolished; the King gave a monopoly to the merchants. Merchants in those times were known as freemen, to be contrasted with craftsmen. A craftsman could become a freeman only if he gave up his craft and got rid of all of this equipment from his house.

A lot of merchants banded together in what was to become the most far-reaching kind of international organization among foreign merchants during that era. It was called the Hanseatic League. The best-known members of this league were the Hansa of London and those of the Teutons. The Hansa of London, for example, by the end of 1350 had gotten all of its members royal protection and a special privilege to trade whenever and wherever they pleased in England for a period of 40 days. In other words, any member of the Hansa League could go to any particular spot in England and stay there for 40 days, all the while trading and making income. The Hanseatic League during the Middle Ages encompassed over 70 towns throughout Europe and England. It was the most far-reaching international organization of foreign merchants. We shall see below that the increased trade among towns and nations was one of the contributors to the downfall of the feudal society.

THE DECLINE OF FEUDALISM

By the beginning of the seventeenth century, feudalism had largely disappeared in Western Europe. In its place was a developing market-oriented economy, which was spreading throughout the world. What accounted for the decline of such a pervasive way of life for such a large sector of the world? Historians have often looked to the Church, religious life styles, and the Crusades to explain at least part of this decline. Let's turn now to the supreme religious adventure in medieval times. The end result of that adventure was a society that the Church had opposed for centuries.

SPREADING THE FAITH

If we ignore for a moment the religious aspects of the Crusades, it is obvious that those hardy Crusaders who made it to the East found a startlingly different way of life, one that they were not used to in the medieval economy. In the East, people were far more civilized in some senses of the word; there were luxuries that were unheard of in the West. The Crusaders also came upon a much more money-oriented economy. In other words, a medium of exchange commonly accepted by a majority of the people was in wide use.

We might say that the Crusades had a *demonstration effect*—knights in shining armor tasted a little bit of the "good" life and wanted to continue it when they returned to the West. Urban living seemed much more appealing after they saw what it was like.

When these valiant men returned to their homelands, some left the countryside; they wanted city life. This demand for an urban environment created one of the impetuses for increased urbanization and all that comes with it. It is perhaps responsible for fostering the growth of towns, the increased number of town charters, and the development of an important middle class.

The Crusades were also a source of increased demand for certain products, such as arms and clothing. This was thought to be a stimulating influence on the medieval economy. It at least induced these industries to grow at a more rapid rate than they would have otherwise, and also accounts for royal government support for merchant guilds instead of craft or producers' "locals."

CHANGING RELIGIOUS ATTITUDES

The Church had lots of rules against market exchanges used to obtain "excessive" personal gain. For example, there were rules against usury—

lending out money at interest, even very low interest. Today it is hard for us to imagine such a rule. Perhaps exorbitant interest rates are out of the question, but a zero rate? Why would people continuously be willing to give up the use of their own money for a certain period of time if they are not paid for it? Voluntary exchange must be mutually beneficial. Perhaps some people would be willing to give up the use of their money for awhile because of love or philanthropy, but most didn't then and still don't. Strictures on interest rates are no different from strictures on a positive price being charged for any good or service.

During medieval times, the Church attempted to instill in the populace the notion that life on this earth was only temporary, ephemeral, and one should look to the hereafter. There was extreme disapproval of wealth seeking. Life on earth should be a preparation for eternity, not a time to make things better for the present. Life on earth was supposed to be unimportant.

THE PROTESTANT ETHIC

The Reformation changed all this for many people. According to some economic historians, the advent of **Calvinism** was responsible for the tremendous growth in a capitalistic system where pecuniary gain was the main guiding force of individual economic actors in society. John Calvin preached the Puritan ethic, or the Protestant ethic, as it is sometimes called. He rationalized the change to bourgeois economic life by teaching the necessity of pursuing intense worldly activity. In so doing, a person would be fulfilling his duty to God. Calvin reinterpreted the so-called **division of labor**; that is, specialization, as a way of allowing each person to do his best according to God's calling. And further, for Calvinists, it was a sin to be idle. Also, Protestants were imbued with the idea that abstinence from consumption was a virtue; therefore, it was a virtue to save, to be thrifty. And, of course, when one saved, one was supposed to do whatever he could to make his savings as productive as possible. All of these new ideas that were soon to be accepted by many in society may have been a factor in causing the breakdown of feudal life. But there were certainly other reasons for this to happen, and it is to those we now turn.

THE ULTIMATE DECLINE IN THE MANORIAL SYSTEM

Cities started to develop in Western Europe even during the beginning of the Middle Ages. It was within the city walls that many serfs found their freedom when they decided that they could do better outside the manorial estate, for it was a rule in most situations that if a serf stayed away from the manor for a year and a day, he became a free man. During this time, a commercial expansion started throughout Europe. Fairs were held in different parts of the countryside. The Crusades also added to the desire for wealthy individuals to acquire the finer things in life that were present in the Orient. This induced traveling salesmen to visit towns and manors throughout the countryside to barter or trade for money with interested villagers and noblemen alike. And introduction of the use of money was an important catalyst.

Money is not, of course, necessary for trade. Things can be bartered. A pair of shoes can be traded for 15 buttons. A pot can be traded for four pieces of cloth. Most wandering merchants, however, wanted to get a more universal medium of exchange for the goods they traded with the villeins and the noblemen. They didn't want to be hampered with additional bulky goods that they would have to trade later on. Money, whether it be coins, dollar bills, or some convenient durable commodity, is generally defined as a medium of exchange. It is also a store of purchasing power if it is commonly accepted, and that's why its use is so widespread. It is extremely inconvenient to resort to barter when trying to obtain what one wants. You need to find someone else who has what you want and wants exactly what you have. It's just a lot simpler to sell goods or labor services for a payment in some medium of exchange and then to later on buy whatever goods or services you want. The use of money allows for increased specialization. Increased trade was dependent on the acceptance of money as a means of exchange, and that's exactly what happened in medieval society. The use of money became more widespread and trade continued to expand. However, money brought with it problems that were previously unknown to the manorial economy.

A JUST PRICE AND INFLATION

Previously, everyone was used to a "just" price that was charged for goods and services. Economic activity had been ruled by custom. This is a logical and economical way of doing things in a stationary society. The just price was generally set such that there were no shortages or surpluses for the goods involved. And why not set such a price if, after all, nothing changes? However, once money was introduced and trade became more widespread, just prices simply weren't good enough any more. One of the main reasons was the ubiquitous phenomenon we know today as inflation—a sustained rise in prices.

RISING PRICES

For example, during the sixteenth century, the general price level more than tripled because of the tremendous influx of gold and silver from the Americas. Now, why should an influx of precious metal cause prices to rise? Remember first that money is not only a medium of exchange but a store of purchasing power. People want to keep it because they can exchange it later on for goods and services. Suppose that the only form of money is gold. Noblemen and villagers, as well as numerous other people in medieval society, learned to accept gold in payment for goods and services. Later on they paid for other goods and services with this gold. Now suppose that all of a sudden the supply of gold in existence doubled because of shipments from the New World. The people who brought the gold in exchanged it for goods and services. Now, before they came, all of the other gold that was used would merely change hands; the supply was fixed, or constant. That is no longer the case. A lot of people ended up with a lot more gold than they used to have. But gold is what they used to buy real goods and services. When lots of people have a lot more gold and there's the same quantity of goods and services around as before, something's got to give. Individuals end up bidding against each other to get what they want. The price of these fixed supplies of goods and services has to go up in terms of gold. Throughout the rest of this book, you'll find other examples of how a large increase in the supply of the medium of exchange has led to an increase in the price level, or inflation.

INFLATION UNEXPECTED

The manorial lords, just like everybody else, were caught off guard. They wanted to buy some of the finer things in life that were available outside of the manor. These things had to be purchased with the medium of exchange, and in terms of that medium of exchange, they became more and more expensive. The lords were no longer satisfied with their previous relationships with their serfs. Up until then, serfs had been required to do a certain amount of each day's work for the lord. Now the lords wanted them to pay a certain amount of money in exchange for the land and protection that the lord provided. In the absence of any inflation, the lord could set a particular mutually agreeable price for the use of his land and the serfs would willingly agree.

With the rise of a market economy, established prices for goods and services were increasingly known by everyone. Hence, the translation of the value of a certain amount of each day's work into a fixed money payment was relatively easy. The wage payment, however, had been fixed before the unanticipated inflation of the sixteenth century. So when the prices of goods and services the lords wished to buy outside of the manor experienced unprecedented increases, the lords experienced a loss in their economic power. In other words, the value in real terms of the money payments received from the people using their land was falling. This is an important relationship—prices determine the real value of money payments. When we talk about real value, we're talking about purchasing power. Take a concrete, present-day example: If the price level goes up 10 percent and your scholarship remains the same, the real value of that scholarship has dropped by 10 percent. The same thing happened to the manorial lords.

At the same time, the merchant class was gaining more power. Unanticipated inflation provided an opportunity for profitable sale in markets, thus whetting commercial appetites and rewarding producers. Additionally, we must realize that the manorial system could not support a increasing population.

A GROWING POPULATION

At the beginning of the Middle Ages, fertile land was relatively abundant. As population grew and manors became overcrowded, new ones could be formed in the untilled regions of Europe. Population continued to grow until the middle of the 1400s, when the Black Death came. Population stagnated for awhile, but then started taking off again. Population pressures started to be felt by the increasingly crowded manors, which could no longer easily expand or multiply into regions where land was still fertile. All of this was happening at the time when merchants were becoming an increasingly economically powerful class.

THE MARKET ECONOMY EMERGES

Workers started to be paid with money instead of being required to do a certain amount of work in exchange for use of land. In other words, this factor of production—labor—was monetized, as it were. Around the same time, especially in England, another factor of production— land—was also being monetized. As land became more valuable, lords attempted to make a higher income by making better use of their lands. In England, for example, there was the beginning of what was later termed the Enclosure Movement. The English had an immensely profitable trade in wool. That meant that land which could be used to raise sheep was more valuable than other land. Hence, it was decided that those peasants who might use land to the detriment of sheep raising should be prevented from such acts. Land was therefore enclosed with fences. A certain number of landless peasants were therefore unable to make a living using the lord's **common property** grounds as they were used to doing. This led to the English Poor Laws, which essentially involved a tax to raise revenues, to round up the poor, and put them to work.

Land, like labor, was no longer conceived as a certain aspect in an explicit social and material relationship within a society. Labor, for example, had become a good or commodity to be disposed of in the marketplace just like any other good. One man did not have to work for a lord or guild master in return for the mere assurance of subsistence. He could attempt to shop around in order to get the best price or wage possible for his labor services. The same was true for land. Land used to be thought of as inviolable, the territory of some great master. Now it had become another commodity to be sold or rented.

A monetized market economy brought with it a lot more than the explicit creation of factors of production such as land and labor. It brought with it a system in which *information* became less costly to obtain. The information we are referring to is considered completely natural today—the prices of goods and services, where they can be bought and sold, what their quality is, and so on. Prior to the development of the market economy, the sources of information were myriad. Mainly, though, they came from the producers, who wished to sell their products at the most favorable prices. To do so required that many potential buyers be aware of price and availability. Moreover, such information provided clues to producers as to where greater profits might be made. If it is well known that a certain type of hat is selling for a specific price in Pisa and a hat maker in Venice had discovered a way to produce them cheaper, the hat maker knows immediately where potential profit-making opportunities lie.

A RECAP

The Middle Ages lasted for a millennium, during which time change was constant: clearing of the land, extension of agriculture, and a rise of resources. We also saw very little that was dramatic except occasional famines and plagues. Cities developed gradually, trade developed gradually, the rise and subsequent decline of the manor were gradual, and the so-called commercial revolution was spread over several centuries. During this period of ups and downs a pervasive phenomenon occurred: Population seemed to increase to some natural limit and then fall back, due to some natural phenomena. Several centuries later one astute person developed a theory after observing these phenomena, and, of course, his name was the Reverend Thomas Robert Malthus. His specter haunts us even today, so let us investigate and we will see what his ideas were and where they seemed to make the most sense.

Issue: Was Malthus Right?

In 1798, a little-known English man of the cloth named Thomas Robert Malthus published, *An Essay on the Principle of Population, as it Affects the Future Improvement of Society*. The uncomfortable and, indeed, depressing conclusion of that 50,000 word treatise was that population, when unchecked, doubles every 24 years or increases in a geometric rate, that is, 1, 2, 4, 8, 16, 32 and so on. But according to Reverend Malthus, food production—or more generally, the means of subsistence—only increases at an arithmetic rate—1, 2, 3, 4, 5. Hence, it is easy to see that population tends to increase at a much more rapid rate than food production in the Malthusian Model.

REVISING HIS IDEAS

A few years later, in 1803, Malthus put out a second edition of his now-infamous essay on population. Instead of talking about population doubling at a geometric rate, he indicated that the human species was destined to poverty and a life of misery unless the rate of population growth was retarded by positive checks or preventive checks. He listed as preventive such things as late marriages or no marriage at all, sexual abstinence, and moral restraint.

Even though Malthus preached moral restraint, he realized that "hot passion leads to surplus souls and cold reason leads to sin." And, since he was of strong moral character, he appeared unimpressed by the low fertility of prostitutes, for a "promiscuous intercourse to such a degree as to prevent the birth of children seems to lower, in the most marked manner, the dignity of human nature. It cannot be without its effect on men, and nothing can be more obvious than its tendency to degrade the female character, and to destroy all of its most amiable and distinguished characteristics."

It's understandable, then that Malthus put much more faith in such positive checks as wars, pestilence, and famine.

As you can imagine, Malthus was criticized severely. His fellow clergymen thought he was crazy; politicians and journalists called him a heretic. But then again, others, especially a famous economist of the time named David Ricardo, made good use of the Malthusian theory. Let's delve a little deeper into why Malthus came up with such heretical ideas; we shall see that although his theories didn't predict very well in the industrial society of his time, they did do a great job of describing what happened during the preindustrial European episodes that we have just studied.

A PRODUCT OF TRADITIONAL EUROPE

Even though the Reverend Malthus grew up during the Industrial Revolution, he was a product of traditional Europe—that is, preindustrial, pre-growth society. He believed, as did Adam Smith, the father of much modern economic thinking, that economic life depended on the productivity of land, so that ultimately it was the land that determined the level of our existence. Malthus was convinced, being the clergyman that he was, that the "passion between sexes" would cause men and women to breed so long as there was enough food around to feed a growing family. According to Malthus there is a relationship between the population size and the real wage rate per person or standard of living. Notice here the emphasis on the word *real*. The real wage rate is essentially the wage rate expressed in purchasing power over all goods and services. Real wage rates are, therefore, an indication of a person's ability to purchase the things he or she wants. We won't have to then worry about problems of inflation, or rather, general changes in the price level. Presumably, if a family does not obtain at least a subsistence level of income (or real wages), then the children will die because they cannot be fed or clothed. According to Malthus, once the population reaches a certain point, widespread famines occur and there are numerous deaths in the society. This was the so-called period of "positive" checks: disease, famine, wars plus an increase in vice, which Malthus thought was degrading but resulted in fewer births.

KEY ASSUMPTIONS

Malthus based his theory on some key assumptions. The most obvious is that population decisions were dependent only on maintaining the real wage rate above the subsistence level of wages. So long as people could obtain a real wage that gave them more than subsistence, the "passion between sexes" would take over and the world would become more peopled. While this may have been true in many situations, which we will describe below, it has not always been the case. There are many primitive societies in which Malthus' "preventive" checks were used, the most obvious being infanticide.

The second key assumption that the Reverend used was one of fixed technology. As we said above, Malthus was growing up in the Industrial Revolution, when this assumption certainly did not hold, but he was a product of an era when technology in fact did not change very quickly. This was certainly true with agricultural societies; technological changes were very slow. For example, English crop rotation and fertilization methods were only slowly adopted during the commercial revolution. This is one of the reasons that Malthus viewed agriculture output as growing at an arithmetic rate instead of at a geometric rate like the population. But, according to Malthus, even if there were some once-and-for-all increase in the food base of a society, this would only lead to inexorable pressure of the population of the increased resources. He felt that when everything got sorted out, the average level of living would be just as low as it was before the great increase in the food base.

MALTHUS AND TRADITIONAL EUROPE

It turns out that Malthus came up with a pretty good description of how things happened throughout Europe for many centuries before he wrote his essay—for example, there were recurrent periods of famine and pestilence. In fact, we can use the Malthusian doctrine to discover what happened during the age of feudalism. Population would increase on a manor until it was no longer worthwhile for the manorial lord to have any additional serfs—for a reason that has to do with an important economic principle called diminishing returns.

DIMINISHING RETURNS

With a fixed amount of land and fixed technology, after a point, additional increases in the number of workers will result in reduced productivity for each additional worker. That is, the additional output brought about by the additional worker will not be as much as by the previous worker. This is sometimes referred to as diminishing returns or productivity of the additional worker. To better understand this concept, look at the situation in which the manor lord has a fixed piece of land of a given fertility. He also has a certain number of plows, which we assume also for the moment to be fixed. He has a certain number of seeds, and whatever else is necessary to grow his crops. The only thing that the manor lord can vary in our little example is the number of men working on his plot of land. After a certain point

say, when he has ten men, he'll run out of plows for each of them. That means that the eleventh man will have to do some other task besides plowing. Or, perhaps he will take turns with somebody else. When the twelfth man comes along to work, he also will have to share a plow, and the thirteenth, and so on. Finally, if the manor lord hires on more than 20 men, each will only be able to use a plow less than half the time. So you see that with a fixed amount of land and tools to work with, as additional men are hired on, it is inevitable that their contribution to productivity or to the total amount produced must diminish. We find, then, that for a given amount of other factors of production, the larger the number of workers in the specific occupation, the smaller the productivity of each one.

The value of each worker to the manor lord is also determined by the value of the output that the workers produce. In a market situation—say, where the manor lord has started to sell some of his crops to city dwellers— the higher the price those city dwellers are willing to pay for his crops, the more valuable each worker becomes. If the market situation is extended to money payments to workers, the manor lord would be willing to raise his workers' wage payments if in fact the price he got for his product in town had gone up.

WHEN TO STOP ADDING SERFS

Before money payments were made to serfs on the manor, they exchanged a certain amount of each day's work for lodging and use of the land and anything else that the manor lord provided. What the lord provided had some value. The labor services that the serf provided did also; the value, as we mentioned above, was determined by the value of the output attributable to each serf. If the manor is fixed in size and there are no increases in agricultural technology, as more and more serfs are added, diminishing returns set in. At some point, the additional output attributable to an additional serf would not be equal in value to the services the manor lord would have to offer the serf. Hence, it would no longer be worthwhile to add serfs to the manor.

Of course, this assumes a fixed amount of usable land with fixed fertility. Manors could extend themselves, and, indeed, they did. However, at some point there would be no more relatively fertile land for manorial extensions. It was more difficult for further increases in population to then spread out into previously uncultivated acreage. The specter of diminishing returns was something that could no longer be escaped by expansion into other territories. At this time, land became relatively more valuable than labor. Since the value of an agricultural worker was dependent upon how much output (and its price) could be attributable to that worker, as relatively fertile land became more scarce, labor became relatively less valuable. Real wages fell in the agricultural sector. This led to an incentive for people to move into nonagricultural pursuits, which constituted a relatively small part of the economy during the pre-1800 European scene.

PLAGUES AND WAR

When looking over the history of the European population during the Middle Ages, we find recurrent periods of famine, pestilence, and war.

In the early 1300s, Europe experienced some of the most serious famines that had ever occurred, and, to top it all off, the famous Hundred Years War between England and France was started before complete recovery was possible. This is when we saw an early example of germ warfare: The enemy got a disease-laden missile sent by catapult.

In the middle of the fourteenth century, the Black Death came. The first wave started in 1347 and continued until 1351. It was of pneumonic type, which was the most infectious and most deadly form of plague. The plague germs were carried by rats and fleas. Relatively dense city centers were the homes of these plague-laden creatures.

During this period, the population was reduced by as much as one-third during a single year over hundreds of thousands of square miles. From the middle of the fourteenth century on. Population was reduced as pestilence continued to recur. For example, in England the plague returned in 1360, 1369, and 1374.

Such horrible crises tended to weed out the physically weak, so after a pestilence occurred, mortality was down, marriages and births were up. Many societies therefore saw surges in population for each generation to come. In fact, if we look at the population before the industrialization of Europe, fluctuations were erratic and sometimes violent, as evidenced by what happened during the Black Death. However, these fluctuations were around some sort of trend. The trend could be stable—up or down.

It is interesting also to note that those who lived in the cities were more susceptible to pestilence than those who didn't. As real incomes rose and the population became more urbanized, the population was more subject to violent death by disease because of the spreading factor that is proportional to population density. The denser the population, the faster infectious disease will spread. In the seventeenth century, for example, the immense town of London lost one-sixth to one-fourth of its population during a period of disease, while in many rural parishes during this period, there wasn't one death attributable to the plague.

WARS

War activities had a lot to do with what Malthus called "positive" checks on population increases. There was a distinct correlation between the fighting of wars (plus the Crusades) and the reduction of population. (There may have also been a correlation between population growth and the start of wars.)

We could go on with further illustrations of periods when population grew until war or pestilence reduced it to some previous level, and then it started to grow again. The Malthusian cycle was indeed at work during the Middle Ages. However, Malthus missed the boat in terms of industrial societies, like the one he was living in.

WHAT WENT WRONG?

What went wrong with Malthus' thesis was that he assumed a fixed technology. In the first instance, we know that starting in the seventeenth and eighteenth centuries, the technological capacity of society increased; whether it was due to the Industrial Revolution, to increased schooling of the population, or to other determinants, it did increase, and that is what the rest of this book is about. Malthus ignored the possibility that technology and productivity could rise. If increases in productivity are a result of increases in technology then the real income per capita of the population can rise even though the population is growing. In this particular simplified scenario there need never be a Malthusian positive check.

Additionally, it turns out that in many situations, as real income rises, the survival rate of children may increase, but the demand for children might fall, or at least might not rise as fast as income does. Stable populations are not unknown in the world today: witness, for example, Japan and

France. We do still find, however, the Malthusian cycle acting up in various developing countries in the world today.

Malthus was right, but only for before his time and perhaps under similar conditions existing today in certain countries.

DEFINITIONS OF NEW TERMS

PREMARKET ECONOMY OR TRADITIONAL SYSTEM A system in which most economic activity is based on custom or tradition, generally where money is not widely used as an intermediate good in exchange, and a situation in which very little trade or exchange takes place relative to more modern times.

INSTITUTIONAL ARRANGEMENTS The customs, laws, and institutions which determine how individuals may conduct themselves in economic and also in noneconomic matters.

CRAFT GUILD An exclusive organization of producer craftsmen. Guilds were run by guild masters who ruled with an iron hand in setting up a system to govern the business and social conduct of all the members.

MONOPOLY In its strictest sense, a single seller of a good or service, but more generally, a seller of a good or service who has considerable control over prices and output. Usury lending money for interest; today usury generally implies lending money at "excessive" interest rates.

CALVINISM A set of beliefs handed down by John Calvin; a rationalization of bourgeois economic life in which a person fulfilled his duty to God by working hard and saving lots of his income, which could be invested in profitable outlets.

DIVISION OF LABOR A situation in which individual workers take on specialized tasks instead of attempting to do everything necessary to produce a product or service.

COMMON PROPERTY Property which is, in a sense, owned by no one but also owned by everyone; the opposite of private property.

Part Two

The Colonial Era

Biographies

A Pioneering Effort in Early Agriculture

Eliza Lucas (1723–1793)

ENTREPRENEUR

In 1737, Lieutenant-Colonel George Lucas, who was stationed in Antigua in the Caribbean, departed for South Carolina with his ailing wife and three daughters. Shortly after settling there, diplomatic negotiations broke down between England and Spain and, with hostilities renewed, Colonel Lucas was recalled to duty in Antigua.

Since Mrs. Lucas was in poor health, responsibility for the family's affairs in South Carolina fell to the oldest daughter, Eliza, who was then sixteen. Not only did she admirably discharge her duties, but she also revolutionized agricultural production in South Carolina.

For her, planting was no mere weekend or holiday business. Having three plantations to oversee, she was rivaled by none in her industriousness and ingenuity.

Like other colonists she spent much time and energy trying to discover which crops were best suited for the soil and climate. Happily, in July 1739, she wrote, in a "coppy book of letters to my Papa": "I wrote my father a very long letter on his plantation affairs . . . on the pains I had taken to bring the Indigo, Ginger, Cotton, Lucern, and Casada to perfection, and had greater hopes from the Indigo." Within three years her hopes were realized and, almost singlehandedly, she successfully introduced and entrepreneured indigo production in the mainland colonies.[1] Additionally, as an active member of the local agricultural society, she helped disseminate her findings to other planters.

Indigo was used as a blue dye to color textiles, and as a complement to textile production it was deemed so valuable in England that Parliament eventually granted a subsidy for its production. By 1770, indigo ranked fifth among the major commodities exported from the thirteen colonies. Three decades earlier, only Eliza had been producing it on the mainland.

In South Carolina, rice and indigo overshadowed all other forms of commercial commodity production. Part of the reason for this was that indigo also complemented rice production. Whereas rice was grown in the low-lying, swampy regions, indigo was grown in high, dry areas. Moreover, the harvesting and planting time for these two crops did not conflict. Consequently, different soil types and work seasons for each permitted plantations to more fully utilize their land and their slaves.

By the time of the Revolution, exports per capita from South Carolina were greater than those from any of the other thirteen colonies. Eliza Lucas, more than any other single person, must be credited with this relative standing. In the process of enriching her family and other South Carolina planters, she hastened the settlement in early America.

Eliza Lucas was certainly one of North America's first great entrepreneurs.

A Man of Common Sense

Benjamin Franklin (1706-1790)

STATESMAN, PRINTER, SCIENTIST, AND WRITER

"Remember that *time* is money. He that can earn ten shillings a day by his labour, and goes abroad, or sits idle, one half of that day, though he spends but sixpence during his diversion of idleness, ought not to reckon *that* his only expense; he has really spent, or rather thrown away, five shillings besides." Such were the words of Benjamin Franklin in his *Advice to a Young Tradesman*, published in 1748. A better example of keen understanding of the opportunity cost of one's time would be hard to find.

To be sure, his aphorisms must have been colored by his strict Calvinist upbringing. The true Calvinist was a driven man, described by British economist R. H. Tawney as: "Tempered by self-examination, self-discipline, self-control, he is the practical ascetic, whose victories are won not in the cloister, but on the battlefield, in the counting house, and in the market." Calvin himself referred to God as the "great task maker" and looked around for tasks man should undertake. Ben Franklin claimed that he was a freethinker, but the continual exhortations he got from his father—for example, "Seest thou a man diligent in his business. He shall stand before kings"—must have had some effect.

Young Ben was born and raised in Boston. Family funds were insufficient for him to aim at Harvard, so he turned his hand to printing and went to Philadelphia in 1723, then decided he needed to perfect his printing knowledge in London, where he spent two years doing so and living like a bohemian. Within a few years, he began to prosper as a master printer. His simple style and great clarity in writing also started to bring in rewards. *Poor Richard's Almanac*, published annually between 1732 and 1757, was one of Franklin's most profitable enterprises, selling 10,000 copies a year. At the tender age of twenty-three, Franklin wrote his first words on economics: *A Modest Inquiry into the Nature and Necessity of a Paper Currency* (1729). Coincidentally, Franklin was the first one to start printing Pennsylvania's paper currency, and he stayed in this business for quite some time.

Franklin was a crusader and also a good businessman. He introduced printing and newspaper publication to many communities throughout the colonies. He also helped start the present University of Pennsylvania in 1751. Then he was named Deputy Postmaster General of the colonies.

Ben Franklin was also one of the first advertisers in America. When he started his *General Magazine,* he became disappointed that business-men did not believe that advertising could bring better results. Franklin himself advertised his own Pennsylvania Fire Place. The copy he wrote was persuasive: He criticized ordinary fire places because they caused drafts that made "women . . . get cold in the head, rheums, and deflux-ions, which fall into their jaws and gums have destroyed early many a fine set of teeth."

During the Revolution, Franklin helped draft the Declaration of Independence, which he signed. He was also the diplomatic agent sent to France for the new republic. Then he was chosen commissioner in 1781 to negotiate peace with Great Britain. Finally, he took part in the Constitutional Convention.

To practical men, especially the officers of savings banks ("a penny saved is a penny earned"), Ben Franklin seemed the summation of good sense and morality. To others, he appeared to be a colorless and materi-alistic opportunist. But as John Adams once said, his "reputation was more universal than that of Leibniz, Newton, or Voltaire, and he was the first civilized American."

ENDNOTES

[1]Many earlier experiments with indigo had been attempted in the southern colonies, but without success.

Four

The Age of Exploration and Spanish Colonization

Europe in 1492

On the eve of Columbus' voyage to the "New World," the wealth and commerce of Europe centered in the coastal regions of the Mediterranean. The most important hubs of commerce were the northern Italian city-states of Venice, Florence, Genoa, and Milan. For centuries these city-states were the funnels of trade between Asia and Europe. Like magnets, they linked three great overland routes from Asia to the markets of Europe. By their superior know-how, commercial skills, and locational advantages, Italian traders were able to dominate most of the world's long-distance trades.

In contrast to the earlier centuries of the Middle Ages, the late sixteenth century was a time of material expansion. This period witnessed the growth of trade, both in volume and in value. In the long-distance trade, the most important items were expensive manufactured products: light cottons and silks from India and China, and jewel-toned rugs from Persia. Even delicate items such as glass from Damascus and porcelain from China were carried on the long routes to the markets of Europe. Another extremely important item in the long-distance trade was spices such as cloves, nutmeg, ginger, and cinnamon. There were eagerly sought to redeem European diets from monotony, and pepper was vital as a meat preservative in these warm climates.

Short-distance trade within Europe was burgeoning as well. Here again Italian merchants reigned supreme, especially in the handling and delivery of Mediterranean goods. A brisk traffic in grain, salt, salted fish, and other bulk commodities such as cheese, wine, and oil arose in the late fifteenth century. By this time, the Mediterranean had become a bustling trade arena.

Clearly the types of commodities carried on the long-distance trade were quite different than those on the short-distance trade. The commodities from distant areas were typically expensive relative to their bulk and weight. This characteristic was due to the high land transportation costs. No cheap water route had yet been discovered to Asia. Nevertheless, Europe was reaching out, and seafaring voyages to the more distant areas were taking place as the decades passed. Of the many motives spurring seafaring adventures into the Atlantic, the primary one was to tap the riches of the long-distance trade from Asia. The most vigorous adventurers in this endeavor, however, were not the Mediterranean city-states. Why should they seek out new paths, since they were already comfortable astride the traditional routes?

THE ATLANTIC PIONEER

The great Atlantic pioneer of that time was Portugal. Indeed, it was almost an accident of history that an Italian sailor in the employ of Spain made the most crucial of all the landfalls. By the time Columbus set sail in 1492, Portugal could already claim more than seven decades of Atlantic exploration and discovery. It was Portugal that discovered Madeira and the Canary Islands, settled the Azores, and made the great daring adventurers along the western coast of Africa. Since as early as 1415, the chain of Portuguese adventures had been given firm and persistent backing by Prince Henry the Navigator, the younger son of the King of Portugal. For almost four decades, he led Portugal through a vibrant period of exploration, and each new probe into the Atlantic added to the seafaring experience and to the stockpile of knowledge about winds and currents. New trades developed in the islands, and in Africa new discoveries were made as the Portuguese relentlessly pushed further and further southward along the African coast. Finally, in 1488, Bartholomew Dias reached the Cape of Good Hope. He might have sailed on into the Indian Ocean, but a mutinous crew stopped further exploration. It was nine years later that Vasco da Gama reached India by the all-water route. The rate of return on the capital invested in that expedition approached 6,000 percent—certainly a lucrative investment. There can be little doubt that in the perspective of that time da Gama, not Columbus, could claim credit for the more celebrated and rewarding discovery. By the turn of the century, Portugal controlled a rich trading realm. The cargoes of spices from Asia; gold, ivory, and slaves from Africa; and sugar from the Atlantic Islands all swelled her coffers.

Of course, the all-water route to the East Indies offered military possibilities as well as economic opportunities. The traditional vessels of the Indian Ocean were no match for the well-armed ships of Portugal. Taking advantage of their military superiority, the Portuguese frequently attempted to block the traditional flows of goods to the Italian city-states in the Mediterranean and to win trading concessions from rulers in the East. It was their ambition to monopolize the trade from the Far East. Despite disruptions, the trade flows along the traditional routes persisted, and Portugal's military excursions in the Far East went in vain.

Although haltingly successful, these ventures proved extremely costly in the long run, and their anticipated goal of complete monopoly was never realized. In the process, Portugal's limited resources were severely strained, and many soldiers, slaves, and ships were lost. Actually, it was not until 1600 that the preeminence of Venice in the eastern trade was destroyed. This was accomplished by the Dutch East India company. The coup was made by economic means: by superior efficiency in shipping and in commercial organization. Superior warfare technology and strength also helped, but they played a secondary role.

SHIFTS IN THE CENTER OF WEALTH

As the realm of Portuguese trade expanded, the relative economic position of the Mediterranean began to slip back. The volume of trade in the Mediterranean continued to increase in absolute terms throughout the sixteenth century, but not in proportion to the size of the Atlantic trade. The centers of commerce and wealth and the balance of power were shifting steadily to the nations bordering the Atlantic Ocean.

In addition to Portugal's colorful seafaring adventures that initiated new southern and far eastern trades, other developments in the North Atlantic were reinforcing the shift of European economic activity. New discoveries of fishing grounds such as that resulting from John Cabot's expedition from England to Newfoundland in 1497 spurred fishing activity in the North. The main force of Northwest European expansion, however, was in the older, established trades. To a disproportionate degree, trade expanded in the cold-zone products—grain, salt, salted fish, woolen cloth, furs, iron, timber, and naval stores. These bulky staple items could withstand the high cost of transportation, since they were transported almost entirely by sea, and unlike the Asian all-water trade, in which vessels were typically full only on the return to Europe, the trade between the Baltic and the northwestern Atlantic regions fully utilized ships in both directions. This had the effect of lowering the average cost of freight and thereby encouraging trade, even in these heavy, bulky products.

As markets widened and trade increased throughout Europe and the rest of the world, greater **regional specialization in production** took place. Areas increasingly specialized in products that they could produce most efficiently and traded these for other goods produced more cheaply elsewhere. In this way, there were **gains from exchange,** and people became better off in terms of material wealth. In addition, the growth of market exchanges during this period encouraged greater **division of labor.** Individual workers slowly but steadily took on specialized tasks instead of performing all tasks necessary to produce an item from start to finish. As each worker specialized in one or a few steps of the line of production, output per worker increased.

ANTWERP

As the volume of trade increased in sixteenth-century Europe, this led to the dazzling preeminence of Antwerp. At this time Antwerp became the **entrepôt** of trade between the traditional city-states of northern Italy, Germany, England, and Holland. Antwerp prospered as the distribution center for German wares of silver, copper, lead, and zinc, and for Italian, Flemish, and English manufactures. Both its shipping and commercial services flourished, and, like a magnet, it pulled in merchants from all over Europe.

The rise of Antwerp was critically linked to the rise of the Atlantic trade. Its commercial superiority was determined primarily by its willingness to enforce contracts and reduce risks of exchange and by its advantageous location. Like the Italian city-states of an earlier era, Antwerp now sat astride the great crossroads of trade. New discoveries of copper, lead, zinc, and silver deposits in southern Germany, Hungary, and Poland further stimulated trade throughout western Europe. The expansion of population and growing **urbanization** also increased demand. Moreover, insurance coverage became more common, and market exchanges became less risky. By the late fifteenth century, the Netherlands had become one of the most densely populated and economically advanced areas in Europe.

Antwerp's zenith was reached around 1560, when it contained a population in excess of 100,000. In the West, only Paris, London, and Seville matched or surpassed Antwerp in size. Trading activity was continuous throughout the year, but four lengthy trade fairs annually provided periods of financial settlement.

Wars and the division of the Netherlands between 1572 and 1585 finally ended Antwerp's supremacy. Its decline paralleled the weakening prosperity of central Europe, which had been sapped by peasant wars in religious and dynastic struggles throughout the middle of the century. By this time, the silver mines of central Europe were cutting back production. The value of silver was decreasing. Now, for the first time, the treasures of America became a truly critical factor in shaping the economic landscape of Europe. The influx of American silver undercut silver production in Europe. The flows of Spanish-American treasure made Cadiz the attractive new entrepôt. In addition, it provided the sinews of war and whetted the Spanish crown's appetite for empire.

The voyages of discovery, together with the swelling tides of commerce, were now exerting heavy pressure on the balance of power in Europe. By the late sixteenth century, dramatic shifts had already occurred. The minor short-run effects of this discovery were giving way to highly significant long-run effects. Although contemporary Europeans had lightly dismissed Christopher Columbus' discovery, later observers were beginning to understand what we know so well: Columbus had placed a bounty of riches at the feet of Spain. He had given Spain an empire that won the envy of Europe.

SPANISH COLONIZATION

The first Europeans to secure a foothold in the New World were the Spanish. They colonized primarily for the dual purpose of extracting wealth and Christianizing the native Indians. To accomplish this double objective, they introduced a practice entitled **encomienda** (commendation), which had been developed earlier in the Canary Islands shortly after the Spanish took over there. To "civilize" the native population and to convert the Indians to Christianity, each populated community was placed under the "protection and authority" of a Spanish overseer. In return for the overseer's "services" and direction, the villagers had to pay tribute in the form of labor services. Of course, the day-to-day direction of encomienda rested with the overseers. They were little influenced in any practical way by the remote authority of the Spanish Crown or the Catholic Church. Therefore, in practice, many abused the system for personal gain. They forced people to give many hours of labor in slave or prison-gang fashion.

The first several decades of Spanish colonization were concentrated in the islands of the Caribbean. It was there that encomienda was the most damaging, with effects even more harsh than slavery. Because the overseers had no rights of ownership in the natives, they had little incentive to care for them properly. Nevertheless, they had "legal claim" to their labor services and this gave ample incentive to work them relentlessly. The combination of poor care, bad nutrition, overwork, and the spread of European diseases (mainly smallpox, typhus, and measles) virtually wiped out the islands' populations. For instance, within several decades, the native population of Española, which today forms the nations of Haiti and the Dominican Republic, fell from approximately 300,000 to several hundred. The populations of Cuba and Puerto Rico suffered similar declines, and other areas, such as the Bahamas and some of the leeward islands that were not settled, had their populations stripped to work the mines of Puerto Rico. The excesses of this system on the islands were gradually curbed on the mainland, and *encomienda* was finally outlawed in 1549. Nevertheless, harsh treatment and disease continued to take their toll. Within two decades of Cortez's conquest of Mexico in 1518–1519, the pre-conquest population of twenty-five million there had been halved. It had been estimated that, in 1500, the population of Spanish America approximately matched that of western Europe. By 1600, the relative numbers were merely one-tenth of Europe's. The forced exchange of Christianity for bullion and treasure was costly for the natives of Spanish America.

The dramatic decline of the native population was offset only to a minor degree by Spanish settlers. By 1650 there were about one-half million residents who were white or predominantly white. Most of these were Spanish-born males of working age, since few women and children were attracted to the New World. Although black slaves had begun to be imported as early as 1503, it was not until the seventeenth century that large numbers arrived in the New World. By the mid-seventeenth century, approximately one-half million black slaves from Africa were working the sugar islands of the Caribbean. In addition, there were another one-half million people of mixed blood. However, in all of Mexico and the central regions of Peru and Bolivia, there now remained only two million pure-blooded Indians.

NEW CROPS

Although the great treasure flows and the striking demographic shifts were the most dramatic changes brought by the Spanish, important cultural and organizational changes also affected the daily lives of people in the Americas. Imported European techniques, commodities, and animals altered economic activity in America. Despite Spanish attention to the mining of precious metals, the basic structure of the economy remained agrarian. This sector was sharply influenced by new European crops, including wheat, barley, rye, sugar, onions, cabbage, peas, apples, and peaches. Having only the llama, the dog, and the turkey as original livestock, the natives discovered that horses, cattle, and oxen afforded possibilities for heavy plowing and better land transportation. In addition, these European livestock were accompanied by hogs, chickens, and sheep, which led to herding activities and improved diets. Of course, European advances in metallurgy and the use of guns and powder had significant effects as well.

In return, a variety of new crops was also introduced to the Europeans. These included tobacco, Indian corn or maize, beans, peanuts, white potatoes, squash, pumpkins, tomatoes, chocolate, vanilla, and avocados. But none of these items became commercially vital. The first cash crop of any significance in the trans-Atlantic trade did not develop until almost a century after Columbus. That crop was sugar, produced in the depopulated islands of the Caribbean. The new labor supply used to produce sugar in these islands was imported. By the mid-seventeenth century, the islands were crowded with African slaves working Spanish-run sugar plantations.

The character of Spanish settlement was altered to a degree by this new cultivation. The extraction of mineral treasure by forced labor had been on a "take and go" basis. The sugar plantations, however, required

Economics at Work

Incentives Matter

The common notion that Native Americans had a reverence for natural resources at any cost is misleading. Economic principles teach us that individuals regardless of race, sex, or time are concerned with improving their own lot. When resources are very scarce people tend to conserve more and when resources are more abundant they tend to conserve less.

For example, the Plains Indians were great buffalo hunters. But before the arrival of horses and guns in the seventeenth century, the tribes of the Plains had to rely on agricultural goods and the few buffalo they could kill. One labor intensive technique the Indians would use was "cliff drives." This is where a band of warriors forced the buffalo off the side of cliffs. Alternatively, buffalo hunters would disguise themselves as wolves and sneak up on the herds with their bow and arrows. But either way the downing of a buffalo was a heralded event.

Early on when the buffalo was scarce (difficult to kill), it was managed carefully with very little waste. For example, the hide was used for moccasins, tepees, drums, and clothing; the hair for ropes, pillows and game balls. The stomach liner was used to make waterproof containers. And the bones made excellent hide scrapers, shovels, knives, war clubs, and sled runners (the large rib bones). Even buffalo droppings (also known as buffalo chips) were used for fuel in cooking and heating.

However, when the Spaniards introduced the horse to the Plains Indians, agricultural pursuits were shed for the nomadic life of the hunter. As Native Americans improved their riding skills, the killing of a buffalo became a common event.

Did the Plains Indians use of this resource change as the cost of acquiring a buffalo fell? Yes, at the lower cost of obtaining a buffalo, only the most desirable portions of the buffalo were valued (hump ribs, tongue, and the intestines); the remainder were left for the coyotes and vultures.

permanent settlement. Forced labor was still used, but now the roots of Spanish occupation sank deeper and became more lasting. As the plantations prospered, both Spanish immigrants and African slaves poured in, and implanted agrarian capitalism. In this way, the commercial link between the New and the Old World was solidly forged.

Issue: American Treasure, European Prices, and the Rise of Commercial Capitalism

CAPITAL FLOWS

Spanish colonization involved numerous special features. Perhaps none was so unique as that involving the direction and magnitude of capital flows. Ordinarily, one might suspect that the taking of a new frontier would require substantial subsidization from the older, established regions and commercial center. To be sure, in the first years of Spanish conquest, Spanish nobles and merchants did supply financial support for ships and stores. By 1506, however, several Spanish colonists had accumulated sizable fortunes from gold mines worked on the islands of Española. These, in part, financed the exploration and settlement of Cuba, Jamaica, and Puerto Rico. In turn, the profits from investments in Cuba supported a series of mainland expedition that, after 1516, led to the conquest of Mexico by Cortez. Further conquests were financed by wealth extracted from Mexico. In this stepwise fashion, fortunes acquired in the Americas led to further expansion and widened the Spanish hold on the new frontier. Consequently, it was only in the first decade or two after Columbus' discovery that Spain made any significant net investment in America. By the mid-sixteenth century, investments were steadily and sizably proceeding in the opposite direction.

These capital flows had profound repercussions in Europe. The flow of gold and silver from America to Europe was large. The lion's share of these Spanish imports was in silver and came after 1516. Compared to the supply of money at the beginning of the sixteenth century, these imports approximately tripled the total supply of money in Europe.

Besides raising Spain to a position of military dominance, the influx of treasure led to higher and higher prices throughout Europe. Inflation became the order of the day. Spanish prices swept upward, and, in 1600, were 340 percent above their level in 1500. Similarly, England experienced a rise of almost 260 percent over the century, and France experienced one of 220 percent.

THE HAMILTON THESIS

The phenomenal impact of American treasure on European prices, commerce, and growth has been analyzed in a pioneering study by Earl J. Hamilton. Hamilton summarized his conclusions as follows:

> It is difficult . . . to see how anything else could have been more important than the great lag of wages behind prices in certain economically advanced countries during the price revolution. Capitalism required capital, and it would not be easy to imagine a more powerful instrument for providing it than forced saving through a highly favorable price-wage ratio. The high rates of profit when prices were rising and wages, the chief cost, were lagging gave a strong inducement to invest savings in productive enterprise. Rising prices penalized delay in investment and by lowering the effective rate of interest encouraged borrowing for investment in anticipation of earnings. In short, rising prices and lagging wages provided capital and gave strong incentives to use it capitalistically. Other things anywhere near equal, capitalism could hardly have failed to flourish.[1]

In short, Hamilton argues that the influx of treasure drove up both prices and wages, but prices more rapidly. As real wages declined, income and wealth were distributed increasingly to the favor of merchants and capitalists. Since these classes supposedly had unusually strong inclinations to save and invest, this led to higher rates of capital formation and ultimately to economic growth throughout Europe.

A great deal of the evidence strongly supports Hamilton's thesis. The large increase in the money supply and the tremendous rise in prices are certainly without doubt. Real wages in Spain, England, and France fell dramatically over the course of the sixteenth century. But the upward march of prices relative to wages did not favor industrial or manufactured goods. Hamilton's analysis did not go far enough and was left at too aggregate a level. The main cause of the general price index rising was the soaring prices of food and items related to agriculture. The prices of finished goods rose less than the prices of raw materials. Consequently, the redistribution of wealth was not so much from workers to capitalists as from the nonagricultural to the agricultural sectors.

In light of the high rates of population growth, it is not surprising to observe a redistribution of income between these sectors. Increasingly, land became relatively more scarce in Europe: Labor–land ratios increased with the rise of population. In all likelihood, average output per agricultural worker declined, as output from additional workers fell to very low levels. Large increases in the supply of labor tended to hold wages down, while the swelling population exerted upward pressures on prices for agricultural goods. Meanwhile rents on land soared higher and higher as agricultural prices rose. As a result, it was landowners, not merchants or industrial capitalists, who gained from the relative price movements of the period.

It is important here to distinguish between relative and absolute price changes. The influx of treasure and the consequent increase in the money supply did spur inflation. This had the tendency to push all prices higher, over time. But general inflation—a rise in average prices—tells us little about changes in relative prices. Some prices moved up faster than others, and for these differential movements we need to look at the condition of supply and demand for various goods and productive resources. The general forces of inflation fail to explain differences in relative price movement, but relative price changes lie at the heart of Hamilton's thesis.

The influx of American treasure did not by itself cause a redistribution of income among economic classes or sectors that led to economic development. It did, however, enrich Spain relative to other nations, at least temporarily. But there is little indication that this advantage raised the productivity or soundness of the Spanish economy. The flood of wealth may even have encouraged Spain to undertake the many ill-fated military ventures that eventually led to its decline. With the exhaustion of American mines around 1650, Spain's vital resource influx dried up, and Spain quickly slipped to a second-rate power in the league of nations. No empire of similar dominance has ever undergone such a rapid rise and fall. No other has rested on such a temporary base.

DEFINITIONS OF NEW TERMS

REGIONAL SPECIALIZATION IN PRODUCTION Regional specialization in production results from the opportunity to trade and from different conditions for production among areas. Each region will tend to produce and trade more of the items they can produce at lowest cost (relative to other regions).

GAINS FROM EXCHANGE Gains from exchange are produced when the personal value or satisfaction of the goods received exceed the personal value or satisfaction of the goods (or money) given in exchange. Note that in most voluntary exchanges, both parties to the exchange gain; that is, they "feel" better off from the trade.

DIVISION OF LABOR In division of labor, individual workers take on specialized tasks instead of attempting to do everything necessary to produce a product or service.

ENTREPÔT An entrepôt is a main center for trade and commercial activity, such as New York today or Antwerp in the sixteenth century.

URBANIZATION When a larger fraction of the total population lives in towns and cities (urban centers), urbanization is said to exist.

ENCOMIENDA Encomienda is an arrangement whereby Spanish overseers extracted labor services from the native population. It was similar but not identical to slavery.

ENDNOTES

[1] Earl J. Hamilton, "Prices as a Factor in Business Growth: Prices and Progress," *The Journal of Economic History,* Volume 69, 2 (Fall 1952): 338–339.

Five
Opening Up North America

The First British Colonies

The most difficult times by far were the first years of settlement. The North American wilderness initially proved disastrous to settlers and investors alike, and the art of survival and the lessons of taking the frontier were learned at great cost and amidst great hardship.

Compared to other nation-states, England was slow to colonize. By the time the British established their first settlements on the mainland, the Dutch were already in North America and in the East and West Indies, the Spanish had been in North and South America for over a century, and the French were already in Canada and the West Indies. The first English attempts at colonization were clear-cut failures. Sir Humphrey Gilbert and Sir Walter Raleigh failed dismally in their attempts in the 1580s to establish bases in Newfoundland and the Carolinas. Raleigh's outpost on Roanoke Island in North Carolina was designed to harass Spanish treasure ships, but, after a necessary departure for supplies, Raleigh's captain, John White, returned in 1590 to find no one or no records whatsoever. Roanoke is therefore referred to as the "lost colony."

This "lost colony" forcefully accents the great hardships faced by newcomers to America. A majority of the earliest settlers in the seventeenth century died within two years of their arrival. Starvation, disease, Indian attacks, and other calamities were commonplace.

In 1607, the Plymouth Company landed a group of settlers near the mouth of the Sagadohoc River in Maine. Those who survived the winter ordeals packed up and returned to England. In that same year, the London Company landed a party of 105 men at Jamestown, Virginia. Of these, 67 died within the first year, but 400 new arrivals in 1609 added to their numbers. By the spring of the next year, frontier hazards had cut their number to 60! All cattle, horses, chickens had been eaten and one man had reputedly dined on his wife.[1] The disheartened survivors were actually heading down river to leave for England when new supplies and more settlers on three ships arrived to change their plans. In this way, Jamestown eventually won the dubious honor of being the first permanent British settlement in North America.

Much of the problem was that the earliest settlers had not yet discovered any commercial enterprise to enrich them materially or any way to provide for themselves, and many were more adventurers than settlers. Vital energy and time was often futilely spent on get-rich-quick schemes; for example, in 1607 and 1608, shiploads of mica and yellow ore were sent to England. Later, the word came back; the minerals were worthless.

In 1622, an Indian uprising near Jamestown resulted in the massacre of 347 settlers. The very next year another 500 died from disease, and this prompted a "royal investigation" of the state of things in the colony. The investigation revealed that 6,000 people had left England for Virginia between 1607 and 1623. Of these, 4,000 had perished. Archeologist Ivor Noel Hume writes, "It is hard to image how much hope, regret, fear, hatred, hunger, pain and dying were experienced at this place [Jamestown]." In short, the odds of surviving in early Jamestown were slim.

By 1620, the Plymouth Company had established the first New England colony, and in 1630 the Massachusetts Bay Company established a second outpost in New England. Then followed Rhode Island, Connecticut, New Hampshire, and the rest.

There can be little doubt that the human costs of taking the colonial frontier were enormous. As the distinguished historian, Charles Andrews, has said, "This was the 'Starving Time' for Virginia, just as there were to be starving times for Bermuda, Plymouth, and Barbados, when men suffered and died, because they had not yet learned the art of colonization, and had come to America inadequately supplied and equipped and unfamiliar with the method of wresting a living from the wilderness."[2]

There can be little doubt that during the earliest years, the white man's economic vitality in North America was at the barest minimum to sustain life. Certainly, it was below that of the resident Indians and provided only the fewest essentials of a subsistence livelihood.

Mercantilism and the Quest for Empire

Colonization was pursued for the purpose of strengthening the parent nation-states, and it greatly affected the balance of power among the nation-states. As we observed with Spain and as we know today, the basis of power is economic strength. At the time of British colonization in North America, the policies of mercantilism were the order of the day.

Mercantilist policies put into practice the idea that the greater the wealth a nation had, the more power it had. Wealth and precious metals were viewed as one, and, in order to increase the inflow of precious bullion, governments encouraged exports and discouraged imports. When exports exceeded imports in value terms (a "favorable balance of trade"), the difference was paid in gold or silver (specie). Accordingly, government intervention took the forms of taxing goods coming into a nation, of expanding colonial territory, and of providing incentives to encourage the sale abroad of domestically produced goods. In other words, there was an attempt to force exports from the mother country to be greater than imports. However, mercantilist precepts ignored a common principle: both parties gain from voluntary trade, whether that trade be between individuals, states, or nations. As an afterthought, we might say that the goal that government intervention should have had was the increase in both exports and imports—a balanced increase in all trade with all nations. But in the hostile world of that era, it was best to develop and trade with one's own colonies. Trade with other nation-states risked the possibility of being cut off from needed goods by war (which was frequent) or by an adverse change in policy.

Differences in Colonization Techniques

Whereas Spain was able to exploit an existing population, using the infamous encomienda system, the British (and others) were unable to force the elusive North American natives into slavery. Nor were there any get-rich-quick opportunities, despite hopes to the contrary. Only permanent settlement and commercial production (for export) could wring wealth from this region.

Even though some of the original English colonies were started with government help, most of them were private ventures in which the English Crown did not directly participate. The lure of profits induced joint stock companies, such as the Virginia Company and the Plymouth Company, to raise money to finance these colonies. The stockholders felt they were entitled to a return on their investment. As it turned out, however, there were dismal financial failures. For instance, capital costs for Jamestown before 1621 exceeded £200,000 (over $20 million in today's prices), but none of this principal or any interest was ever repaid. Several colonies, such as Maryland, founded by Lord Baltimore, and Pennsylvania, founded by William Penn, were started as individual proprietorships. They, too, were unable to turn a profit. They tried to secure revenues from the settlers by annual payments, called quit rents, but these generally proved futile to collect.

It may seem hard to believe that the original profit-seeking entrepreneurs who set up colonies in the New World were unable to profit or generate large rewards. After all, wasn't the New World filled with untold natural riches? Weren't there abundant lands full of timber and rich soil? Yes, indeed, but it takes more than one factor of production to yield a product.

The Problem of Scarcity

Land was abundant, but labor was scarce. So was capital. Originally there were few tools, very little equipment (such as those needed to clear land), and almost no manufacturing implements. Normally, when land is abundant relative to labor and capital, as in early America, land is relatively low priced. Labor and capital were relatively scarce and, hence, relatively high priced. The colonists originally could do little with the raw land except work some of the already-cleared areas that the Indians had abandoned. Later, as tools, horses, and other livestock were imported and better crop-planting methods were developed, more land was tilled, but even then there was a limit to output because that depended primarily on the number of hands available.

WAYS TO GET WORKERS

There was always a problem of obtaining inexpensive labor, and several methods were used to induce more people to come to the New World. By peopling North America, England was assured strong colonies, a great empire, and more power. Basically, England employed four methods to attract laborers to the New World.

HEAD RIGHTS Many, although not all, of the British colonies lured workers by offering "head rights" of land ownership. Under the head right system, approximately fifty acres were promised to each person who paid his own way to the colonies; an additional fifty acres was due one who paid the way for others. But because the costs of transport were exorbitantly high, relatively few individuals could afford the expense.

LAND GRANTS Whole groups of settlers could obtain land grants for organizing their own communities. Generally, this happened when a religious minority wanted to escape persecution in Europe. The Pilgrims are a good example.

WHITE INDENTURE Many who yearned to come to the New World but could not pay their own way solved the problem by selling their labor in advance, for a specified length of time. Four years was probably the most common period, although terms ranged from two to seven years, depending on the relative skill of the worker or the desirability of the location. The indenture contract was generally signed with a shipowner or with the owner's recruiting agent. As soon as the servant was delivered alive at an American port, the contract was sold to a planter or merchant.

Servants bound by indenture worked at their employer's demand in return for room, board, and certain "freedom dues" of money or land to be received at the end of the indenture period. Indentured servants generally came from the ranks of farmers, unskilled workers, artisans, and domestic servants; occasionally, better educated and more skilled people also became indentured servants. With very few exceptions, they came voluntarily, drawn by the prospect of owning land, which in Britain and on the Continent was an impossible dream for most. It is estimated that 50 percent of the total white immigrants to the Northern Colonies came as indentured servants. This figure is even higher for some colonies such as Virginia, Maryland, and Pennsylvania where as many as 75 percent of the white immigrants came over as indentured servants.

As the nineteenth century approached, higher wages and lower transportation costs reduced the average duration of service and ultimately led to the demise of indentured servitude in America. In the final analysis, indentured servitude closely resembled a highly competitive labor market.

MIGRATION Although migration was a major source of labor in the earlier years, the largest numbers crossed the Atlantic in the eighteenth century. Nearly 100,000 Germans came between 1710 and 1770, most of them to Pennsylvania, and between 100,000 and 125,000 Irish and Scots also arrived, with the Scots tending to prefer the South. Many English came as well, but the largest English migration took place in the seventeenth century. The total of 250,000 to 300,000 whites who came between 1700 and 1775 contributed between 15 to 20 percent of the total increase of the white population. Consequently, the primary source of the white populations' increase, from as early as the mid-seventeenth century, was due to natural factors.

BLACK SLAVERY Slaves were first introduced to North America by Dutch traders in 1619. Eventually, slaves were imported in British and American ships. The slave population was concentrated in the South rather than the North for several reasons; the nature of the crop, the size of the average landholdings, and the climate. Both the rice grown in the South Carolina area (which was almost exclusively done by slaves) and the tobacco grown in the Chesapeake Bay region required lots of labor. Consequently, the major markets for slaves were Virginia and South Carolina.

The average landholdings were typically larger in the southern colonies than the northern or middle colonies because of liberal land policies (recall the head right system) and primogeniture. Primogeniture is the legal right of the eldest son to inherit the parent's estate (a common practice in the Colonial South). Consequently, primogeniture prevented the large landholdings from being divided into smaller parcels among all the children upon the death of their parents.

Slave labor was bought for a fixed sum of money. Since workers were not paid by the hour, there was reason to keep the slaves working as much as possible, which was more practical in the South, where the climate permitted outdoor work almost every day, summer and winter. In addition, the crops that could be grown in the South required a great deal of unskilled labor that could be done under limited supervision. Everything about the plantation system favored slavery.

Although just beginning on the mainland colonies, elsewhere in the seventeenth century slavery was expanding at a rapid rate, especially in the sugar islands of the Caribbean. Only 6 percent of the total number of Africans involved in forced immigration through the Atlantic slave trade were imported to North America. The majority of slaves in the slave trade were sent to Brazil and the Caribbean.

Slavery was actually unimportant in North America for almost the first century of settlement. Before 1730, for example, there were fewer than 100,000 slaves in the mainland colonies. By the Revolution, that figure had grown to over 500,000. The slave trade was booming, and the total number of incoming blacks matched that of immigrant whites. Accordingly, the black population which was around 4 percent of the total in 1650, grew to more than 20 percent by the time of the American Revolution. Initially, the import of slaves was the most important source of increase in the slave population. But by 1720, and throughout the eighteenth and nineteenth century, the natural rate of increase dominated the growth of black population. At the end of the colonial period, the concentration of blacks in the population varied widely among the colonies. In the northern colonies, blacks averaged less than 5 percent of the population, but in the rich rice fields of South Carolina their proportion was 70 percent, and it was 47 percent in Virginia, and 33 percent in Maryland. In contrast, the proportion of blacks in the British and French sugar island of the Caribbean approached 90 percent.

What to Produce and Where?

At first, of course, there was little question of how the colonists should spend their working time. It was either produce or die. Later on, however, it was no longer a question of just surviving, but of rising above the subsistence level. Historically, this has been accomplished by finding one's *comparative advantage*. It was obvious in most of the colonies, at least at first, that their comparative advantage lay mainly in agricultural production, and so almost all of the population was engaged in this endeavor. The colonists were not self-sufficient, however. They may have been able to produce the agricultural products they wanted, but there were certain manufactured goods that they could obtain only by trade with other countries.

Of course, the most obvious country to trade with was England. The colonists spoke the English language, were familiar with their customs and the system of prices, and could do business in a relatively easy manner. In other words, the *transactions* or *business costs* involved in trading with England were generally less than those with other countries.[3] As the English trades and other overseas trades developed, specialization in production in the various colonies became more and more apparent.

THE SOUTH

The South had a relatively large population. By 1770, there were over 1.4 million southern colonists as opposed to nearly 600,000 in New England and a similar number in the middle colonies.

The South developed exports that were complementary to English production. These included tobacco, indigo, rice, and other items that were not produced in England. By 1770, over one-half of the exports of the colonies were accounted for by southern production. In fact, even thereafter, trade with England was dominated by southern staples.

TOBACCO Tobacco use in England spread slowly. It was first introduced by traveling Spaniards, but King James I dubbed the habit "a vile and stinking custom." Nevertheless, Sir Walter Raleigh and others popularized it, and when it was found that good-quality tobacco could be grown in Maryland and in Virginia more cheaply than in most other parts of the world, the English were delighted. Even the English Crown was glad to be free of Spanish tobacco imports—so happy, in fact, that England banned its production at home and gave the Chesapeake Bay area monopoly rights to tobacco production in the empire.

It is easily understood why slavery and the plantation system developed once it was found that tobacco could be grown in the warm southern climates. Tobacco cultivation required only very crude implements and much unskilled labor. If the old land lost its fertility, there was much new land available. The plantation system, with its large numbers of slaves, was well suited for such production. Here the task system could be used, and supervision over each slave's "piecework" was relatively easy.

From the outset, productivity advances in tobacco were so remarkable that prices of Chesapeake tobacco fell from around 28 pence (sterling) per pound before 1620 to between 3 and 6 pence per pound 10 years later. Another productivity surge between 1640 and 1670 pushed the price downward almost to 1 penny per pound. There it remained, except for short-run cyclical variations, for the remainder of the colonial period. These striking reductions in costs resulted not from falling wages or rents, but rather from efficiency gains that sharply raised output per worker (and per acre). By the end of the seventeenth century, the Chesapeake population had expanded to almost 100,000, and the area was exporting more than 36 million pounds of tobacco annually.

Developments in tobacco production showed that mercantilism was not only pervasive among the great nation-states of that time, it also was practiced by the southern colonies themselves. A free enterprise environment sometimes was thought to hinder the wealth of the southern colonists. For example, by community effort, one-half of the Virginia tobacco crop was burned in order to maintain prices in 1639, and in 1733 the growing of tobacco was again restricted.

Actually, the burning and restricting of tobacco was not as foolish as it may sound. Planters believed that the demand for tobacco, like that of many agricultural products today, was relatively **price inelastic;** that is, the quantity purchased was relatively unresponsive to price changes. Therefore, a rise in the price of tobacco would not lead to a drastic reduction in the quantity demanded. Conversely, a fall in the price would not lead to a drastic increase. Given this type of demand situation, a bumper crop of tobacco could only be sold if the southern colonists were willing to accept an extremely large decrease in the price. To avoid this in 1639, planters burned portions of their tobacco crops; such "burnings" have been periodic occurrences in our history.

Also, it is interesting to note that most farms, even the highly specialized tobacco plantations, were self-sufficient in most foodstuffs, especially Indian corn, vegetables, and livestock. As the growth of demand for tobacco slowed in eighteenth-century Europe, the Chesapeake region complemented their tobacco production with wheat production which became another important commercial crop.

RICE Rice became a major export crop of South Carolina by 1700. It was grown in low-lying fields and sometimes in swamplands. These could be irrigated with some control by allowing tidewater rivers to flood them. Like tobacco, it required a warm climate and considerable unskilled labor. Of all the mainland colonial products, it was the most conducive to a plantation system.

INDIGO Indigo, another major crop of South Carolina, was first introduced on the mainland in 1743 by Eliza Lucas, one of America's first female entrepreneurs. She had imported the plants from the Caribbean. Indigo was useful to the British as a dye for the textile industries. Because of their influence in Parliament, the British paid a special subsidy, or bounty, to indigo producers. In other words, any colonist who produced indigo was assured a specific subsidy payment from the British in addition to whatever the crop fetched in sale on the open market in Britain.

Indigo proved to be a useful and convenient crop to grow because it was complimentary to rice in its use of labor services; that is, the peak seasonal periods, when most of the unskilled workers were needed in the indigo fields, were different from the peak seasonal periods when the workers were engaged in the rice fields.

NAVAL STORES The southern colonies, and other colonies as well, produced significant amounts of accessories and materials for ships, or *naval stores,* as they were called. These were items such as pitch, tar, and turpentine, which were true forest derivatives.

THE MIDDLE COLONIES

The middle colonies (dubbed the "bread colonies") comprised the fertile agricultural areas of Pennsylvania, Delaware, New York, and New Jersey. Here livestock and grain could be more cheaply produced than in New England or the South. That is, the middle colonies' comparative advantage lay in the production of various grains and livestock. There was much less direct trade with England from these colonies, because their comparative advantage was essentially the same as that of the English, and England also produced these goods relatively cheaply. The middle colonies, in fact, tended to import more than they exported to England. What they did to balance their trade deficit was to trade with southern Europe, the West Indies, and other colonies. Nevertheless, often this was not enough, and English merchants commonly granted short-term loans (of a revolving type) to finance trade.

NEW ENGLAND

The New England area consisted mainly of very small farms that produced only for local town markets. The comparative advantage of the New England area was fish and ships. New Englanders had easy access to ocean waters, which were filled with fish, as well as to vast forest lands. They exported ship timbers, especially white pine for ship masts, and whale oil and codfish. Later on, the New England colonists became extremely efficient shipbuilders, and many New Englanders became world traders and sailors directly in competition with the mother country. In fact, their most important economic activity was providing shipping services, which they provided throughout the Atlantic, the Caribbean, and other seas.

Colonial Population

From 1650 to 1775 the colonial population growth rate averaged roughly 3.5 percent per year. This is an extremely rapid population growth rate, very similar to those rates we see today in less-developed countries. In some societies, the large population growth might be detrimental to economic growth as the larger population places greater demands on fertile farmlands. This was surely not the case in the mainland colonies where land was fertile, plentiful, and waiting to be developed. Colonial living standards rose despite a population boom. To be able to escape the so called "Malthusian Trap" (discussed in Chapter 3) was an unprecedented outcome in economic history.

Most of the white population increases in the colonies after 1700 were due to natural increases (an excess of birth rates over death rates). As a result of the high birth rates, family size tended to be large. For example, Benjamin Franklin was 1 of 17 children and Patrick Henry was 1 of 19 kids. Patrick Henry must have enjoyed being part of such a large family because he was the father of 17 children and the grandfather of 60. The typical colonial family was not as large, on average six to seven children (slightly higher in the rural areas) as compared to four children on average in England. However, because of the high fatality rate associated with childbirth, a man might have to remarry a couple of times to have a family of seven or eight. In fact, complications associated with pregnancies was one of the leading causes of death for colonial women.

One important factor that led to the high population growth rate in the colonies was early marriages. The North American colonists tended to marry young, in their early twenties. This was not the case in Europe, where people were not likely to marry until their late twenties. Most colonists chose to marry and those that did usually had children. Under these circumstances, it is not difficult to see why birth rates were high in the colonies. With a labor shortage in the colonies it made good economic sense to have a large family, especially in the rural areas. Children were a good investment—they covered their rearing costs at a very early age—especially on the farm where children could help with daily chores such as: fencing, clearing property, making candles, or feeding the livestock.

But high birth rates are only part of the reason for the natural population increase; the other reason being, of course, low death rates. Death rates were lower for the northern colonies than they were in the Mother Country. The abundant food supply, the low population densities, and the ample supply of wood for heating were all important factors that contributed to the low death rate. However, parts of the Lower South, especially in the seventeenth century, did not fare as well. With the presence of malaria, dysentery, and typhoid fever the death rate in this region was higher than the other regions of the mainland colonies.

The black population in the Mainland colonies also witnessed high birth rates and low death rates. This was in sharp contrast to the experience in the Caribbean. In the Caribbean, black population failed to expand through natural increases. The lack of a nutritional diet, a high rate of disease, and strenuous work on the sugar plantations translated into higher mortality rates for Caribbean blacks. The low black birth rates in the Caribbean were mostly due to the unequal sex ratios—males outnumbered females three to one.

Technology

The colonial era was one of painstakingly slow progress in technology. Adapting crops to the best-suited soils (and climates) raised output per acre and per worker in agriculture, and capital accumulation and other learning-by-doing efforts did as well. But compared to later times, there was little advance in knowledge and, especially within agriculture, the mainstay of colonial economic activity, there were no apparent technological improvements. The types of tools used, the care of animals, and the methods of agricultural production in general showed only minimal signs of change. Of course, there were some exceptions. For example, the Dutch farmers in Pennsylvania used various techniques to increase or maintain the fertility of their soil.

The lack of major technological advances was typical of other sectors as well. Few breakthroughs in knowledge led to advances in output relative to inputs. Yet output did increase relative to inputs as market participation increased, as business and economic organization improved, and as risks declined. For instance, cost reductions in shipping led to a fall in freight rates by almost one-half between 1675 and 1775. Most of this decline was due to the elimination of piracy and because of shorter port times for ships. As piracy was eliminated, dual purpose defense and cargo carrying vessels were gradually converted to simple all-cargo carrying vessels. They used simpler rigs and eliminated armaments and men to "man the guns." And once the British Navy had ousted most of the pirates from the western Atlantic, insurance rates tumbled. In addition, growth in the volume of trade led to centralized warehousing of goods, which reduced long and costly delays in ports. This saved on crew costs and reduced underutilization of capital.

The Principal-Agent Problem: A Historical Perspective

The principal-agent problem arises when the owner of a business or the chief executive officer (the principal) hires a manager (the agent) to perform stipulated tasks when the principal cannot know with certainty what the manager actually does. What keeps agents (managers) from pursuing their own narrow self-interest at the expense of the principal? For example, an owner might want a manager to work much harder than the manager wishes. This situation exists because imperfect and uncertain information often allows agents to pursue their self-interest through hidden agendas. The result is opportunistic behavior on the part of the agent, whether it is clerks pocketing money from customers or managers pocketing the frequent flier miles from corporate travel. Is there a way to deter such opportunistic behavior at a reasonable cost? One approach might be to write a detailed contract specifying to the letter in each possible situation. However, not only would such a contract be costly to write and negotiate, it might be prohibitively costly to monitor and enforce. And its far from a recent phenomenon.

Let's see how the Hudson Bay Company handled this principal-agent problem over three hundred years ago.

The Hudson Bay Company was a fur trading firm chartered in North America by the English Crown in 1670, with offices in Amsterdam

Vessel characteristics similar to those of the Dutch flute (first produced in 1595) diffused and spread once piracy was eliminated. This obstacle to **technical diffusion** was eliminated near the turn of the eighteenth century. Rapid changes in shipping, such as those just mentioned, soon followed, but **technological change**, in the sense of advances in knowledge, did not take place. Rather, change was the result of applying known techniques to new and now favorable circumstances. In general, this was characteristic of many of the improvements of the colonial era.

MANUFACTURING

Because of the high costs locally of wages and capital, and because of a limited and scattered domestic market, manufactured and other capital- and labor-intensive items were usually imported. Small-scale manufacturers such as homespun woolens, flour production, rum distilling, and iron production for domestic use were common regional activities, but not for major commercial enterprises. It was the immigration of skilled shipwrights to the new world and the availability of inexpensive raw materials in the fast forests which made shipbuilding a viable and major and London. Agents were so far away, it was very difficult to deter their opportunistic behavior. In order to discourage their managers from taking advantage of their chances to benefit themselves at their employer's expense, the Hudson Bay Company paid their managers well, gave them generous housing, food and travel allowances, and rewarded them with a bonus program based on productivity. They also closely monitored their managers' activities. The ships were searched often for smuggled goods and agents were required to keep accurate accounts of all transactions and inventories. While these ship ledgers reduced the potential for theft, they also provided valuable information for manager promotions or firings.

One major area of principal-agent conflict involved managers trading for themselves as well as for the company. Specifically, a manager could claim the more lucrative "deals" for himself, diverting what would have been company profits into his pocket. As an additional safeguard to policies such as ship searches, detailed ledgers, etc., the Hudson Bay Company required that their managers take an oath stating that they would not trade privately. While even the elaborate safeguards adopted were less than completely successful, the fact that the Hudson Bay Company is still in operation more than 300 years after its founding indicates that they have been reasonably successful in overcoming their principal-agent problem.[*]

[*]For a more detailed discussion of agency problems in early chartered companies, see Ann M. Carlos and Stephen Nicholas, "Grants of an Earlier Capitalism: The Early Chartered Companies as Modern Multinationals," *Business History Review*, Vol. 62, Autumn 1988.

manufacturing enterprise in the Northern colonies. In this instance, the locational advantage of low-cost materials offset the high-cost disadvantages of labor and capital.

Overseas Trade

From the very beginning, the colonists depended on overseas trade. Even by the late colonial period, overseas trade comprised between 15 and 20 percent of American incomes. This figure was probably even higher during the early colonial period.

The five leading commodity exports in the 13 Colonies (1768–1772), by value were tobacco, £766,000; bread and flour, £410,000; rice, £312,000; dried fish, £154,000; and indigo, £113,000. But shipping services, which earned foreign exchanges totaling nearly £600,000 annually at this time, were a source of exchange earnings second only to tobacco.

Throughout the colonial era, the colonies were not allowed to trade unimpeded in the world market, and the intensification of British controls on colonial trade finally spurred the outbreak of the Revolution.

Restricting the Colonies

The earliest general restrictions on colonial activity dated back to 1660 with the passage of the Navigation Acts. These acts were passed in response to Dutch supremacy in shipping and trade. As mentioned earlier, in 1595 the Dutch developed a commercial sailing boat called the *flute*, which was as good as any trading ship to be developed for centuries. To oust the highly efficient Dutch from British trades, the Navigation Acts imposed the stipulation that only English ships (including ships of its colonies) could be used for trade within the British Empire. Since the colonies were part of this empire, the laws applied to them also.

The period from 1763 onward was a period of intensification of British restrictions, repeated crises, and ultimately revolt. After the Seven Years War (1756–1763) between the English and the French, a series of edicts on the political and economic freedom of the colonists were handed down by the British Crown. For example, the Proclamation of 1763 declared that all colonial settlement must cease at the crest of the Appalachians. In order to raise money in the colonies to pay for the wars that Britain had waged to a significant degree on their behalf, the Sugar Act of 1764 assessed a tax on three pence per gallon on molasses.[4] However, much opposition arose in the colonies, and very little of this duty was ever collected. The colonists were unsympathetic to the plight of the British treasury.

Still attempting to obtain money from the colonies, the English promulgated the Stamp Act of 1765, providing for internal taxation— or, as the Stamp Act Congress in 1765 called it, "Taxation without representation." As a result of a boycott in the colonies, the British backed down and William Pitt made his famous appeal to Parliament to repeal the Stamp Act and also to modify the Sugar Act. It is important to note that the Stamp Act crisis generated a feeling of unity within the colonies, because the Act applied uniformly to all of them. When the Townshend Acts were passed in 1767, imposing duties on glass, paper, tea, and lead in paint, the colonists again followed with a boycott of English commodities. The results were impressive. By 1769, purchases of British goods were reduced by about 50 percent. This caused the British to back down again and to retreat into an uneasy truce that lasted until the Boston Tea Party of 1773. This escapade was in response to Parliament's attempt to aid the British East India Company, which was facing financial difficulties. Parliament had given the company the exclusive rights to the sale of tea in the colonies and allowed tea to be directly shipped from the East; previously it had to be brought to England first and then reexported. The result was a fall in the price of tea (and presumably happier customers in the colonies), but this hurt the traditional handlers of tea in the colonies and also smugglers. Many highly vocal colonists loudly responded that they did not want a British monopoly on the sales of that product, and several showed their wrath by dumping a shipload of tea into Boston Harbor.

Essentially, the period of negotiation ended in 1773. The colonists first found out that they were a fairly unified group after the Stamp Act was countered by the Stamp Act Congress. They also found strength in their ability to boycott British goods. The colonists demanded and eventually won their sovereignty. The "shot heard 'round the world" on April 19, 1775, finally led to political independence. A question remains, however, regarding their economic situation. Were the mercantilist restrictions placed on the colonies by the British Crown actually detrimental to their economic health?

INDEPENDENCE

By the time of the American Revolution, the white population of the colonies had reached almost 2.5 million and the blacks numbered nearly half a million. In 1776, the white colonial population had an average income rivaling and often surpassing that of citizens of the wealthiest, most advanced countries in Europe. Since taxes in the colonies were well below those in the mother country, the colonists' after-tax, or disposable, income was particularly favorable relative to those attainable in Europe. In any case, North America was the best hope for the ambitious poor worker, for wages were highest there and land most abundant.

From Alice Hanson Jones's estimates of wealth in the American colonies, we can derive estimates of average annual levels of income per capita. Gary Walton suggests average per capita income levels were between $1,300 and $1,500 in 2000 dollars and prices. Today, nations that comprise more than one half of the world's population currently have average per capita income levels below that of the free colonists over 230 years ago.

Inequalities in the Colonial Economy

"With liberty and justice for all" summarizes an American ideal. But does "justice for all" refer merely to equal rights before the law, or does it mean more-equal rights to good health, to job security, equal pay, equal leisure; in short, does it mean total equality?

Some people believe that the distribution of income that results from participation in a market economy such as ours is inherently unjust and that the income should be distributed equally. Actually, in the earliest years of colonial life in America, the goal of strict economic equality was earnestly pursued.

JAMESTOWN REVISITED

The Jamestown colony in Virginia originally operated as a collective in terms of both communal production and shared consumption. Belief in the ideals of fairness and equality, however, was not shared by all. Many individuals inevitably shirked assigned tasks, and the human characteristics of self-interest offset incentives to work and to innovate. To see why, consider the following hypothetical case.

Suppose that one out of 100 equally industrious workers suddenly decides to work half as hard as the others. As a result, daily output falls by 0.5 percent. If each worker receives an equal share of the total product, the one who shirks loses almost nothing in consumption, yet his work is markedly easier. Others follow suit, and with each new shirker, the total product continues to decrease. Alternatively, suppose one worker decides to work twice as hard as his or her peers. Total output then rises by about 0.5 percent. For twice the effort, however, this worker receives hardly anything more to consume. In such circumstances, greater work effort is not likely to occur. Now suppose that there are various tasks to be done, and one worker thinks of a way to perform a task better and more quickly. With collective production methods, the worker gains little, for the time freed is not rewarded to this person alone; for the sake of equality, it must be used to help others in the task. As a consequence, collective production methods and shared consumption often lead to relatively low levels of output and limited growth, especially when material gain is the main incentive to work.

Such was the situation in Jamestown in the early years. Single men complained of working, without due reward, for other men's wives and children. The strong and industrious were aggrieved at obtaining no more in food, clothes, and supplies than those capable of much less work. Wives considered tasks benefiting others than their own families a form of enslavement. And since land was owned in common, incentives to care for and improve it were generally lacking. Only with private holdings could individuals expect the *full* return for their efforts to improve the land.

Despite the introduction of tobacco in 1612, which led to commercial production, the organizational difficulties stemming from collective enterprise resulted in continued complaints and low levels of output per worker. The class of the egalitarian ideal with the economic reality of individual self-interest could not be ignored. By 1614, the first step toward private holdings (with three-acre limits) had been taken. In

Intitutional Change in Property Ownership in Plymouth

Like the Jamestown Colony, the Pilgrims suffered from starvation and early hardship. Their response to the situation was similar to the one taken in Jamestown. Governor William Bradford, second governor of the Plymouth Colony had made an institutional change moving from communal ownership to private ownership of property after the dismal harvest of 1623. In Governor William Bradford words, for this community, common ownership

> . . . was found to breed much confusion and discontent and retard much employment that would have been to their benefit and comfort. For the young men, that were most able and fit for labor and service, did repine that they should spend their time and strength to work for other men's wives and children without any recompense. The strong . . . had no more in division of victuals and clothes than he that was weaker . . . .

The Pilgrims were human and responded to incentives in predictable ways. If they worked hard or not at all and received the same allotment of food they would shirk (not pull their weight). So in 1623, each family was given responsibility to provide its own food. The granting of private ownership of property had very good success. Bradford writes,

> and so he assigned every family a parcel of parcel of land...This had very good success, for it made all hands very industrious, so as much more corne was planted than other waise would have bene . . . . The women now went willingly into the field, and took their little ones with them to set corn; which before would allege weakness and inability;

By changing the institutional framework of the colony Governor Bradford was able to overcome starvation and declining morale. Specifically, collective ownership creates a "free rider" problem where the incentive for each worker is to not work since the individual will get the same amount of food and clothes whether he works hard or shirks. So the system creates a workforce of shirkers that leads to lower effort levels and lower total output.

Source: William Bradford, *History of Plymouth Plantation* (New York: Capricorn, 1962).

1619, the head-right system was introduced. This program granted 50 acres of land to anyone paying his or her ocean passage to Virginia. Another 50 acres could be obtained if the person paid the way for someone else. In 1623, the year of the "royal investigation," all holdings were converted to private ownership. The net effect of these changes was to

Exhibit 5.1

Regional Distribution of Physical Wealth, 1774 (in millions of £ Sterling)

	Free Population	Nonhuman* Wealth	%	Total Wealth	%
Southern Colonies	652,585	£40.2	45.6	£60.5	55.3
Middle Colonies	585,149	25.8	29.3	26.8	24.4
New England	582,285	22.1	25.1	22.2	20.3
Total	1,820,019	£88.1	100.0	£109.5	100.0

*Nonhuman wealth does not include value of slaves and indentured servants in probated estates.

Source: Adapted from Alice Hanson Jones, *Wealth of a Nation to Be: The American Colonies on the Eve of the Revolution* (New York: Columbia University Press, 1980), presented in Edwin Perkins, *The Economy of Colonial America*, 2nd ed. (New York: Columbia University Press, 1988), p. 221.

spur individual initiative and to raise productivity to such an extent that Virginia (and Maryland) gained a comparative advantage in the production of tobacco at a time when Europe had developed a seemingly insatiable demand for the crop. The result was to hasten the migration of both labor and capital to the Chesapeake area. The noble but difficult era of economic equality in America was over.[5]

WEALTH INEQUALITIES

Differences in ability, inheritance, legal status, work effort, and just plain luck soon led to a distribution of wealth in the 13 colonies that was far from egalitarian. Not only did differences in people's wealth sharply accent differences in social class in the colonies, epitomized in the contrast between master and slave, but they also revealed very sharp differences in the possibilities of obtaining wealth among the major geographical regions.

As shown in Exhibit 5.1, in the years just preceding the American Revolution, the southern colonies had the largest share of colonial wealth, followed by the middle colonies and New England. This higher relative standing shows up not only in the category of slaves, where we might expect it, but also in all the other components of wealth.

Southern whites averaged the highest wealth holdings per free person in the entire 13 colonies. At the same time, the South domiciled 90 percent of the nation's slaves. In the late colonial period, Virginia's population, for instance, was 45 percent black; in South Carolina, 70 percent of the population was black. Despite their large numbers, the share of total

Exhibit 5.2

Total Physical Wealth, 1774: Estate Sizes and Composition for Free Wealth Holders

	All Colonies	New England	Middle Colonies	South
Distribution				
Bottom 20%	0.8%	1.0%	1.2%	0.7%
Top 20%	67.3	65.9	52.7	69.6
Composition				
Land	53.0	71.4	60.5	45.9
Slaves and servants	22.1	0.5	04.1	33.6
Livestock	9.2	7.5	11.3	8.8
Consumer-personal	6.7	11.2	8.4	5.1

Source: Adapted from Alice Hanson Jones, *American Colonial Wealth: Documents and Methods*, 2nd ed., 3 vols. (New York: Amo Press, 1978), presented in Edwin Perkins, *The Economy of Colonial America*, 2nd ed. (New York: Columbia University Press, 1988), p. 219.

wealth going to those in bondage was only a tiny fraction of the whole. The blacks in Virginia probably received less than 10 percent of the wealth; in South Carolina, they might have held a little more than 10 percent. Yet, as just noted, their proportions of these populations were 45 percent and 70 percent, respectively.

In the New England and middle colonies, slaves were few, and most people had the legal right to share at least potentially in the economic opportunities provided by work and enterprise. As Exhibit 5.2 reveals, however, the distribution of wealth per free person in the colonies was far from equal. In New England, the wealthiest 20 percent of the population owned 66 percent of the total wealth. The degree of inequality was less striking in the middle colonies, where the wealthiest 20 percent held 53 percent of the total wealth. But the highest concentration of wealth was in the South, where 70 percent of the wealth was held by the top 20 percent.

TRENDS IN INEQUALITY IN THE COLONIAL PERIOD

One scholar, Jackson Turner Main, provides evidence that there was growing inequality in wealth and income as a result of the very process of colonial settlement and economic development. In Main's opinion, the increasing commercialization as frontier areas were transformed into subsistence farming areas and ultimately, in some instances, into urban areas resulted in greater inequality in the distribution of colonial wealth and income.[6]

Other studies also suggest a growth over time in the inequality of the colonial distribution of wealth within regions.[7] The inequality was greatest in the major urban centers, such as Boston. Comparing two Boston tax lists, James Henretta found that the top 10 percent of Boston's taxpayers owned 42 percent of the wealth in 1687, whereas they owned 57 percent in 1771. Bruce Daniels surveyed many New England probate records and therefore was able tentatively to support Main's contention that as economic activity grew more complex in the colonies, it tended to produce a greater concentration of wealth. Apparently, as subsistence production gave way to production for markets, the interdependence among producers generated or was accompanied by greater wealth inequalities. This was true both in older and in more newly settled agricultural areas. Alternatively, large established urban areas, such as Boston and Hartford (Connecticut) exhibited a fairly stable (although very unequal) distribution of wealth throughout the eighteenth century until 1776. Smaller towns showed less inequality, but as they grew, their inequality also increased.

Especially high levels of affluence were observed in the port towns and cities where merchant classes were emerging. Particularly influential were the merchant shipowners who were engaged in the export–import trade and who were considered to be in the upper class of society. In addition, urbanization and industrialization produced another class: a free labor force that owned little or no property. Obviously, occupation differences and property ownership were major factors in widening the gap between various social groups in the colonies. Of course, race and sex were also factors. Typically, women owned far less property than men, and women's opportunities to gain wealth were sharply restricted. Similarly, the growing use of indentured and slave labor after 1675 furthered the rise of wealth inequality in the colonies.

It is a statistical curiosity, however, that throughout most of the colonial period up to 1775, a growing concentration of wealth did not occur in the 13 colonies as a whole. Although there was increasing inequality within some regions and localities, the areas in which there was a lower concentration of wealth—the rural and, especially, the new frontier regions, which contained over 90 percent of the population—grew faster than the urban areas, thus offsetting the growing inequality of the urban centers.[8] Whatever the details, substantial inequality of wealth was a fact of economic life long before the age of industrialization and the rapid and sustained economic growth of the nineteenth century.

Issue: Was England Exploiting the Colonists?

MERCANTILIST RESTRICTIONS

THE NAVIGATION ACTS In the seventeenth century, the Netherlands was the supreme maritime nation. By around the turn of the eighteenth century, the English had surpassed the Dutch on the high seas. How was this accomplished?

A series of ocean battles was important, but a primary factor was the English Navigation Acts. These were devised to exclude the highly efficient Dutch shippers from carrying and handling trade within the British Empire.

The Navigation Act of 1661 was directed at shipping and restricted all British Empire trade to British (including colonial) ships. A foreign ship could land goods in England, but only from its own country, not from its own colonies or elsewhere. A British ship was one built, owned, and at least three-quarters crewed by British (including colonial) citizens.

Other acts in 1660 and 1663 regulated the movement of many goods. Imports into the colonies from continental Europe were required to pass through England first. Certain items, such as salt and wine from Spain, were made exceptions and could be shipped directly. Most of the vast array of colonial imports from the continent, however, had to be landed in England and then reloaded before heading on to America. In addition, key colonial products were to be shipped only to England; at first, tobacco, sugar, and indigo. Others were later added to the list, mainly naval stores such as pitch, tar, turpentine, and masts. These were called **enumerated articles** and could be reexported to the continent only after landing in England. Of course, this procedure made transportation and other distribution costs much higher.

Some of the mercantilist controls encouraged production of certain "essential" items. Other laws actually prohibited production. Indigo and some of the naval stores were subsidized by a per unit bounty. Various other manufacturers were outlawed. For instance, the production of finished woolens outside of England was outlawed in 1699. Later, in 1732, imports of fur hats (mainly beaver) from the colonies were forbidden, as was finished iron in 1750.

THE ECONOMICS OF BRITISH CONTROLS

While a simple tabulation of the mercantilist restrictions on colonial trade might lead one to conclude that the colonists were being exploited, this assumption is not necessarily correct. All aspects of the problem must be considered. The colonists, of course, generally only saw the negative side of British rule. As dispassionate observers, however, we should be able to weigh not only the costs that were incurred because of English rule, but also the benefits. Moreover, we cannot reflect only on what actually happened. For a valid analysis, we have to compare what actually happened with what realistically *could* have happened. Would the colonists have been better off if they had been independent at an earlier date? Otherwise stated, would the levels of material well-being in the colonies have been higher if independence had been secured at an earlier date? To address this question, we must first assess the costs of the restrictions and then consider the benefits of membership in the British Empire.

MANUFACTURING RESTRICTIONS The least consequential of the mercantilist restrictions were those on manufacturers. It is hardly surprising to find that these were imposed by Parliament in response to pleas from various vested interest groups at home (the English woolen, hat, and iron manufacturers). They wanted to stop "undesirable" competition elsewhere in the British Empire. Actually, the Woolen Act was aimed primarily at Ireland, but it addressed the colonies as well. American colonists were allowed to produce homespun woolens (bedding and garments), and they imported fine linens and fabrics. This was quite satisfactory to the colonists and would have resulted with or without the law. The English and other Europeans could produce these items more cheaply, so for the colonists the law was superfluous.

The restrictions on fur hat production in the colonies hurt New York hatters, but this was a small group. Overall, it was inconsequential.

Interestingly enough, the restrictions on the production of finished iron were also harmless, because the law was ignored with impunity. Twenty-five "illegal" iron mills were established between 1750 and 1775 in Pennsylvania and Delaware alone, despite the ease of detection.

Given the overwhelming comparative disadvantage of the colonies in most types of manufacturers, these restrictions were not a significant hardship. At most, they were a minor nuisance. There is little case for inferring exploitation from these restrictions.

SHIPPING The controls on shipping had mixed effects in the colonies. Tobacco planters and other producers lost out after 1660, as cheap Dutch shipping was no longer available. But colonial shippers gained, as did colonial shipbuilders. Shipping became a major commercial enterprise in New England and the middle colonies, and shipbuilding developed into the most important colonial manufacturing activity. By 1775, approximately one-third of all British-owned ships had been built in the colonies. Considering both those who were hurt and those who gained, it is likely that the colonists benefitted, on average, from the controls on shipping. After independence, when American shipping was treated as foreign by the British, its exclusion from British Empire trade had catastrophic consequences. American shipbuilders were severely hurt, too, because American-built ships were then classified as foreign.

TRADE The most costly features of the Navigation Acts to the colonists were those influencing the movement of goods. By requiring colonial imports and enumerated articles to pass first through the mother country, English ports were made more active. Of course, this was precisely the purpose of the Acts, and their stimulus made the English ports entrepôts of trade. But they also raised the costs of distribution, and this hit at the pocketbooks of the colonists both coming and going.

The procedure used to estimate these burdens is a tedious business. Essentially, the problem is to figure out how prices and quantities would have changed on goods forcibly routed through England if direct free movement had been allowed. If direct shipment to the continent had been permitted, the prices received and quantities sold of colonial exports would have been higher. Similarly, if goods had come in directly, colonial imports from the continent would have cost less and been more plentiful.

Of course, after the Revolution, direct shipment was allowed, and price adjustments resulting from this change have been studied by a number of scholars to assess the likely magnitudes of these burden.[9] These range from 1 to 3 percent of colonial income; that is, colonists averaged less income by a couple of percentage points because of the trade restrictions.

THE BENEFITS OF BEING A COLONY

We have yet to enumerate the possible benefit that the colonists reaped from being under British rule. Some of the specific benefits of mercantilist regula-

tions have already been briefly mentioned, the most obvious being bounties on indigo, naval stores, silk, and, to a lesser extent, lumber. Although the direct payments to colonists in bounties do not indicate the actual net gain to them, we can get an upper estimate on the benefit from bounties. The data obtained by Lawrence Harper show that, in total, the bounties paid on colonial products totaled about 65,000 pounds sterling, or, at the approximate exchange ratio of pounds to dollars in those days, $325,000.[10] This particular benefit was dwarfed by an even larger one, which came from military protection.

MILITARY PROTECTION Before the Revolution, the colonists had little to do with the protection of their property and life. Almost all of this was provided by the British government. In the beginning, the British helped fight the Spanish, the Indians, and the French, Moreover, American ships were allowed to sail to the Barbary Coast without fear of the infamous Barbary pirates, for Britain had, in effect, bought off the pirates from attacking its own ships as well as the ships of its colonies. One measure of the benefit of British protection to the colonies is obtained by looking at what the new government spent for national defense after independence. Its annual outlay was in excess of $2 million, an outlay that continued to grow as the population grew. Had the colonists become independent earlier, they would have had to provide for their own military and naval protection. The burden of defense would have been on them alone.

Additionally, Britain took care of much of the administrative work in the colonies. The colonies did not, for example, have to conduct their own foreign policy, pay for missions abroad for ministers, and the like.

When these benefits are compared with the costs, any net burden is reduced to insignificant proportions, at least on average.

Don't Just Look at Averages

Of course, we also have to be careful about looking only at averages. We have calculated that the average net cost of British control was probably less than 1 percent. This hardly seems enough to warrant a revolution. However, the costs bore differently on different sectors of the economy. For example, the restriction of no further colonization west of the Appalachians hurt New England merchants the least and young frontiersmen the most. Not only did it eliminate the possibility of obtaining increased land for cultivation, but it also destroyed the possibility for continuing speculation in land sales. Perhaps it is not surprising that George Washington, who was one of the biggest landowners in the colonies and who had wished to own lots of land in Ohio, was one of the staunchest supporters of the Revolution.

Exploitation or Self-Determination

There is a general agreement among historians that the only argument for

the existence of exploitation stemmed from the indirect routing of goods and from trade controls. Note, however, that these controls were never mentioned in the list of grievances sent by the colonists to the British Crown. More importantly, they were more injurious in the seventeenth century than in 1775, and the colonists had lived with these Navigation Acts, quite harmoniously, for more than a century. Expectations, land values, and values of other assets had long since adjusted to the Acts. There is little connection between exploitation and the Revolution.

The numerous changes after 1763, however, are another matter. These changes did incite antagonism in the colonies. Many of them concerned economic matters, such as controlling the money supply and restricting settlement in western lands and the like. But in these and other concerns, especially in the question of taxation and in matters of the courts, the essence of the confrontation was who was to rule. Actually, the new nation adopted many of the British ordinances after independence, particulary those concerning land and currency. Would this have been done if these laws had imposed great burdens? The main problem was that the colonists had lived too long under conditions of relative neglect and *de facto* freedom. The British attempt to intensify control after 1763 stirred the colonists to rethink the matter of their British ties. Ironically, the defeat of the French in North America in 1763 increased the probability of independence. The threat of a French takeover was greatly reduced after 1763. When the various crises erupted, epitomized in the three boycotts between 1765 and 1775, each new British reversal prodded the colonists onward. After all, they won out on each confrontation. By 1775, they were ready, and as we know, ultimately able to free themselves from British rule. However, as we shall see in Chapter 6, independence was not a smooth road. British economic and military influence in North America did not end with the Revolution.

DEFINTIONS OF NEW TERMS

ENUMERATED ARTICLES Enumerated articles were colonial exports that could be shipped only to England; after unloading, shipment elsewhere was permitted.

PRICE INELASTIC A characteristic of demand in which a price rise leads to a less than proportionate decrease in quantity demanded or vice versa.

TECHNICAL DIFFUSION Technical diffusion is the spread of new or known techniques from one product area to another or from one use to another.

TECHNICAL CHANGES Technical change is an advance in knowledge that permits more output to be produced with an unchanged amount of inputs.

ENDNOTES

[1]See George Brown Tindell, *America: A Narrative History,* Volume 1. (New York: W.W. Norton and Company, Inc., 1984), p. 151.

[2]Charles M. Andrews, *The Colonial Period of American History,* Vol. 1, (New Haven: Yale University Press, 1934), pp. 110–111.

[3]A very close, and sometimes superior, competitor in certain trades was Holland. As discussed later, the English legislated trade controls to counter this competition.

[4]The Sugar Act replaced the earlier "Molasses Act" of 1733, which had higher duties, six pence per gallon, but was widely evaded and seldom enforced. This authoritative neglect set an important precedent in the relations between England and America.

[5]Although eventually abandoned, collective activity in early New England had fewer negative results. Undoubtedly, this was because of a more cohesive society there, based on common religious principles (Puritan beliefs). Similarly, the Mormon pioneers, and to a degree their

descendants, fruitfully combined collective enterprise with individual motivation. Again, these successes apparently result when strong religious or social forces tend to counter individual motivation based on self-interest.

[6]Jackson Turner Main, *The Social Structure of Revolutionary America* (Princeton: Princeton University Press, 1965).

[7]James Henretta, "Economic Development and Social Structure in Colonial Boston," *William and Mary Quarterly*, 22 (January 1965), pp. 93–105; and Bruce D. Daniels, "Long-Range Trends of Wealth Distribution in Eighteenth-Century New England," *Explorations in Economic History,* 11 (Winter 1973–1974), pp. 123–135.

[8]Jeffrey G. Williamson and Peter H. Linden, *American Inequality: A Macroeconomic History* (New York: Academic, 1980), pp. 21–31.

[9]These studies are surveyed in Gary M. Walton, "The New Economic History and the Burdens of the Navigation Acts," *Economic History Review,* 24, 3 (November 1971), pp. 533–542.

[10]Lawrence Harper, "The Effect of the Navigation Acts on the Thirteen Colonies," in R.B. Morris, ed. *The Era of the American Revolution* (New York: Columbia University Press, 1939).

Part Three

The Rise of a National Economy

Biographies

The Man Who Faced the Jacksonians

Nicholas Biddle (1786–1884)

PRESIDENT, SECOND BANK OF THE UNITED STATES (1822–1836)

Faulty strategy in his fight against President Jackson and the Jacksonians certainly was not in keeping with the brilliant career that Nicholas Biddle had led up until the time he took over the presidency of the Second Bank of the United States in 1822. Biddle came from a prominent Philadelphia family. James Biddle, his father, was a U.S. Naval officer, commander of the *Ontario*, and the man who took formal possession of Oregon Country for the United States in 1818.

Young Nicholas was a precocious student; he entered the University of Pennsylvania at ten and graduated at the tender age of thirteen. He also received another degree from the College of New Jersey (now Princeton) at age fifteen. He was a student of the classics and French literature and became the editor of America's first literary periodical, *Port Folio*. In 1815, he helped prepare Pennsylvania's reply to the Hartford Convention, in which numerous proposed amendments to the Constitution had been offered. Most of these proposals attempted to limit the power of Congress and the executive. He went on later to compile for the State Department a digest of foreign legislation affecting U.S. trade.

Among his published works was *A History of the Expedition Under the Command of Captains Lewis and Clark,* which he prepared from the explorers' notes and journals.

By the time Biddle was appointed a director of the Second Bank of the United States in 1819, he was considered brilliant, debonaire, and versatile. At the age of thirty-seven he had already been a child prodigy, a writer, a lawyer, a state senator, and a diplomat. And Biddle added to these traits tremendous pride and an uncompromising attitude toward others. These latter two qualities seemed to serve him well when he took over the presidency of the Second Bank.

As president he showed that he could discipline any other bank by forcing it to pay debts to the Second Bank of the United States and its branches in hard specie. But such behavior did not win Biddle many friends in the newer sections of the country or in the Old South.

Biddle's cavalier demeanor did not enhance his chances of winning over President Jackson's veto of the Bank's charter in 1832. Jackson claimed the Bank was unconstitutional and was merely a monopoly that used public funds to enrich a few already wealthy men. Of course, Jackson's veto prevailed and from 1834 to 1836 Biddle had his bank concentrate on how to liquidate itself. This, of course, meant moving all of its capital to the East, where the banking center of the nation still lay. However, a state charter was drawn up giving it a new name and allowing it to continue in existence. With this new lease on life, Biddle attempted to peg the world price of cotton because he felt it was crucial to American credit abroad. His first cotton pool earned a cool $800,000. The second one, however, failed to the tune of over $900,000. The Bank closed its doors in 1841.

Biddle died disgraced and discredited by many, but he left behind principles that could be used later in the formulation of a true central banking system in the United States. Some observers believe that the monetary and banking reforms of Franklin Delano Roosevelt and the original creation of the Federal Reserve System were in part based on some of the principles established by Biddle.

The Man Who Made Cotton King
Eli Whitney (1765-1825)

INVENTOR AND MANUFACTURER

In 1790, cotton production in the United States was about two million pounds. Ten years later, it had risen to thirty-five million. In the early 1790s, several northern states introduced gradual emancipation schemes, and the trend toward voluntary abolition of slavery was increasing: For example, Washington and Jefferson provided in their wills for their own slaves to be set free. This trend was soon reversed, however, and slavery in the United States grew until the Civil War.

What was responsible for the tremendous increase in the production and sale of cotton and for the newfound profitability in slaves? A simple but monumental invention—the cotton gin. And it was invented by an inveterate tinkerer, Eli Whitney.

As a boy, Eli used to putter around in his father's workshop on their family farm in Massachusetts. Eventually he started to make and repair violins in the neighborhood. When he was only fifteen, he was a manufacturer of nails in his father's shop, even hiring helpers to fill part of his orders. Then he turned to hat pins. But by the time he was eighteen, he decided he wanted more education. Working his way through Leicester Academy in Massachusetts, he finally was able to enter Yale in 1789 at the age of twenty-three. Not able to live on the funds offered by his father, he repaired equipment and apparatus around the college. A carpenter who had lent Eli his tools remarked after watching him work, "There was one good mechanic spoiled when you went to college."

Then he decided to go into law. Having been invited as a tutor to stay with the widow of General Nathaniel Green, he overheard a conversation at one of her dinners on the Savannah plantation. The men there pointed out the deplorable state of cotton cultivation in the South. Except in certain coastal areas the only variety that could be grown was short-staple, upland cotton, which was extremely difficult to clean, requiring one whole day to obtain a pound of lint. A machine was needed to remove the tenacious seed from the cotton. In ten days Whitney had invented that machine; a cylinder barely two feet long and six inches in diameter, with rows of combing teeth to separate the lint from the seeds and a brush with a fan to remove the clean cotton. This little model was fifty times as efficient as hand labor. News of the cotton gin soon spread, and the curious and interested flocked to find out what it was all about. It was soon stolen, carried off, and copied. Given the ease of duplication and weakly enforced patent laws of the time, there was little Whitney could claim for his efforts and ingenuity.

Nevertheless, his invention changed the entire history of the South, and indeed, the United States. Most southern planters went into cotton production, and land that was once considered worthless soon became valuable. Slaves were now a much sought-after part of the cotton production process, and the price of field hands doubled in twenty years.

Whitney did not stop with the cotton gin, however, and in later years, he invented another process that perhaps proved to be even more important for the history of the United States. Whitney looked at the manufacture of firearms and decided he could do better. Having never built a gun before, he brashly contacted Treasury Secretary Oliver Wolcott in 1798 and took on the task of manufacturing 10,000 or 15,000 stand of arms at a price of $ 13.40 each. Whitney proposed to make the guns by a new method and in so doing invented the standardization of parts. He once wrote, "One of my primary objects is to form the tools so the tools themselves shall fashion the work and give to every part its just proportion—which when once accomplished, will give expedition, uniformity, and exactness to the whole. . . . The tools which I contemplate are similar to an engraving on a copper plate."

After a slow start, Whitney perfected his method. He was able to use relatively unskilled mechanics to fashion the precise parts that when put together made a very good gun. As it was, Whitney took eight years to fulfill a contract that he promised would be done in two. During this period he had to withstand prejudice and ridicule, but in the end he won out, and his method of machine milling of parts that could be used interchangeably revolutionized the entire manufacturing process used throughout the world. As late as 1840 the British were amazed at the use of interchangeable parts, which had already begun to revolutionize industry in America.

College apparently did not spoil the mechanic in Eli Whitney.

Six
From Unification to Secession: Nonagricultural Development

The year 1776 produced the Declaration of Independence, but it was not until 1783 that the Treaty of Paris formalized the termination of hostilities with England. During the Revolution, the new nation was continually faced with the economic problems of war; among the most pressing of which was how to finance it.

Financing the War

Even though the total cost of the war for the United States was only $100 million—taking probably less than 10 percent of national income per year from 1775 to 1783—the Continental Congress had great difficulty raising even that sum. The very weak Articles of Confederation did not give the Continental Congress the power to tax. However, Congress was able to borrow almost $8 million in gold from abroad, over three-fourths of it coming from France and the remainder from Holland and Spain. Domestically, about $10 million was raised through loans from individuals and businesses. By requisitioning money from the states, the Congress obtained only $6 million, because the states usually ignored the requests. From the viewpoint of any particular state, it often seemed wise to hold back and let the other states pay. When each acted this way, of course, little revenue was raised.

CONTINENTAL DOLLARS

The Continental Congress authorized an issue of almost $200 million in paper currency during the four-year period commencing in 1775. But during that period, this paper money actually accounted for little more than $40 million in terms of gold. Since nobody was really sure whether these "Continentals" were going to be redeemed in gold or silver after the Revolution, their value steadily declined. Congress was not empowered to declare that these notes could be used as legal tender. Instead, it merely asked the states to penalize persons who refused to take them in exchange for goods and services. By 1781, Continentals were worth 1/500th of their original face value. Part of this **devaluation** was caused by people's uncertainty and lack of faith in the government, but a large part was caused by the tremendous increase in the amount of contintential currency issued.

Generally, there is a relationship between large changes in the money supply and the price level. This has been called the **quantity theory of money and prices.** Basically, it states that, for a relatively fixed amount of output, if people did not alter their habits about using money (or cash), changes in the money supply will lead to proportionate changes in the price level. (Remember this in reference to the sixteenth-century influx of American gold and silver into Europe.) Before the Continentals fell precipitously in value, however, other schemes did allow the government to purchase substantial amounts of war materials.

Struggling Under the Articles of Confederation

When peace was resumed, the Treaty of Paris gave the United States all of the territory west to the Mississippi between Canada and Florida, in addition to the right to navigate the Mississippi. However, this was worth little, since at that time Spain controlled the mouth of the river at New Orleans. Additionally, the United States received fishing rights within British territorial waters in the North Atlantic.

Except for these highlights, there were few bright spots. The United States suffered many economic hardships stemming from the war and independence, and the Articles of Confederation added to the difficulties because of its weak political framework.

The first major peacetime goal was to reopen trade with overseas areas. Here the United States faced great problems, for American ships could no longer trade legally with the British West Indies, and ships built in America lost this market in England because of the Navigation Acts.

Overall, exports did not bounce back to their former levels, and yet imports were vital, because Americans were far from being self-sufficient. Consequently, there was a deficit in the U.S. balance of trade with the rest of the world, as the value of exports remained below the value of imports.

In order to pay for this excess of imports over exports, the United States temporarily shipped large amounts of specie—gold and silver—to other countries. The result was a reduction in the U.S. money supply and with it a fall in prices. This caused many American merchants grave concern because they were hurt when the British resumed large-scale exports to the United States. In fact, the British were accused of **dumping**—that is, selling their goods in our country at prices below cost. This undercut domestic production.

What happened in the United States was a "depression" between the years 1785 and 1786. This was limited primarily to the commercial sector and one should be careful not to equate the depression of those years with depressions (or recessions) of more modern times. Today a depression is usually felt by the vast majority of Americans, but, in those early years, most of the population was engaged in farming. The fall in prices hurt people, but few became unemployed. Changes in business activity were not generally catastrophic.

The export sector, however, did suffer. The real value of exports per capita right after the war was probably less than one-half of that just before it. As Table 6.1 (on page 98) shows, annual averages of real exports per capita fell by 30 percent between 1768–1772 and 1791–1792. This lower level was still evident after several years of business recovery in the late 1780s. Most of the difficulty, as Table 6.1 indicates, was with the southern states. The markets in Europe and elsewhere had stagnated. In addition, the United States had not yet secured much political power internationally.

Few countries had yet accepted the United States as a viable nation in the world economy. As a result, trade discussions and treaties were less fruitful than they might have been.

The Effects of Deflation

As the price level fell in the early and mid-1780s, there was growing unrest among debtors in the nation. The main problem was that these price declines were not generally expected. And when the principal and interest on loans had to be repaid, debtors found that they had to pay with dollars of greater value. In real purchasing power, they had to pay back more than they had bargained for. On the other side of the coin, of course, creditors were made better off.

SHAYS' REBELLION AND THE NEED TO REVAMP THE ARTICLES OF CONFEDERATION

By 1786, in the city of Concord, Massachusetts, the scene of one of the first battles of the Revolution, there were three times as many people in debtors' prison as there were imprisoned for all other crimes combined. In Worcester County, the ratio was even higher—20 to 1. The prisoners were generally small farmers who could not pay their debts. In August of 1786, mobs of musket-bearing farmers seized county courthouses and did not allow the trials of debtors to continue. The rebels encouraged Daniel Shays, a captain from the Continental Army, to lead them. Shays' men launched an attack on the federal arsenal at Springfield, Massachusetts, but were repulsed. The rebellion did not stop there but continued to grow into the winter. Finally, George Washington wrote to a friend, "For God's sake, tell me what is the cause of these commotions?

Exhibit 6.1

Average Annual Real Per Capita Exports from Colonies and Regions of the Thirteen Colonies, 1768–1772, and from States and Regions of the United States, 1791–1792 (Pounds Sterling, 1768–1772 Prices)å

Origin	1768–1772	1791–1792
New England		
New Hampshire	0.74	0.23
Massachusetts	0.97	1.14
Rhode Island	1.39	1.72
Connecticut	0.50	0.62
Total, New England	0.82	0.83
Middle Atlantic		
New York	1.15	1.51
New Jersey	0.02	0.03
Pennsylvania	1.47	1.34
Delaware	0.51	0.44
Total, Middle Atlantic	1.01	1.11
Upper South		
Maryland	1.93	1.51
Virginia	1.72	0.91
Total, Upper South	1.79	1.09
Lower South		
North Carolina	0.38	0.27
South Carolina	3.66	1.75
Georgia	3.17	1.17
Total, Lower South	1.75	0.88
Total, All Regions	1.31	0.99

The difficulties of adjusting to independence and new peacetime circumstances were felt unevenly throughout the nation. The 30 percent decline in real per capita exports for the entire United States between 1768–1772 and 1791–1792 was largely due to catastrophic declines in the export of the major southern staples. The northern states fared better than the southern states in their ability to recover.

Source: James F. Shepherd and Gary M. Walton, "Economic Change After the American Revolution: Pre- and Post-War Comparisons of Maritime Shipping and Trade," *Explorations in Economic History,* 13 (October 1976): 413.

Do they proceed from licentiousness, British influence disseminated by the Tories, or real grievances which admit to redress? If the latter, why were they delayed until the public mind had become so agitated? If the former, why are not the powers of government tried at once?"

What Shays' Rebellion did was demonstrate the chaos and weakness of the government under the Articles of Confederation. In order for the nation to grow and prosper in the world economy, it was necessary that a stronger central government be organized. So the Constitutional Convention, which originated as a commercial convention, was convened in Philadelphia in May 1787. The completed Constitution went into effect in March 1789. It was a critical factor in the economic development of the nation.

The Economic Aspects of the Constitution

Article I, sections 8, 9, and 10 contain the main economic provisions of the Constitution. These sections reaffirmed the permanent nature of private property in terms of federal support of the institution. The additional three major categories of the economic provision were taxation, control over money and credit, and restriction over commerce, as well as the ability of the federal government to establish treaties with foreign powers, which were to be held paramount over all laws made by the several states.

TAXATION

One of the major weaknesses of the Articles of Confederation was the inability of the Continental Congress to levy taxes against the population. Although this problem was perhaps more political than economic, without the power of tax, the United States never could have had a large, organized central government.

MONEY AND CREDIT

Even though state banks were allowed, the federal government now was empowered to "coin money, regulate the value thereof, and of foreign coin, in addition to fixing the standard of weights and measures." Implicit in this section of the Constitution was the ability of the federal government to issue a national currency. Eventually this was important for the development of commercial activities and a market in which the buying and selling of debts and shares in companies could occur. This kind of trading occurs in a **capital market.** The Constitution also allowed the federal government to redeem the debts of the "several" (individual) states. This further allowed a capital market to develop.

The Constitution also decreed that all import duties should be the same for all of the several states, and further, that there would be no export duties. This was to ensure that the states did not establish barriers to trade among themselves. This was a way of fostering interregional trade, as well as intraregional trade. The Constitution effectively gave the federal government the right to police interstate commerce, which was at that time limited mainly to coastal trade.

Recovery and the Growth of Shipping

The situation at the end of the 1780s was one of incomplete economic recovery from the depression of 1785 and 1786. In 1789, a revolution began in France. Then, in 1793, the French and English became embroiled in war. The series of battles between the two arch enemies lasted until 1815.

By necessity, both the British and French quickly relaxed their normal mercantilist restrictions. As their demand for U.S. goods increased, American export activity soared; by 1795, exports of American goods had doubled over the 1793 level.

In addition, British and French ships, which normally carried cargo, were now deployed on sterner business. U.S. shipping was ready and able to fill the void created, and the United States quickly became one of the main shipping concerns in the world.

The United States also began to reexport numerous goods because it was a neutral power. Goods of other nations were shipped to the United States and then shipped to the belligerents. For example, in 1790 the United States reexported only three percent of the goods imported, but by 1805, it was reexporting 60 percent.

The reexport trade grew by leaps and bounds. So, too, of course, did total exports, until certain political actions in 1807 prevented further U.S. trade expansion. In 1790, almost 60 percent of U.S. trade was carried on in American ships; in the years 1805 and 1806, it was nearly 100 percent. This was, in fact, an era of unusually intense commercial and trading activity, as well as shipping activity. For Americans, the war in Europe was fortunate, at least initially. It stimulated the U.S. economy and brought prosperity to American businesses and workers.

Nevertheless, the prosperity of these times was not necessarily a basis for long-term development. There was no similar increase of prosperity in the interior of the United States, and a large nation cannot generally grow by merely becoming an efficient shipper for the rest of the world. Yet, the profits made from commercial endeavors during this period were a major source of investment funds that financed later development, and the market sector of the economy was growing in importance.

THE END OF THE COMMERCIAL BOOM

England and France had a temporary peace during 1803, and the U.S. commercial shipping boom plummeted. When the European powers started fighting again, they renewed the economic stimulus for American shipping until both belligerents decided to deny neutral ships entry to enemy ports. Nearly 1,500 American ships were seized after 1805 until Congress enacted the Embargo Act late in 1807. This prohibited American vessels from sailing to foreign ports, in the hope of forcing England and France to respect American neutrality. The results of the embargo were impressive indeed. Reexports fell drastically; similarly, total exports dropped by almost 80 percent when the embargo was enacted. Pressure from merchants, sailors, and commercial interests led to the repeal of the act in 1809. Instead, the Non-Importation Act was passed, prohibiting trade specifically with Great Britain, France, and their territories.

Nevertheless, further difficulties continued, and eventually the War of 1812 erupted. The United States went to war with England again. It was largely a naval war, one in which the British navy blockaded the entire coast of the United States and seized more than 1,000 American ships. Exports fell to practically nothing.

The Rise of Industry

The blockading of American waters gave a strong boost to American industry. Before 1812, there had been almost no manufacturing in the United States. Only seven percent of the population lived in urban areas. The young nation did have a small textile industry in 1800, but even by 1910 two-thirds of it was based in homes. Heroic attempts by Samuel Slater developed the mechanized weaving industry in Providence, Rhode Island, in the 1790s. None of the increased commercial activities or promise of fortune stirred anyone's interest until the embargo of 1807. Resources flowed into areas where they had the highest relative rates of return. Entrepreneurs in the day before the embargo saw their highest rates of return in reexporting, shipping, and general trading. Suddenly this changed. Manufacturing was the new growth sector.

The Textile Industry and Technological Adaptation

In 1808 there were only 15 textile mills in the United States, but by 1909, there were almost 90. The rapid multiplication of mills demonstrated how little capital was needed to start one. Few of these new mills survived, however, once the Peace of Ghent in 1814 brought the War of 1812 to a close and Britain resumed massive exports to the States. The textile industry faltered, but certain large-scale concerns, such as the Waltham system of cloth weaving developed by Francis Cabot Lowell, survived and grew. His use of water-powered mills and a system that used relatively low-cost, well-supervised labor spearheaded the growth of the industry.

Britain was the front-runner in the Industrial Revolution, and American businesses borrowed English know-how in order to make certain products. However, most British technology was relatively capital and labor intensive, whereas the United States had to contend with conditions of relative labor scarcity. The great desire of American businesses for labor-saving machinery may have led to the initial U.S. emphasis on standardized parts, such as occurred with firearms. Moreover, in the early days, U.S. manufacturing development depended largely on water power, which was relatively plentiful and inexpensive compared to the more capital-intensive steam power used in Britain.

Through the forces of supply and demand we can summarize the expansion in the cotton textile industry in America during the period 1815–1860. The following factors led to an increase in demand for American cotton textiles in the antebellum period.

1. *Tariffs* imposed on British products. These increased the demand for American cloth in the short run. That is, since the price of British cloth rose, the demand for the American cloth (a substitute), increased.

IRON PRODUCTION AND TOTAL MANUFACTURERS

The U.S. iron-making industry grew very slowly but eventually developed into one of our major manufacturing activities. After the introduction of puddling and rolling techniques (which had already been in use three decades in England before being used in the United States), our technology of iron making did not change until the introduction of the Bessemer converter in the late 1870s and the open-hearth furnace methods in the 1870s and 1880s.

2. *Population growth* of roughly 3 percent a year. An expanding population implies an increase in the demand for clothing.

3. *Growth in income.* Per capita income during this period was growing at least 1 percent a year. People were able to buy more clothing, especially cotton clothing produced in factories.

4. *Improvements in transportation.* Lower delivery prices for cotton textiles were a direct result of transportation improvements (the introduction of the steamboat and the completion of the Erie Canal). The falling transport costs shifted out the demand curve for cotton textiles particularly for those areas outside the New England states.

5. *Tastes.* American consumers in the antebellum period increasingly preferred cotton to woolens, increasing the demand for cotton cloth.

Recent findings suggest that demand factors alone caused cotton cloth sales to rise roughly 20 percent a year from 1815 to 1833, and thereafter around 4 percent annually until 1860.[1]

Other factors influenced suppliers to produce more cotton cloth.

1. *Technology.* The cost of weaving fell by 75 percent with the introduction of the power loom.

2. *Suppliers' input prices.* The price of raw cotton fell steadily until the 1840s. This drop lowered the cost and raised the quantity of production.

3. *Improvements in organization and machinery.* Better methods of production reduced costs, thus increasing profits and raising output.

The traditional view is that technical change (the supply side) was by far the dominant force leading to industrial development in early America. But by applying the laws of supply *and* demand to historical data we can see that all the foregoing factors probably worked together in the transformation of this particular industry.

By the start of the Civil War, manufacturing had become a substantial part of national output. In fact, it had risen to 60 percent of the product generated by the agricultural sectors. By 1850, the productive capacity of the United States that was devoted to the making of **capital equipment**—machines and the like—represented a higher percentage of total production than in any other nation in the world. Prior to the Civil War, we were indeed on the way to becoming fully industrialized.

Money and Capital

Remember a key provision of the Constitution was that the federal government regulates coinage. In 1791, when Alexander Hamilton was 34 years old, he was appointed Secretary of the Treasury. He wielded a power in this nation that was second only to that of the president. His financial program reflected his belief in a powerful national government. He had great influence, particularly in commercial and banking sectors. In the 30th Federalist paper, he had pointed out that "Money is, with propriety, considered as the vital principal of the body politic; as that which sustains its life and motion, and enables it to perform its most essential functions." He suggested that a basic unit of value be established, and so the Mint Act of 1792 was passed. The dollar was to be that basic unit of value, and the decimal system was to be used (we fortunately did not use the old British pounds, shillings, and pence).

Hamilton also wanted a national bank: "The tendency of a national bank is to increase public and private credit. Industry is increased, commodities are multiplied, agriculture and manufacturing flourish, and herein consists the true wealth and prosperity of a state."

FIRST U.S. BANK

Largely due to Hamilton, the First Bank of the United States was chartered in 1791 for a period of 20 years. It was a private corporation governed by 25 directors and had a capital of $10 million, of which the federal government provided 20 percent. This bank served as the government's depository. It also made loans to the government and to private individuals and companies. It was profitable, averaging an eight percent per year rate of return for those who invested in it. It died, however, when its charter was not renewed in 1811; the assets of the bank were bought by Stephen Girard of Philadelphia.

This was an unfortunate time for the bank to close its doors because, during the War of 1812, treasury finances were in a poor state and no central depository existed. At that time, there was a great increase in unregulated local banking. In general, specie payments were abandoned; that is, nobody was willing to pay off their debts in hard currency—gold or silver. The cry went up for a second U.S. Bank, which appeared in 1816.

THE SECOND BANK OF THE UNITED STATES

This bank was also chartered for a period of 20 years. It started with a capital stock three and one-half times that of the First Bank and the government again provided 20 percent. Soon after it had been chartered, difficulties arose as the price of cotton dropped, and farmers began to have troubles. Instead of countering these problems with expansionary activities, the bank from 1818 to 1819 contracted its deposits. This put pressure on state banks, especially in the west. At the same time, the U.S. had to pay off the debt for the Louisiana Purchase. So quite a bit of specie flowed overseas, helping contract the U.S. money supply in a way that the public did not anticipate.

Finally, there was the Panic of 1819. The bank completely stopped the payment of specie, and there were bank failures throughout the economy. The price level was falling drastically at the time. However, the extent of this crisis should not be exaggerated in a country that was highly agricultural. True, the commercial sector was hit very hard, but certainly not the largely self-sufficient agricultural sector. The first president of the bank, who was considered incompetent, was ousted after the Panic of 1819. Two later presidents, Langdon Sheves (1819–1823) and Nicholas Biddle (1823–1836) were viewed with more esteem, but Biddle, too, eventually faced difficulties.

BANKING AND POLITICS

Meanwhile, there were political currents in motion, particularly toward the end of Biddle's appointment. When President Jackson took office in 1829, he immediately began to attack the Second Bank of the United States. He wanted to close it, but a committee that was formed in the House of Representatives affirmed the constitutionality of the bank in spite of Jackson's request that it do otherwise. During the 1820s, the Bank had developed a sort of national currency because it had a large number of branches, and U.S. Bank notes were in circulation everywhere. The rate of exchange between U.S. Bank notes and all other Bank notes was approximately stable throughout the nation. Congress apparently saw this as a good thing, and Jackson's attempt at that time to block recharter on the grounds of unconstitutionality failed.

The Second Bank was unpopular in some quarters. Of course, it was not like a modern central bank. It could not legally regulate the reserves of commercial banks, and the support it could give to others in periods of financial crises was limited. But by virtue of its size and the number of branches it had, it could exercise some control over the economy. For instance, it would ask for specie redemption from other banks from time to time, to keep them "honest."

Biddle's big political mistake was to apply for a recharter four years before the end of the Second U.S. Bank's original charter. His purpose was to get rechartered and at the same time to embarrass Jackson in the 1832 election and maybe cause him to lose it. Biddle backed Henry Clay in the 1832 campaign. The recharter was passed in Congress in July 1832, but it was vetoed by Jackson. For Biddle, the whole scheme backfired.

INFLATION

The demise of the Second U.S. Bank brought with it many changes in the American banking scene. However, the inflation of 1835, 1836, and part of 1837 and about the depression from 1839 to 1843 were not entirely a result of the bank's closure. Many historians believe that the inflation was caused by the fall of the Second U.S. Bank, which allowed for a rapid increase in the amount of paper currency available through a proliferation of wildcat banks. (These banks got their name from the fact that they were so far out in the boondocks that it was said only wildcats frequented them.) The evidence concerning the increase in the money supply and the increase in prices is fairly impressive; the money supply did indeed increase after Jackson's veto.

At this time, Jackson began withdrawing funds from the Second Bank and placing them in state banks called "pet banks." Biddle's powers were curbed severely.

But was wildcat banking, resulting from the demise of the Second Bank, the cause of the sharp money increase? No, wildcat banking with unchecked expansion of credit and paper currency did not occur. The ratio of bank-held reserves to credit outstanding did not rise. Banks on the whole were fairly cautious, and they did not overlend. What then caused the money supply to increase?

INTERNATIONAL ECONOMY

The United States was part of an international economy, adhering to a gold and silver standard that involved shipments of gold and silver in and out of the country. These formed the basis of the circulating money supply. Moreover, there was a large increase in specie imports from Mexico. England and France were also periodically sending specie to the United States. There was a tremendous specie jump between 1833 and 1837. Therefore, the demise of the Second Bank alone did not cause the inflation of 1835 and 1836.

THE SECOND BANK ONCE AGAIN

Still, the bank was a factor. In the early 1830s, people became very trusting of banks, largely because the Second Bank helped maintain sound banking practices. This confidence let to a sharp reduction in the proportion of specie people held as money. Paper money would serve just as well, people believed, as long as the banks were sound. But after the demise of the Second Bank, people's confidence declined. The proportion of their money that they wanted in specie form went up. Also, the Specie Circular 1836, requiring that most federal land sales be paid in gold, also increased specie holdings by individuals. People went to the banks for specie and, when some of the banks could not convert bank notes into specie, banking panics occurred. Then everyone wanted to convert, which put great strains on the banking system. The end result was the worst depression of the century, lasting from 1830 to 1843.

By this time, the effects of a depression, especially one as wide and as deep as that from 1839 to 1843, was felt much more severely by the general population. To some degree, this economic contraction was international in scope, like the one to follow nearly a century later. Particularly hard hit was the new class of workers, those tied to the mills and factories. The process of mechanization and systematic production controls were just arriving on the American economic landscape. To these new pressures were now added sharp declines in employment and real wages throughout the business downturn. To the hardships of labor was added the hardship of forced idleness.

Issue: Did Government Spur Economic Growth?

TRANSPORTATION

One of the main deterrents to interregional trade in colonial times was the lack of cheap transportation among the colonies, except along the coast. This had to change if the United States was to become an integrated and ever-expanding market in which specialization could continuously occur. At first we turned to the development of the most obvious methods of transportation: waterways and roads. There was rarely any federal assistance for the development of highways in those days because of constitutional objections. Nevertheless, private companies did build a number of turnpikes. By 1810, there were 180 turnpike companies in New England alone. By 1813, there were about 1,400 miles of privately built roads in New York, and by 1832 Pennsylvania had over 2,000 miles.

THE RIVERS

By far the most important part of the early transportation network was the natural waterways, especially the great Mississippi, Ohio, and Missouri rivers, as well as the Great Lakes. First flat-boats and barges (keelboats) carried all of the freight and passengers on these arteries. By 1815, however, the steamboat was successfully introduced on the western rivers, and keelboating, which had made most of its revenues on the laborious trek upriver, was quickly eclipsed. Comparatively, steamboats were much more efficient on the upstream run. Flatboats did not disappear, however, and these downstream crafts remained active throughout the period. Actually, the steamboat helped flatboating by lowering the costs of the crew's return upriver.

The steamboat was a vital force in early westward expansion, and a stream of improvements between 1815 and 1860 greatly increased its efficiency and safety. Steamboat boiler explosions, which brought Americans the first hazards of industrialization, were fairly uncommon after 1850, and various changes in the hull and design greatly increased the steamboats' carrying capacity and length of useful service in shallow water seasons (and areas). As a result, freight costs on the rivers tumbled between 1815 and 1860, and as late as 1845, the rivers still carried more traffic than all of the other transportation mediums combined.

Most of the gains in efficiency in steamboating resulted from many minor modifications and improvements in the design and structure of the vessel and in the handling and operations of the vessel. The sum of these many small improvements was more significant in reducing the cost of river transport than was the major but single technological advance of introducing steam power.

CANALS

Canals, like the natural waterways, had disadvantages, such as freezing in the winter, but they also had many advantages. Mainly, they allowed for relatively cheap transportation among fixed points. The greatest canal-building activity occurred between the late 1820s and the Panic of 1837. The most famous canal, of course, was the Erie, which ran from the Hudson River near Albany, New York, to Buffalo on Lake Erie. Completed in 1825, it extended some 360 miles and could accommodate 30-ton barges. There were many other canals as well, such as those built in Pennsylvania, Delaware, Maryland, Ohio, Illinois, and Michigan.

THE RAILROADS

By tapping the interior, New York's successful Erie Canal posed a threat to other eastern cities and their commercial interests. To counter this, Baltimore emphasized the railroad, because canals were not completely practical due to engineering difficulties, terrain, and the high cost of construction there. Of course, there were to be many mistakes with the use of this new transportation mechanism. For example, Baltimore tried to build its railroad over a mountain pass in a period when steam locomotives were not completely worked out in their design and application. Railroads did have advantages, though, and they were soon to be realized. They were speedier than canal transportation, they could be used in almost all weather, and they certainly had advantages for overland routes. These features were particularly advantageous in the provision of passenger services when the railroads were first built.

In the following section, we examine whether government action was important for railroad development and the development of the United

States. We also analyze the impact of government promotion in general. For example, were government investments a key stimulus to growth?

GOVERNMENT INVOLVEMENT IN THE ANTEBELLUM ECONOMY

Today, when over 20 percent of national output is consumed by government at the federal, state, and local levels, it seems almost unthinkable to question whether or not government has any direct impact on the economy. However, this relatively high percentage of government involvement was unheard of in earlier days. In the nineteenth century, for example, no more than five percent of **gross domestic product (GDP)** was accounted for by government expenditures. Most of government activity was much more decentralized than it is today. In particular, the state governments were much more active than the federal government. Nevertheless, government intervention in economic affairs was not insignificant, and from the very beginning government was active at all levels. In particular, it was responsible in one way or another for much of the development of the transportation system and the manufacturing sector where important changes were occurring.

CLEANING UP THE RIVERS

The backbone of the transportation system before the Civil War was the natural waterways. The main hazards of the rivers were "snags," trees that fell from the shore and became lodged in the river bed. Pointing downstream and largely submerged, they endangered many steamboats coming upstream. Between 1811 and 1849, 830 steamboats were lost on the western rivers of the Mississippi, the Missouri, the Ohio, and their tributaries. Fifty were lost by collision, 150 by burning, 184 by explosion, and 446 by snags.

Of course, it did not pay private individuals to clean up the rivers. Had they done so, they would have borne all of the costs, while most of the benefits would have gone to other steamboaters. Similarly, since most river transport was interstate, state and local governments had little incentive to spend money for snag removals. There again the benefits from cleaning up the rivers were widely dispersed and tolls could not be charged by the states on interstate traffic. The rallying cry was "Let the federal government do it!" But for most of the period, the federal government did little. Sporadic expenditures to clean up the rivers occurred, but the government contribution was less than 1 percent of total resources expended in river transportation. The development of the western river transportation system as a whole stemmed almost entirely from private enterprise.

HELPING OUT THE CANALS

Overland travel was a relatively expensive form of transportation for shipping goods across country. Therefore, the idea of a network of canals was thought of very early in American history. One of the earliest and most successful of the canals, the Erie, connected the Hudson River with Lake

Erie, a distance of 363 miles. New York State did indeed intervene in this particular venture—100 percent. The governor, DeWitt Clinton, was an early advocate of the Erie Canal. In 1817, the state legislature set up a fund to build that famous waterway. They estimated the cost then would be a little bit under $6 million. "Clinton's Ditch" was finally completed in 1825, costing closer to $8.5 million. Even before the canal was completed—that is, while only sections of it were being used—the tolls exceeded the interest costs on the debt used to pay for its construction. In the first nine years of its existence, the tolls summed to almost $17 million.

The effect of the canal on the movement of goods was dramatic. Much of the produce of Illinois, Indiana, Ohio, and western New York could have an easy route to the Atlantic Coast. Freight rates from Buffalo to New York fell by almost 85 percent, and the shipping time was cut to one-half of what it had been previously. By 1853, tolls reached a cumulative value of $94 million on the great Erie Canal.

In the beginning of the canal era, state intervention was great. Between 1815 and the start of the Civil War, almost $140 million was provided by state governments. This amounted to almost three-fourths of the total investment in canals during that period. Some states used indirect financial aid. For example, instead of giving money directly, New Jersey provided a banking privilege to get some of its canals started. After an auspicious beginning, however, direct state intervention in canal efforts dwindled, and there was a tendency to have a mixed government–private system.

HELPING THE RAILROADS

Just as with the canal system, state aid was greater at the beginning of the development of railroads than at the end. In fact, toward the latter part of the nineteenth century, there was almost no government help for railroad systems.

In the 1830s, however, the government engaged in some less ambitious and less successful railroad schemes that may have set the foundation for further development of the Iron Horse. In the South, for example, during the period before the Civil War, state financing accounted for 55 percent of total railroad expenditures, of which 75 percent was directly in cash. By the 1850s, private financing of the railroads had taken over most of what the states had done in the beginning (although after the Civil War, land grants altered the picture). In this early period, the only assistance from government was at the state and local level. When a state financed a railroad, it provided entrepreneurial aid. When local governments helped finance a railroad, it did no such thing.

The plethora of local aid in the South and the North during this time seemed to induce some weird configurations of railroad lines. One historian, commenting on a railroad in the state of New York, said that it zigzagged across the countryside "in search of municipal bonds."

Comparing Government Investments

Government expenditures accounted for very different proportions of total expenditures among the different modes of transportation. Most of this activity was undertaken by state and local governments, especially in canals and railroads. By these expenditures, they hoped to stimulate regional development. Land values and business activity jumped with the advent of railroads and canals, so it paid state and local governments to become involved. The benefits were internalized by the community to a large degree, unlike benefits from snag removal on the rivers. One noted historian, Harry Scheiber, has termed such involvement "local mercantilism."

The period of greatest involvement was before the Civil War, especially by the state and local governments. Overall, this intervention created an atmosphere that induced private investors to risk their capital in these ventures. For canals, the government stimulus was highly significant; for railroads, it was important; for river transport, it was minor.

Land Grants and Aid

States and the federal government did allow a few land grants to help the railroads. Before the Civil War, they were not very important. During the pre-Civil War period, only two railroads were completed with the assistance of land grants. However, a total of 130 million acres was eventually given to railroads by the federal government and over 50 million by state governments.

Did Intervention Spur Growth?

An answer to whether or not state intervention spurred the growth of the American economy still eludes us. Many historians have labeled the system of mixed government–private enterprise building of canals and railroads "The American System." One historian maintains that during this period, the government "everywhere undertook the role put on it by the people, that of planner, promoter, investor, and regulator."[2] This, in fact, was only the case in certain very specific examples, such as the Erie Canal. At any rate, the government's role in the transportation system declined as we approached the Civil War. However, this still does not answer the question, "Would the rate of worth of the United States have been lower if the government had not participated even to the limited extent it did?" Using economic data, historians have yet to come up with a definitive conclusion. Certain, very obvious examples suggest that this intervention did yield positive benefits. Some have said, for example, that the Erie Canal had effects on the development of the United States that "ramify almost into infinity." But we can just as easily find some spectacular failures of government intervention, such as occurred with the Pennsylvania Canal System. If fact, on the whole, canals were financial failures and a considerable misuse of resources because technological obsolescence occured so quickly. One prominent investigator has concluded that perhaps as much as 85 percent of canal investments was a social waste.[3] Ironically, most of these financial failures were due to the arrival of the railroad, which diverted canal traffic to overland routes.

With regard to transportation improvements, the case for critical growth stimulus via government involvement is shaky at best. In river transport, there was no significant involvement. In canals, the influence was probably negative; in rails, it was positive. Overall, perhaps it was neutral.

What about Government and Manufacturing?

From the very beginning, the government did not carry through Alexander Hamilton's suggestions listed in his "Report on Manufacturers." There he suggested that the state undertake a number of promotional activities, such as subsidizing important industries. Up until the Civil War, however, there was very little subsidy of manufacturing. There was also not an overwhelming amount of "protection" in the form of relatively high tariffs, although for a short period we did have rising tariff rates.

The first tariff was put into effect on July 4, 1789, with an average rate of only 8.5 percent. It grew steadily larger, reaching a peak in the late 1820s and then falling thereafter.

The United States during this period had a system of no quotas, no currency regulations, very little allocation of scarce resources by the government, and few subsidies paid to manufacturing. We had a more or less freely functioning market mechanism in which changes in relative prices and relative rates of return induced resources to flow in directions that would yield the highest rates of return both to the individual and to the nation. Where the state did have some effect, probably the most important effect of all on the growth of the economy, was in its Constitutional provisions that generated an atmosphere conducive to the development of large and well-functioning markets.

Establishing the Atmosphere

The key articles in the Constitution— giving power to Congress to tax, provide for a common currency, regulate tariffs, and so on—were of vital importance in providing a framework for a large market system. The Constitution also provided an atmosphere of political stability in which the states would not be imposing restrictive duties on each other's goods. On the other hand, powers left to the states, such as the power to incorporate, often proved beneficial. Certainly the flexibility of state-chartered corporations was conducive to industrial expansion in the United States.

It was perhaps in the development of an atmosphere in which everybody knew what the ground rules were, who owned what, and how well it would be protected that the growth of the nation could continue for years to come.

DEFINITIONS OF NEW TERMS

DEVALUATION Devaluation is a reduction in the exchange value of money.

QUANTITY THEORY OF MONEY AND PRICES The quantity theory of money and prices is a theory that can be used to predict changes in the price level. Basically, if the economy is fully employed and if we assume that people's habits concerning the use of cash (and the number of transactions) remain unchanged, then an increase in the quantity of money in circulation will lead to a proportionate increase in the price level.

DUMPING Dumping is selling goods abroad lower than costs.

DEFLATION Deflation is a continuing fall in the price level.

CAPITAL MARKET A capital market is one in which loans can be obtained or in which shares in companies can be bought and sold.

CAPITAL EQUIPMENT The term capital equipment applies to machines, buildings, and other productive goods.

GROSS DOMESTIC PRODUCT (GDP) The gross domestic product is the market value of all final goods and services. When GDP is corrected for price level changes, it is called real GDP.

ENDNOTES

[1]For a detailed explanation, see R. Zevin, "The Growth of Cotton Textile Production After 1815," in *The Reinterpretation of American Economic History,* Robert W. Fogel and Stanley L. Engerman, eds. (New York: Harper & Row, 1971).

[3]Robert A. Lively, "The American System," *The Business History Review,* 39, 1 (March 1955): 81.

[4]Roger Ransom, "Canals and Development: A Discussion of the Issues," *American Economic Review,* 54 (May 1964): 375.

Seven
Agriculture, Cotton, and National Growth

From the very beginning, the staple crops from the South account-ed for a large percentage of the total exports from America. In the colonial era, rice, tobacco, and indigo accounted for more than one-half of the exports of all the colonies combined. However, a new staple crop was soon to take the place of all the others and to become the leading source of national income for many years to follow.

King Cotton

Back in 1793, cotton was an insignificant feature of the southern land-scape. In fact, since the importance of southern exports had fallen after the Revolution, there was little southern furor when the Constitution stipulated that slave imports would be stopped after 20 years. This was all to change, partially because Eli Whitney invented the cotton ginning machine. The cotton gin removed the bottleneck in the preparation of short-staple cotton and enabled one worker to remove the seeds from more than 50 pounds of raw cotton a day. By hand, a worker could clean only one pound a day. This lowered the cost of American cotton at the same time that England's textile industry was growing by leaps and bounds. King Cotton was on the rise.

JUMPS IN COTTON PRODUCTION

The South increased its production of cotton at a phenomenal rate, dou-bling almost every decade until 1840, after which it still continued to grow, but at a slower rate.

A NEW SOURCE OF EXPORT INCOME

Cotton quickly became the major export not only for the South, but also for all the United States. Cotton exports as a percentage of all U.S. exports rose from 38 percent during the period from 1815 to 1819 to 65 percent just before 1840. Although the absolute volume continued to rise, relatively it fell to 51 percent by the start of the Civil War.

There are numerous reasons why the South became so highly spe-cialized in cotton production. First, the southern climate and terrain were particularly well suited for such a crop. This was especially true in the New South, the cotton states of Alabama, Mississippi, Arkansas,

Louisiana, and eastern Texas. These new lands were highly fertile and easily cultivated. Moreover, the land policy of the federal government was becoming increasingly liberal over this period. Western lands were becoming easier to obtain for small and large farmers alike, as federally set minimum land prices fell and credit availability increased. Second, from the plantation system inherited from colonial times, the South had the necessary know-how and entrepreneurial skills. Third, it also had a large pool of unskilled labor, in bondage, to pick and carry cotton. Finally, inexpensive transportation was another important reason why cotton became king in the South. There was a vast network of waterways that could carry the cotton to ocean ports—the main port, of course, being New Orleans. This well-established transportation system allowed cotton farmers merely to cart their bales of cotton to a nearby river and to have them shipped down to large vessels waiting at the dock in New Orleans, Savannah, Charleston, or Mobile.

It is fairly obvious that cotton was what the South would produce best. Since there was the possibility of both interregional and international trade, the South was able to specialize in its comparative advantage: cotton production.

The Antebellum South

Although cotton was king and there were numerous plantations around the southern countryside, the vast majority of people were engaged in yeoman farming that was either subsistence or that left a slight surplus that could be sold to the plantation owners for their own consumption and that of the slaves.

There was very little urbanization in the South, with the obvious exception of New Orleans and perhaps Mobile, Charleston, Savannah, and Richmond. This meant that there were few local industries, but that did not mean that the South was stagnating, as some historians have said. Table 7.1 shows that per capita income in the South, although more unequally distributed, was certainly not much lower than the national average, and in some areas, such as in the West South Central, it was much higher. It was also higher in all cases compared with the North Central region of the United States, a region that historians have customarily indicated as having a high level of living at that time. If we consider the per capita income of only the free population in the South, we see that in 1840 and 1860 it exceeded the national average.

Moreover, the South certainly was not stagnating in terms of its growth rate. Per capita income grew at an average rate of 1.7 percent a

Per Capita Income Before the Civil War (1860 prices)

	Total Population		Free Population	
	1840	1860	1840	1860
National Average	$ 96	$128	$109	$144
North	109	141	110	142
Northeast	129	181	130	183
North Central	65	89	66	90
South	74	103	105	150
South Atlantic	66	84	96	124
East South Central	69	89	92	124
West South Central	151	184	238	274

Source: Robert W. Fogel and Stanley L. Engerman, "The Economics of Slavery," in *The Reinterpretation of American Economic History,* New York: Harper & Row, 1971, p. 335, Table 8.

year, which exceeded the national average of 1.3 percent a year. It also exceeded the growth rate of the North Central states. The South was far from being an underdeveloped region.

Cotton was not the only crop that was grown in the pre-Civil War era. Corn accounted for the most acreage, but it was not a commercial crop, and there was rice in South Carolina and sugar in Louisiana and Texas, as well as tobacco in Virginia. In fact, sugar was one of the staples that was grown on the new lands of the westward migration, which we will talk about in the following section. Lastly, there was abundant livestock for consumption in the South.

The South was not a well-diversified economy. It was quite clear to Southern planation owners that their comparative advantage lay in cotton production or, to a lesser extent, the production of sugar, rice, or tobacco. We find, for example, that in the Old South, the states along the Atlantic coast, where the costs of producing cotton were much higher than in the New South, there was almost no shift to other types of production. Cotton was still the best thing that a landowner could produce, even when the cost of producing it went up. So, during the pre-Civil War era, there was little tendency for industry to grow in the South.

DIVERSITY OF INCOMES

Although the average income of free people in the South was, in fact, as high as or higher than that of most other regions of the country before the Civil War, there was more diversity or inequality in income and wealth than in other sections of the country. To be sure, one of the main reasons for this great inequality was the large number of slaves in the southern economy. For an average slave, more than one-half of his or her income went to the owner rather than to the slave.

In the period just before the Civil War, almost one-half of southern personal income went to just 1,000 families. There were some blatant examples of concentrated wealth. The Hairstons had 1,700 slaves on all of their plantations. In Georgia, a Mr. Howell Cobb had over 1,000 slaves on his lands. In rural Louisiana, the top 10 percent of families held 96 percent of all wealth!

LITTLE INVESTMENT IN EDUCATION

One aspect of the southern economy that was not favorable to its further development was the limited amount of investment in education. This was partly because much of the population consisted of slaves. It was not generally worthwhile for a slave owner to provide education for those in bondage. In some states, it was even illegal! Most were bought specifically to do tasks that required very few skills. However, it is not certain why the free white population in the South lagged so far behind the rest of the country in obtaining educational resources. In the post-Civil War era, even up to the present, this had grave consequences, because *investment in human capital,* as it is called, is important for increasing the productivity of individuals, regions, and the nation as a whole.

Schools available for each white person in the South averaged almost 20 percent fewer than in the North. There were almost 50 percent fewer students (per person) going to school in the South than in the North. So small an investment in education is perhaps understandable if most Southerners felt that cotton would remain king. After all, there was little need for a highly educated population if the only productive activities would involve growing staple crops.

Cotton and Interregional Trade

THE SOUTHWEST

The issue of whether or not the cotton economy helped increase the growth of the national economy is an important one. First, how did cotton affect the Southwest (Alabama, Arkansas, Florida, Louisiana, and Mississippi)? Whether or not the movement into the Southwest increased national growth is, of course, a debatable issue, but it is clear that cotton caused westward migration on a scale that far exceeded what would have happened in its absence.

As already mentioned, cotton required fertile lands; and cotton, like most crops cultivated for a long time, takes fertility out of the land. Once the natural fertility of the soil has been depleted, it is necessary either to fertilize and/or rest the land or to move on to new lands. Moreover, in the quest for profits, southern cotton growers moved on to new, fertile lands as the price of cotton rose relative to other crops. There was a lag of one or two years between increases in the price of cotton and a new thrust in westward migration. The main surges to the Southwest occurred during the periods from 1816 to 1819, from 1833 to 1837, and to a lesser extent, in the 1850s.

When the relative price of cotton rose in the American economy, a common scenario generally followed.

1. The relative price of cotton goes up.

2. New plantations are started, taking three to four years to clear the land.

3. The supply of cotton rises.

4. The relative price of cotton falls.

5. Some of these plantations shift to growing corn, but whenever the price of cotton goes up, they shift back to cotton.

6. The demand for cotton rises so much again that most of the cultivated land is being used for cotton production.

7. The relative price of cotton goes up again as demand outstrips supply.

8. A new cycle starts again; more thrust into the West.

There is little doubt that the cotton economy did propel the growth of population into the new Southwest. It also had some effect on the development of manufacturing in the North, but to a decreasing extent as the North branched out into industries other than textile manufacturing.

THE NORTHEAST

That the availability of relatively inexpensive cotton was vital for the development of the New England textile industry is, of course, a well-known historical fact. Moreover, each fall in the price of cotton in the South was an additional stimulus to the North, because cotton was a major input into its manufacturing sector. So, to some extent, the cotton economy did encourage the growth of industry in New England. Also, southern demand for shoes and cheap textiles to clothe slaves further spurred northern industry, and northern shipping and commercial activities were stimulated as well. In the late antebellum period, the Northeast accounted for over 70 percent of the country's manufacturing employment.

However, it was not just cotton that spurred northern industry; there were other factors as well. One rather obvious reason was the lack of fertile agricultural areas. Another reason was the presence of **economies of scale** as New England moved from a host of small artisinal shops to large factories.[1] Economies of scale exist when a firms average costs fall as they increase production. This may be due to factors like mass production (such as assembly lines of production) or through greater division of labor and specialization.

In addition, the wages of women workers were partly responsible for the high concentration of manufacturing in the New England area, especially in the early 1800s. Female workers were relatively more productive in the manufacturing sector than in the physically demanding agricultural sector (the cultivation of northern grains was indeed strenuous work). Since female productivity (and hence wages) was higher in manufacturing than it was in agriculture, the factory was a rather obvious employment choice. And as manufacturing expanded, so did female hirings.[2]

THE NORTHEAST AND INTERREGIONAL TRADE

Some economic historians, most notably, Douglas C. North,[3] have maintained that the demand for foodstuffs by the South spurred the development of the western regions by providing a ready market for products such as wheat. North's argument goes as follows: As the demand for cotton increased, the South would export cotton to New England and foreign ports and buy imports from New England and the West; the West would sell foodstuffs to the South and the North and buy certain products from the North. This allowed for a very complete and ever-increasing trade among all parts of the nation. In the process, each region became more specialized and more efficient.

However, when closely examined, the data indicate that even prior to the Civil War, the South was almost entirely self-sufficient in foodstuffs.[4] The trade link between the agricultural West (today it is the Midwest)

Resolving the First Energy Crisis

The fuel involved in America's first energy crisis, not much more than a century ago, was whale oil. It was used for lighting, both in the United States and abroad. Because the supply of whale oil could not keep pace with increasing demand, the price rose from 23 cents a gallon in 1832 to $1.45 a gallon in 1865. But the quantity demanded fell only slightly, despite the large increase in price, because no good substitute was available; the demand was price inelastic (that is, over a significant range of the demand curve, a price increase or a price decrease would only have a minimum affect on the quantity demanded).

The growth in the demand for whale oil was stimulated by increases in population and in income between 1830 and 1860. During this time, the number of easily accessible whales diminished. In the early 1800s, New England whalers had to travel only short distances to make a catch, but as supplies dwindled, whalers had to go farther and farther from the Nantucket area, out into the Pacific and the Bering Sea. These extended voyages raised the costs of whaling. Other forces, however, acted simultaneously to counter this trend; new and improved technology increased the productivity of the whaling industry, thus tending to lower costs and increase supply.

With these two supply factors offsetting each other, it is hard to know which dominated. Therefore we will assume that the shifts in the supply curve were not that instrumental in the price changes in the whale oil industry. However, we do know that an increase in demand had occurred, which by itself would drive prices higher.

The discovery of petroleum in 1859 coupled with the high whale oil prices prompted producers to develop a refining process for crude petroleum. The end product of this research and development was a substitute fuel—kerosene. By the mid-1860s, consumers were substituting away from the higher priced whale oil to the lower priced kerosene. Hence, prices provided the appropriate signal to the market and forestalled a long-term energy crisis.

and the Cotton South was minimal. For example, in 1840, the importation of western corn into the South added a grand total of one percent to the Southern corn supply. Even the large specialized plantations raised most of their own corn and pork. Most of what the West sent to the South in 1839 was reexported. By 1850, only about 14 percent of the West's exports were consumed in the South. The key to growing interregional trade, then, contrary to North's assertion, was not the link between South and West.

The main element of growing regional interdependence was the East–West connection spurred by the westward expansion in the 1850s of the railroad and other transportation improvements. It was the industrializing East that was short on food, and western shipments paralleled the rise of eastern demands. By 1860, the West–North trade flows were more than ten times greater than those between the West and the South. With the railroad tying the West to the North, it is no surprise that the West threw its political support to the North after the South seceded and the Civil War commenced. By 1860, nearly 40 percent of the nation's population resided west of the great Appalachian barrier. Increasingly, as the decades passed, the West took on greater significance both politically and economically. It was unrivaled in grain production, but it was also well diversified in numerous manufactures—mainly in processing agricultural products. And the difficult question of slavery in the new western territories was a critical political issue that added dimension to the rising North–South, slave versus free, conflict.

Issue: Slavery—The Peculiar Instutition

Some historians have argued that on the eve of the Civil War, slavery not only was unprofitable but was "on its last legs" as an institution. In other words, the Civil War was apparently unnecessary. However, recent evidence indicates that this was not true. This is not to say, of course, that slavery should have been allowed to continue. Nevertheless, it is important that we set our history and our economics straight.

THE RISE OF SLAVERY

Slavery was relatively unimportant for almost the first century of settlement in mainland North America. Over 90 percent of all blacks taken as slaves from Africa went to South America (mainly Brazil) and the Caribbean islands. Most of these were engaged in sugar production. In contrast, few slaves went to North America. Before 1730, there were fewer than 100,000 slaves in all of the thirteen American colonies. However, between 1730 and the time of the Revolution, that number doubled and more than doubled again. As in the sugar islands, America's interest in slavery was, of course, economic. The discovery that tobacco could be grown cheaply in Maryland and Virginia encouraged the use of large numbers of unskilled workers to cultivate many acres of land. The same held true for growing rice and indigo in South Carolina.

The Dutch were the first to develop the slave trade with the American colonies, but soon England entered this profitable venture. Slave investments simply returned higher profits than their next best substitute—indentured servants.

While the southern contribution to total exports remained high until the Revolution, there was a reversal in the trend immediately thereafter until cotton became king in the South. At the time the Constitution was written, the forefathers of the nation agreed not to import slaves. As part of one of the great compromises of the Constitution, therefore, slave imports became illegal after 1808. The demand for slaves, which temporarily stagnated, soon expanded, however, as the demand for cotton expanded. While slavery declined in the North, it was being intensified in the South.

NORTHERN EMANCIPATION

As we see from Table 7.2, various northern states emancipated slaves between 1780 and 1804, but the living population of slaves were not freed. Emancipation would have been very costly to their owners. Even the abolitionists recognized the substantial wealth losses that owners would incur if slaves were freed. As part of a political compromise, "gradual emancipation" policies were adopted. Newborn babies would be freed at adulthood (unless they were sold in the South). Table 7.2 shows the ages at which the

Northern Emancipation for the "Free-Born"

State	Date of Enactment	Age of Emancipation Male	Age of Emancipation Female
Pennsylvania	1780[1]	28	28
Rhode Island	1784[2]	21	18
Connecticut	1784[3]	25	25
New York	1799[4]	28	25
New Jersey	1804[5]	25	21

1. The last census that enumerated any slaves in Pennsylvania was that of 1840.
2. All slavery was abolished in 1842.
3. The age of emancipation was changed, in 1797, to age 21. In 1848, all slavery was abolished.
4. In 1817, a law was passed freeing all slaves as of July 4, 1827.
5. In 1846, all slaves were emancipated, but apprenticeships continued for the children of slave mothers and were introduced for freed slaves.

Source: Robert W. Fogel and Stanley L. Engerman, "Philanthropy at Bargain Prices: Notes on the Economics of Gradual Emancipation," *The Journal of Legal Studies*, Volume 3, 2 (June 1974): 341.

newborns were freed. Of course, child rearing imposed costs on owners, but by working slaves until their mid-twenties, owners were able to recover (with interest) those costs. In this way, slave owners escaped almost all of the "costs of emancipation."[5]

NOT EVERYONE WAS A SLAVE OWNER

Although there were many more slave owners in the South than in the North, it was far from true that everyone in the South had slaves. By the start of the Civil War, there were 1.4 million free families in the southern states. Only 380,000 of them owned slaves, which meant that only about one-fourth of all southern families were slaveholders. Of this particular group, however, less than one-fourth held ten or more slaves, which means that not even four percent of the southern white population had ten or more slaves on their farms. This four percent held over three-fourths of the total number of slaves at that time. Hence, slavery was not the all-pervasive institution that one usually thinks it was in the pre-Civil War South. However, those who held power in the southern states were more likely than not to be the owners of slaves, for slaves were a significant part of the southern wealth. It is therefore understandable that they would object to any threats by the North to emancipate the blacks.

Plantation Agriculture

Until the Civil War, the distinguishing feature of southern social and economic structure was the great plantation. Scattered throughout the South, these spreading domains made functional by slave labor were far more productive than small farms or larger ones cultivated by free workers. In fact as shown in Table 7.3, farms working 16 to 50 slaves were 33 percent more effi-

TABLE 7.3

Comparisons of Efficiency in Southern Agriculture by Farm Type and Size

Index of Free Southern Farms = 100.

Number of Slaves	Indexes of Output per Unit of Total Input
0	100
1-15	101
16-50	133
51 or more	148

Source: Robert W. Fogel and Stanley L. Engerman, "Explaining the Relative Efficiency of Slave Agriculture in the Antebellum South," *American Economic Review,* 67 (June 1977): 285, Table 7.

cient, and those with more than 50 slaves were 48 percent more efficient, than farms without slaves.

To explain such an advantage, we must look to economies of scale and to the way in which crops were grown and harvested. The large plantation in the antebellum South more closely resembled a factory than a farm, and the organization of labor was very much like the assembly line method in use to this day. Slaves were often organized into production units called gangs, with each worker carefully selected by skill for a specific task. Moreover, the intensity of work per hour was far greater than on smaller farms. Contemporary writers described work on the great plantations in these terms.[6]

> The cotton plantation was not a farm consisting, as the farm does, in a multiplicity of duties and arrangements within a limited scope, one hand charged with half a dozen parts to act in a day or week. The cotton plantation labor was as thoroughly organized as the cotton mill labor. There were wagoners, the plowmen, the hoe hands, the ditchers, the blacksmiths, the wheelwrights, the carpenters, the men in care of the work animals, the men in care of hogs and cattle, the women who had care of the nursery . . . the cooks for all . . . No industry in its practical operation was moved more methodically or was more exacting of a nice discrimination in the application of labor than the Canebrake Cotton plantation.
>
> When the period of planting arrives, the hands are divided into three classes: 1st, the best hands, embracing those of good judgment and quick motion; 2nd, those of the weakest and most inefficient class; 3rd, the second class of hoe hands. Thus classified, the first class will run ahead and open a small hole about seven to ten inches apart, into which the 2nd class (will) drop four to five cotton seeds, and the third class (will) follow and cover with a rake.

To recoup strength for such hard-driven work, the slaves on large plantations needed, and were granted, longer rest breaks and more time off on Sundays than workers on smaller holdings. Although specialization of tasks enhanced productivity, it is obvious that much of the plantations' superior efficiency resulted primarily from the extent to which labor was forced to produce. No free-labor plantations of any size emerged during the period, and after emancipation the organization and efficiency of plantation production declined sharply.

THE ECONOMIC EXPLOITATION SLAVERY

Slavery is a special case of **monopsony**—where there is a single buyer of an input. The ordeal of black slaves in the two and one-half centuries before the Civil War may be viewed as a case of monopsonistic exploitation. Slavery is a system whereby property rights in human capital are altered to allow one group of persons (slave owners) to derive extraordinary profits at the the expense of another group (slaves). In a free, perfect labor market, people can move around between employers, going to the highest bidder. In slavery, by contrast, mobility is forbidden and the slave has only one employer, who literally owns him or her. Hence, the monopsonistic exploitation is real and substantial. Workers, indeed, can be paid any "wage" the slave owner wishes, subject only to the constraint that an excessively low wage might affect the amount of physical productivity of the slave.

How badly were American slaves exploited on the eve of the Civil War? While some controversy on this point exists, Professor Richard Vedder suggests that the **marginal revenue product** (added revenue from the use of an additional unit of labor) of a slave of average productivity was about $85 a year with the figure ranging from zero (very old and very young slaves) to several hundred dollars (male field hands in their peak working years).[7] The subsistence wage given slaves in the form of food, clothing and shelter had a value of perhaps $30 a year. Therefore, some 65 percent of the $85 marginal revenue product of slaves was taken from them by slave owners. In a free market, the wage would be equal to the intersection of demand and supply for labor, roughly a wage of $85 a year, but slave owners in fact only paid wages equal to a subsistence level of $30. The remaining $55 was exploitive profit. Slave exploitation did not only come in the form of salary. In fact, much of the work exploitation came in the form of intensity of work rather than the number of hours worked (northern farmers worked at least as many hours).

SLAVE TREATMENT

Slave treatment varied from owner to owner. Some were cruel and others paternalistic. In short, there was no uniformity in the treatment of slaves. Most slave owners did use a combination of fear and small rewards to provide incentives and disincentives to try to get the most from their workers. However, we would think from purely economic considerations that many slave owners would not overly abuse their workers for the obvious reason that their slaves were an investment worth close to $300,000 (in 2000 prices).

Slaves did not have political rights; in fact, they had no role in shaping the rules of the economic game and did not have education opportunities. In fact, many owners were paranoid that if more slaves were able to read and write that it would increase the possibility of slave rebellions. Slaves could not change slave owners or move to another area to pursue other economic opportunites. In addition, most slaves had either been whipped or witnessed a whipping and on some plantations would constantly work under the threat of the whip; the harshest penalties went to those who tried to escape, were caught stealing, or poor work effort. Pregnant women were overworked and many slave children were subject to malnutrition. And family break ups were not uncommon; a 16 year old male slave had a 20 percent chance of being sold.[8] The owner had unresticted power over the slaves—slaves that caused trouble could be sold and separated from family and friends.

While the standard of living was certainly low compared to today's standards, it was sulf-sustaining and clearly better than in the Caribbean and Brazil where the slave population was on a continual decline from malnutrition and the especially brutal conditions for slaves.

Was Slavery Dying Out?

It is sometimes believed that the South was stagnating before the Civil War and that, since slaves seemed to be unprofitable and less productive than free workers, the institution of slavery would have died of its own accord. But if we examine what was actually happening in the South, slavery does not appear to have been moribund, for the South itself was far from stagnating.

The South was a growing economy, one in which its inhabitants anticipated that things would continue to improve, not worsen. Table 7.4 shows that the price of slaves was rising generally throughout this period. Clearly, slave values were increasing, not decreasing. This increasing price indicated that slaves had rising economic value to southern plantation owners. Farm and household slaves also provided leisure time for owners—another reason, then, why they were desired.

Were Slave Owners Losing Money?

Until quite recently, some historians hypothesized that by the end of the 1850s, slave owners were losing money on their investment in slaves. To understand how the price of slaves was determined, we have to view slaves as a **capital investment**. That is, the

---

Exhibit 7.4

Slave Prices in the Upper and Lower South

Period	Upper South Price	Lower South Price
1830–1835	$521	$948
1836–1840	957	
1841–1845	529	722
1846–1850	709	926
1851–1855	935	1,240
1856–1860	1,294	1,658

Source: R. Evans, Jr., "The Economics of American Negro Slavery," *Aspects of Labor Economics*, Princeton, NJ: Princeton University Press, 1962, p. 216.

potential owner would decide how much to pay for the slave by determining what the current value of the slave's future net income was.

PROFITABILITY COMPUTATIONS

Slaves provided owners with a stream of income. That income was the value of the product that the slave produced for the owner minus the cost of the slave's maintenance. For example, a slave could help the owner increase his cotton production by, say, three bales of cotton. Let's say that those bales could be sold in the open market for ten cents a pound, or $50 a bale. That would mean that the total revenues of the plantation's owner would go up by $150 if he hired this additional slave. We cannot accept that as the first year's net revenues on the slave purchase, because we have to subtract out the cost of maintaining the slave, say $25 per year. That meant that the net profits to the owner from having the slave would be $125 per year. This stretched over the expected lifetime of the slave. Let us add all this up and properly account for the fact that some of it occurred in later years. Having done this, assume our answer for the current value of the future streams of net profit from hiring the additional slave would be equal to $1,250. The maximum price that a slave owner would pay for an additional slave, then, would be $1,250. That is indeed how the price of slaves was determined in the open slave market. It was a function mainly of the price of cotton and the productivity of slaves. Ignoring the latter, we find that the price of cotton

was, for the most part, either stable or rising. Slave owners anticipated that the price of cotton would continue to be high for many years in the future. So, on the eve of the Civil War, they were far from pessimistic about the profitability of slavery.

COTTON PRICES NOT FALLING

The price of raw cotton in cents per pound, corrected for general changes in the price level grew from 7.4 cents in 1840 to 12.4 cents in 1850, then fell again during the first few years of that decade, but started to rise again in 1857. Any drop in the price of cotton was viewed as temporary by plantation owners. They anticipated continuing high revenues from having slaves on their plantation. The price of slaves reflected the slave owners' anticipations of future prices for cotton. The price of slaves in the upper South, for example, was only $521 during the period 1830 to 1835, but by 1856, it had risen to over $1,200. In the lower South in 1860, a prime slave could have fetched $1,800. In Table 7.4 the various prices of slaves as five-year averages are shown.

SLAVES: A PROFITABLE INVESTMENT?

What did all this have to do with the profitability of slavery? A correct investigation of the data shows that the average rate of return on the slaves was as high as or higher than on any other capital investment that was available to Southerners during that period. In the lower South, for example, it was 12 percent during the period 1830–1835, falling to about 10 percent on the eve of the Civil War. This was at least as high as rates of return that prevailed elsewhere in the economy. So long as the rate of return on investment in slavery was as good as or better than the rates of return that existed in other capital investments, we would expect that the institution of slavery would expand. That is exactly what happened.

The Viability of Slavery

Slavery was indeed profitable and, at least for the foreseeable future, clearly viable. A slave was economically viable when the value of the slave's output exceeded the costs of the slave's reproduction. This was certainly so if slavery was still profitable and could be so even if it were not. However, some important facts tend to counter this position. At that time, new competition in the world cotton market from India and Egypt was appearing. Moreover, there were the beginnings of a worldwide emancipation movement that was certain to reach the United States sooner or later. Perhaps slavery would have died out of its own accord at some time in the late nineteenth century. Was some type of strong coercive measure necessary to abruptly terminate the existence of this institution? The Civil War did not begin as a war to end slavery, but emancipation was one favorable outcome of that bitter, costly conflict.

PROFITABLE BUT HORRIBLY RETROGRESSIVE

According to Nobel Laureate Robert Fogel, "Markets don't guarantee that evil systems will collapse, because sometimes they're very effective and only political intervention can bring them to an end. The system was economically profitable but horribly retrogressive in its social, political, and ideological aspects." And the recent research by Professor Richard Steckel and others on the welfare of slave children should put to rest any notion that the slave system was benign.

DEFINITION OF NEW TERMS

ECONOMIES OF SCALE Economies of scale occur when there is a reduction in the average per unit cost of producing something due to production on a larger scale. Strictly speaking, economies of scale exist when an increase in all inputs leads to a more than proportionate increase in output.

MONOPOSONY A single buyer of an input.

MARGINAL REVENUE PRODUCT Added revenue from the use of an additional unit of labor.

CAPITAL INVESTMENT Capital investment is investment in a productive asset that is, an asset that will yield a stream of income in the future. The purchase of a slave was a spatial investment.

ENDNOTES

[1]See Kenneth L. Sokoloff, "Was the Transition from the Artisinal Shop to the Nonmechanized Factory Associated with Gains in Efficiency? Evidence from the U.S. Manufacturing Censuses of 1820 and 1850," *Explorations in Economic History,* October 1984.

[2]See Claudia Goldin and Kenneth L. Sokoloff, "The Relative Productivity Hypothesis of Industrialization: The American Case, 1820 to 1850," *The Quarterly Journal of Economics,* August 1984.

[3]See Douglas C. North, *The Economic Growth of the United States 1790–1860* (Englewood Cliffs, NJ: Prentice-Hall, 1961).

[4]The question of self-sufficiency may depend on how one defines the South. For example, are the border states of Kentucky and Tennessee southern or northern states? For a detailed discussion see Robert L. Sexton, "Regional Choice and Economic History," *Economic Forum,* Volume XVI, Number 1, Winter 1987.

[5]There was a small possible loss to owners of female slaves since newborns would eventually be freed and would not be the property of the white master. About ten percent of the value of female slaves was due to the economic value of their offspring. Females were about 37 percent of the total value of slaves. Hence, the maximum loss to owners was 10 percent of 37 percent, or 3.7 percent. The loopholes of selling South, working slaves harder, or reducing maintenance costs probably erased this small amount, however.

[6]For complete citations and quotations, see Jacob Metzer, "Rational Management, Modern Business Practices, and Economies of Scale in Antebellum Southern Plantations," *Explorations in Economic History* 12 (April 1975):134–135.

[7]See Richard K. Vedder, "The Slave Exploitation (Expropriation) Rate," *Explorations in Economic History* 12 (October 1975): 453–458.

[8]See Stephen Crawford, "The Slave Family: A View from the Slave Narratives," in *Strategic Factors in the Nineteenth Century American Economic History: A Volume to Honor Robert W. Fogel,* eds. Claudia Gloden and Hugh Rockoff (Chicago: Chicago University Press, 1992) pp. 331–350.

Eight
Secession, War, and Economic Change

During the decades just prior to the Civil War, incomes per free person were higher in the South than in the North, and per capita incomes in the South were rising faster than the national average. Investments in slaves continued to be profitable, and the "peculiar institution" remained viable. No natural forces were leading to the collapse of slavery in the United States, and it could end only by political or military means.

It seems clear in retrospect that secession after the election of President Lincoln was not entirely without cause. The politically dominant slaveholders feared the northern abolitionists and the uncertainty of a newly elected president opposed to slavery. Except for these anxieties, slaveholders were optimistic on the eve of the Civil War. They anticipated a continuation of their social order and also a new era of increased prosperity. In short, the South seceded out of economic strength, not weakness.

The Outbreak Of War

The outbreak of hostilities brought with it the usual problems of obtaining labor and paying for that labor, ammunition, and all the items necessary for war. Because the North was fighting to hold the union together, it was forced to attack. In contrast, the military goal of the South was much more modest: Obtain a draw or a stalemate.

What Happened in the South?

At one time or another, almost one million soldiers served in the Confederate Army. At the height of the war, there were perhaps over one-half million engaged in combat. This represented an impressive 50 percent of the white male population between the ages of 15 and 50. As can be expected, the economy suffered from a scarcity of food, clothing, and war materials. The North had quickly set up a naval blockade—a disaster for the South, which had engaged in extensive trade with the East and with foreign ports. At the beginning of the war, only one-tenth of the total value of manufactured products used in the South were made there. Self-sufficiency would indeed be difficult; trade was important. Despite these and myriad other problems, the southern economy supported a large army for four years of extremely heavy fighting.

SHIFTING PRODUCTIVE CAPACITIES

Among the South's greatest problems was the shifting of the productive resources out of cotton—which was no longer a useful industry because the output could not be traded for needed manufactured goods and foodstuffs—into providing increased foodstuffs and supplies for the armies, as well as other manufactured goods for the civilian population. To this end, cotton production was cut back sharply in 1862. The government did not need to enforce this cutback. After all, the southern cotton growers were not going to continue increasing production if they could not sell it. They quickly shifted their capital into areas where relative rates of return were higher. Reduction of the crop continued: In 1863, it was well below one million bales, as compared to four million a few years earlier, and in the following years the output was halved again. Tobacco production also was reduced, again because the surplus over what was consumed in the South could not be sold.

Entrepreneurs made a valiant effort to produce substitutes for the manufactured goods that the South had previously imported. A noteworthy achievement was the development of homespun cloth.

URBANIZATION

The rise in the manufacturing industry in the South dramatically increased urbanization. Before the Civil War, the South had remained overwhelmingly rural, with only one major city, New Orleans. After the war started, Charleston, Atlanta, Richmond, and Wilmington all became increasingly crowded, for there industrial and administrative employment were available. Southerners were seeking out areas where they could earn the most income, and that no longer was on the farm.

Were the Southern Forces Defeated from Within?

Many observers of the defeat of the Confederacy maintain that the government policy of inflationary finance and inept foreign trade policy caused the downfall of the South during the Civil War. However, the evidence in support of this view is mixed.

TRADE POLICIES

The Confederacy did make a number of mistakes in trade policy, at least in retrospect. The northern blockade really did not take effect until 1863 and 1864, so before that time, that is, during the first two years of the war, the South could have continued exporting cotton to obtain needed munitions, manufactured items, and foodstuffs. However, the Confederate government discouraged any export during this period, so out of a four-million-bale crop from 1861 to 1862, only 13,000 bales were reported to have left the South. The government was so sure that cotton was king that by withholding it from the North and foreign countries (especially Britain), the South hoped to obtain support for the Confederacy by all the industrialists who would be hurt. Obviously, the South would have been better off had they exported as much cotton as possible in order to obtain supplies for the army and the civilian population.

INFLATIONARY FINANCE

The Confederate government, of course, somehow had to obtain part of the civilian output for use in fighting the war. Foreigners were unwilling to lend very large sums to the Confederacy and, certainly after the northern blockade on trade came into effect, there were very few import duties that could be used to support the war effort. The South did obtain a certain amount of federal government property and that of Union citizens when the war broke out. The most noteworthy acquisitions were the Harpers Ferry arsenal and the naval shipyard at Norfolk. There was a certain amount of confiscation of privately produced goods in addition to internal taxes and loans, but that accounted for less than one-half of the total outlays of the Confederate government during the war. These outlays were valued then at about $3 billion. How was the rest made up? By **inflationary finance.** That is, the Confederacy issued large amounts of paper notes (printed money). This led to a situation called **hyperinflation**—that is, a dramatic overwhelming increase in the price level over a short period of time. As prices begin to rise very rapidly, consumers start anticipating this rise: They realized that the dollars—in this case, Confederate notes—are going to lose purchasing power because of inflation. That means that it becomes more expensive to hold cash and so people attempted to spend their dollars before they lost value.

In this way, people bid up prices even faster than would occur otherwise. During these periods, some people think there is a scarcity of money. In fact, it is just the other way around. The reason that prices are going up so fast is because there is too much money in circulation and it is turning over too fast.

The Confederacy also faced a problem not encountered by most countries during hyperinflation: Toward the end of the war, it was assumed that Confederate notes would have a zero exchange value if there was a Union victory. Clearly, a Confederate dollar would be worth little or nothing if the South lost the war.

That is the main reason that the inflation reached astronomical proportions by the end of 1864.

The Collapse

Valiant as the Confederate forces were, their ultimate collapse was inevitable given the steady drain on southern resources. The physical base on which the southern economy rested was slowly but surely whittled away by the military efforts of the Union.

Union forces were continuously making inroads into the western and coastal fronts of the South. By 1861, there were almost no Confederate forces in Missouri; Kentucky and West Virginia were held by the Union. One of the key southern disasters of the war was the loss of New Orleans to federal amphibious forces in the spring of 1862. During that same year, western Tennessee was captured. This event closed off much of the South's access to the Mississippi. Many of the ports were unavailable, such as Savannah and Jacksonville. Then, in 1863, the Union conquered Mississippi. The Confederacy was cut in two. In 1864, Sherman marched through Georgia, breaking up the Confederacy into fourths. Atlanta fell. This continuous loss of territory prevented a Confederate military stalemate. The Union would be preserved, but at great cost to both the North and the South.

The Federal War Economy

MILITARY LABOR

About 15 percent of the labor force was involved in the Union effort. There had to be some way to procure these men. In 1863, the North passed the Enrollment Bill for troop conscription. However, this system of draft was quite different from our recently defunct system of conscription. It allowed those who were drafted to pay someone to go in their stead. Thus, even though the method of conscription was somewhat arbitrary, the final determination of who would go to war was quite a bit more flexible.

Obviously those whose civilian incomes were relatively high found it useful—indeed, advantageous—to hire replacements whose civilian incomes were relatively low. And apparently many of the less well-to-do found the "bribes" advantageous, since they accepted them.

This method of conscription tended to trade off equity for efficiency, and some may view the scheme as unfair or unjust. Nevertheless, it is clear that those whose incomes are high suffer a greater dollar cost if they are drafted than those whose incomes are low. From society's economic point of view, then, it is more efficient to allow high-income earners to pay low-income earners to fight the war, because income is generally (though not always) a reflection of a person's productivity in society. As such, if high-income people are left to do their jobs and low-income people fight the war, the total output of the economy will be higher than otherwise. In a situation like this, fairness and efficiency conflict. The North's means of manpower procurement emphasized the latter.

FINANCING THE NORTHERN EFFORT

With the declaration of war in 1861, there was an immediate financial panic as banks suspended specie payments, and business failures occurred. The federal treasury was almost empty; federal credit was at a low point, as the government itself suspended specie payment. The Union had to finance the war somehow, and it did it by increased loans, taxation, and paper money.

LOANS With respect to the first form of war finance, J. Cooke, a Philadelphia banker, floated many loans for the government. He popularized bond issues by emphasizing the advantages of the investment and the patriotic duty of the citizens of the North. Over $2 billion were raised in this manner. Cooke's fee was 1 percent on sales up to $10 million and three-eighths of 1 percent on sales that exceeded that figure. He made a mint.

TAXES The North probably used taxation to raise funds more than did the South. Excise taxes were raised in 1862 and extended to numerous goods and services. They produced almost $300 million. The Morrill Tariff, passed in 1861, raised another $300 million. And then there was the income tax, which produced about $55 million.

MONEY CREATION As in the South, large amounts of paper money were created. Almost half a billion dollars in United States Notes, otherwise called **greenbacks**, were issued. These bills were not backed by gold or silver; they were merely promises on the part of the government to redeem them. Their value fluctuated widely in terms of gold. By 1864, the rate of exchange was one greenback for 40 cents of gold. By 1864, the price index had risen to two times its pre-1860 level.

NORTHERN INDUSTRY DURING THE WAR

While it is true that some new manufacturing occurred during the war that would not have occurred otherwise, it is not obvious that total output in the North was any greater during the Civil War than it was before or than it would have been without the war. There are no extensive data for that particular period, for the censuses then were taken in ten-year intervals. However, New York and Massachusetts did take censuses for 1865, and these show that in both states there were declines in real output between 1860 and 1865, and also between 1855 and 1865. It appears that these two key manufacturing states, which accounted for over one-third of total manufacturing value added in 1860 and a little over 30 percent in 1870, did not have a rapidly expanding manufacturing sector during the war years.

LITTLE CAPITAL INVESTMENT

Estimates of residential construction during this period indicate that after the war, there was twice as much residential building as during the war. Moreover, sales of McCormick reapers showed a boom after the war, not during it. And there was certainly not a large surge in what we normally call war industries. Generally, the Civil War was not a period of intensive capital investment. For example, the iron needed for the small-arms production during the war was only 1 percent of total U.S. iron output during the four years starting in 1861—one small factory could have done that. At the same time, the iron used in laying railroad track decreased by seven times this figure. Another often-cited war industry was the manufacturing of boots for servicemen. However, at the same time that more boots were needed for federal soldiers, fewer boots were sold to the South. For example, in Massachusetts, employment in the boot and shoe industry fell from almost 80,000 to 55,000 during the Civil War. Output fell from 45 million pairs to 32 million.

THE NORTHERN BUSINESS ATMOSPHERE

It is true that northern business was booming after the first few disorganized months of the war. However, good business does not necessarily imply economic development. Many profits may be derived merely from speculation, and this is just a transfer from one sector of the economy to another. Also, with all the good businesses, there was just as much poor business in some sectors. In fact, there were more poor businesses than good in the northern cotton textile industry because it suffered after the blockade of imports from the South. Numerous mills closed down and others were forced into the production of wool, which, as can be expected, grew as an industry to replace the cotton textiles that could no longer be spun. However, there were costs involved in shifting over, and these costs contributed to the reduced productivity in that sector. Moreover, even during the Civil War there were in the North severe pockets of unemployment. To be sure, the conscription of that time did ameliorate to some extent this problem of unemployment, but not completely.

GOVERNMENT EXPENDITURES

There is also the idea that large amounts of government expenditures caused a rapid increase in the manufacturing sector, especially in the North. This, however, was not true. Government expenditures went mainly for bounties, salaries, and food—especially beef—and for various types of unsophisticated weapons. In any event, the total amount of northern government expenditures during the Civil War represented a minor part of total output, and these expenditures were generally substitutes for what the private sector would have spent anyway. In other words, the private sector did not spend as much of its income because the government obtained part of it through loans, increased excise taxes, a new income tax, and inflationary finance.

Postwar Recovery in the South

After the war, the southern economy recovered faster in manufacturing than in agriculture. By 1870, manufacturing production approached the prewar level and transportation and railroads also had recovered. Manufacturing could recover faster than agriculture because the whole makeup of the agricultural society had been altered by the Emancipation Proclamation, while in manufacturing there had been predominantly a free white labor force before the war anyway.

There is no doubt that in the postwar years, the South was burdened by large material and human losses, as well as by an incalculable amount of social disorganization caused by the unquestionably changed status of slaves. Although the full cost of the war can, of course, not be seen in the statistics, Table 8.1 (on page 138) shows the commodity output per capita by region from 1860 to 1880. The South, even after 15 years of recovery from the Civil War, still had a per capita commodity output that was less than before the start of the Civil War. Clearly, the South was hurt badly and took many years to recover. Outside the South, however,

Exhibit 8.1
Real Commodity Output per Capita (1879 dollars)

	Outside the South	South
1860	$ 74.8	$77.7
1870	81.5	47.6
1880	105.8	61.5

Source: Stanley Engerman, "The Economic Impact of the Civil War," *Explorations in Economic History* (Spring 1966) p. 181.

was another story; per capita income increased over 40 percent between 1860–1880.

Of course, much of the South's productive capacity had been destroyed; not only its capital, but also its labor. Nearly 259,000 Confederate soldiers had been killed and another 261,000 wounded. These were almost all men of working age and were a direct loss to the Southern labor force. Many were planters or sons of planters, and the loss in entrepreneurial skills and human capital, as well as raw labor, was very high.

In addition, there was the great problem of how to reorganize the entire agricultural system and contend with the social disorganization of a large, politically free, but still economically dependent, black population. With the new rights of freedom, many blacks, especially the women and children, retreated from the fields. And males also typically chose to work fewer hours. In the cotton belt, the overall reduction in labor effort was about 30 percent. No wonder output fell. And of course, the highly efficient plantations were a thing of the past.[1]

In the North, there were no such problems of economic reorganization. Nevertheless, 360,000 Union men had lost their lives, and 365,000 had been wounded. The Civil War was more costly in blood and human suffering than any other war the U.S. had ever fought.

The National View in Long-Term Perspective

The growth rate of total commodity output from 1859 to 1869 was only 2.0 percent per year, the lowest it had been in decades. In fact, examining the long-term trends, total commodity output rose at an average annual rate of 4.6 percent between 1840 and 1860, dropping to an average annual rate of 4.4 percent between 1870 and 1900. With respect to industrialization, the shift out of agriculture into manufacturing was as rapid during the two decades before the war as it was during the two decades after the war. If we look at how much manufacturing contributed to the increases in output, we find that while value added in manufacturing grew at about 7.0 percent per annum from 1840 to 1860, it grew at only 6 percent per annum from 1870 to 1900. There was also a relatively large decline in the productivity of labor in the manufacturing sector from 1860 to 1870.

Rather than being a decade of tremendously increased production in industrialization, the Civil War decade marked a departure from the general output, productivity, and income trends that had existed prior to it. At least in part, this should not be surprising, given the fact that out of a labor force of 7.5 million, one million men were involved in the fighting. This is a reduction of about 15 percent. How could the economy have experienced an industrial renaissance with that kind of depletion of the work force?

Although the evidence presented strongly suggests that rapid economic expansion did not stem from the war, some historians have argued that the Civil War was a type of second political revolution. It supposedly removed the "backward South" as a political force and allowed the northern Republicans to pass legislation favorable to economic growth. To assess this proposition, we must carefully assess the economic consequences of the legislation passed by the Republican Congresses.

Issue: Did the Civil War Legislation Stimulate Growth?

The War and Government Legislation

Perhaps because of faulty data or perhaps because of the general notion that war is sometimes good for the economy, early students of the Civil War were convinced that it spurred economic growth and industrialization. However, as discussed in the preceding paragraphs, it now appears that the Civil War did not itself stimulate growth rates in the North and reversed them sharply in the South. But this would provide too facile a view of the potential impact of the Civil War on future U.S. economic development. During the war period, several innovative pieces of government legislation were passed that may have influenced the future course of the economy. Some historians have argued that the Civil War was necessary to rid the Congress (especially the Senate) of the southern voting block, which fought legislation allegedly essential to economic development. After their removal, the all-Republican Congress had a free hand, and a series of economic measures were passed. One of the most significant pieces was the National Banking Act.

ENACTMENT OF THE NATIONAL BANKING ACT

Prior to the federal legislation in 1863 and 1864, which established a national banking system, the banking atmosphere was one of considerable freedom throughout all of the states. In this era of free banking, state bank charters were easily obtained in just about any state. The main intent of the National Banking Act—at least that which was aired in public—was to establish a national system that would unify all of the banks in the entire United States. However, the original legislation that provided for the chartering of national banks was based on the free banking charters of that day—in almost all respects. The several exceptions made all the difference in the world, as will be explained below. The result was *not* a national banking system that would foster further development by greatly expanding credit markets and credit availability.

THE WAR AND THE NEED FOR MORE MONEY

Congress enacted the banking legislation primarily, although not exclusively, in order to increase the government's borrowing power during the war. It did this by requiring all national banks to invest a portion of their capital in government bonds. The capital that was necessary to open a national bank was, it turned out, substantially higher than most banks actually had, especially in the rural areas. As a result, the system of national banks did not in fact become established as the one and only institution for banking throughout the United States. In the agricultural areas of the country, the average capital of non-national banks was less than the minimum required to open or be transformed into a national bank, and national banks were forbidden to make real estate loans. Moreover, state-chartered banks had their note issues taxed by the federal government. Taken together, these conditions hindered the growth of rural banks. The consequence was higher rural interest rates in the South and West.

NO NATIONAL SYSTEM CREATED

Even by 1900, there were still about 9,000 non-national banks, as opposed to about 4,000 national banks. Obviously, the Civil War legislation did not give the United States a single, unified banking system. Because of the differential treatment of non-national banks, which slowed their growth, it seems likely that there was actually a restraint on the number of banks that were started after enactment of the legislation as compared to what would have happened had it never been passed.

A UNIFIED RESERVE SYSTEM

On the plus side of the national banking legislation was the fact that the country's banks were linked together through a reserve system that provided a legally sanctioned formal mechanism for transferring funds between banks. This tended to promote an efficient allocation of loanable funds throughout the country. In other words, it was easier for funds to go to areas where they could yield the highest social product that is, to areas where the rate of return would be highest. This generally meant the transfer of bank funds from agricultural to industrial uses, which helped funnel credit to areas that required large amount of capital, such as railroad investment and large-scale industry. Taking the positive and negative effects together, the net effects of the National Banking Act are unclear. It seems highly doubtful that the act was critical to the economic development of the United States.

Giving Away Land

In 1862, the Union Congress passed the Homestead Act. This provided that 160 acres of land hitherto owned by the federal government could be acquired by a settler if he agreed to live on it or cultivate it for at least five consecutive years. What effect did this magnanimous Act have on the distribution of land holdings in the United States and, consequently, on the development of our open spaces? It turns out that the amount of new land put into cultivation after the Civil War that was attributable to homesteading was less than 20 percent of the total new acres taken up until then. The rest was either purchased from federal, state, or local governments, or was given away in the form of land grants to railroads.

Many historians maintain that the Homestead Act caused a reduced growth of national product during this period because it caused farmers to use inefficient amounts of capital and labor on tracts of land that turned out to be too small. Remember that the Homestead Act provided for only 160 acres. By the time it was passed in 1862, the frontier and most of the land available were pretty far west. Although there was some good land left, most of it was prairie land and good for little more than grazing sheep or cattle. As any rancher will attest, 160 acres of grassland is not much for grazing purposes, and in fact will supply only about 15 or 20 cattle with forage.

HELPING OUT THE RAILROADS

Land grants to railroads were another possible way of disposing of land in the public domain. Other railroad subsidies were also given out during this period, and again we must ask the question: Did federal land grants sharply affect the growth rate?

Remember that during the war years, there was almost a total stop to the construction of new railroad mileage. But the federal government had established a policy of subsidizing the railroads by giving them land grants along their rights-of-way. Five railroad systems accounted for 75 percent of all these subsidies: Central Pacific; Union Pacific; Atchison, Topeka and Santa Fe; Northern Pacific; and the Texas and Pacific railroad systems. The subsidy to the Union Pacific

Railroad, which obtained land grants by the Acts of 1862 and 1864, did indeed turn out favorably. The social rate of return—that is, the return to the investors plus the spillover benefits to society—on that investment was relatively high. So the government subsidies were indeed justified from a social point of view. However, the increase in national income made possible by the Union Pacific was only 0.01 of 1 percent. Similar computations have been made for the Central Pacific Railroad with similar results. Although all of these numbers certainly leave some room for doubt, nonetheless it appears that legislation allowing subsidies to a few railroads provided positive but very minor impetus to growth. It seems likely that the railroads in question would have been built eventually even without the land grants. Such an alteration in the timing of construction due to the subsidies would have had negligible effects on national income.

Protecting Infant Industries

Even before the days of Alexander Hamilton, the first prominent American leader to advocate high protective tariffs to stimulate U.S. manufacturing, it was well-known that certain industries would gain from tariff protection. Under special circumstances, it is alleged, society as a whole may also gain.

By this argument, if certain industries are to be able to start up and become technologically efficient so that they can eventually compete in the world market, they must be "protected" in their infancy. That is, a tariff wall must be erected around that "**infant industry**." The tariff wall causes the price of imports to rise high enough so that the less efficient "infant" producer can compete. Later, by learning through doing and by developing better technology, the infant will eventually become a full-grown adult. Then the tariff walls can be lowered.

However, the usual case is that when the infant has grown up, the tariffs are not taken off. Nonetheless, the argument is often used when discussing the economic impact of legislation during the Civil War.

It should be remembered that the two decades prior to the Civil War saw the price of manufacturing and economic growth under a low tariff policy. The Republicans, however, came into power in 1861 committed to making sure that there were higher duties to "protect" American manufacturers. Since there were no southern congressmen to fight them, the Republicans raised the tariff even before Lincoln took office. Then, using the excuse that they needed to raise more war revenues, they raised the tariff even higher. By 1867, the average duty on imports reached a whopping 47 percent. It was not clear at that time which industries benefitted and who was hurt.

DISTORTIONS CAUSED BY TARIFFS

What is clear is that, in almost all cases, a tariff causes a distortion and a misapplication of resources. After all, the highest economic value from scarce resources is obtained by using them where they have the highest comparative advantage. If other countries can produce goods at a lower price than U.S. producers, consumers can take advantage of that if they want to maximize their economic welfare. Of course, certain industries may be hurt in the short run, but others end up producing goods for which other nations do not have a comparative advantage. We export the latter and import the former. The results are gains from trade, and that is why so many economists (and consumers) are against setting up tariff walls.

Even though the tariff was raised substantially during the Civil War, it is not at all obvious that the northerners benefitted and that economic growth in general was increased. No doubt some of the manufacturers benefitted, and no doubt the economy as a whole suffered.

This is just another instance where there is no positive evidence to show that legislative actions during the Civil War helped promote the growth of the United States. Considering the package of Civil War legislation as a whole, it also appears that the growth stimulus was very weak, especially from the national perspective.

Technological Advance

Finally it should be emphasized that this was a period when technological advance and diffusion was increasing sharply. The loss of labor from the farms (for the war effort) encouraged the substitution of capital for labor, such as McCormick's reaper. In addition, the 1860s and 1870s were decades of sharp increases in animal power—often in place of human energy.

Not only the spread of advanced technologies, but also the development of new ones in ever-widening scales of application added to the growth impetus of the period. Increasingly, technological changes and innovation (or technical diffusion) became commonplace in transportation, manufacturing, mining, and construction. And the development of more perfect capital markets, in conjunction with higher overall levels of investment, readily channeled these advances in technology into the production process. Technological change was increasingly becoming a vital part of the story of U.S. economic growth, especially by the last half of the nineteenth century.

DEFINITIONS OF NEW TERMS

INFLATIONARY FINANCE Inflationary finance involves the issuance of large amounts of money to help finance government expenditures, usually during wartime.

HYPERINFLATION Hyperinflation is a consistent rise in the price level that attains astronomical rates, such as a 1,000 percent increase a month!

GREENBACKS Greenbacks were U.S. Bank Notes that were not backed by gold or silver; they got their name from their color.

INFANT INDUSTRY ARGUMENT The infant industry argument is used in support of high tariffs. Presumably an industry, if protected by a high tariff, can improve its technology and efficiency so much that later on, when it is full-grown, the tariff can be removed, but it will still be able to compete in the world market with other full-grown competitors.

ENDNOTES

[1]See Philip Graves and Robert L. Sexton, "Development, Mobility and Slavery: Real Income and Spatial Equilibration in the Postbellum South," *The American Economists,* Spring 1986.

Part Four

New Strides Toward Economic Progress 1865–1919

Biographies

The Ruthless Businessman Par Excellence

Jay Gould (1836-1892)

RAILROADS AND GOLD MANIPULATIONS

Can you imagine that one man caused a major panic on what Wall Street called Black Friday (September 24, 1869)? It may sound impossible; still, it actually happened. That one man was Jay Gould, who with the help of his flamboyant sidekick, Jim Fisk, cornered the market in gold, sold out, and watched it fall. Gold was a very precious commodity after the Civil War, for the issuance of greenbacks, which could not be redeemed at par in specie, brought great speculation in all precious metals. However, the growth of confidence in the government, improvement in the U.S. trade balance, and perhaps the postwar prosperity brought the price of gold down again in terms of greenbacks. By 1869, $131 in greenbacks bought $100 of gold. Gould bought $7 million worth, helping send the price up to $140. Since Jim Fisk seemed to have similar ideas, they banded together and started to buy all the gold they could, with as much money as they were able to get out of a Tammany Hall–controlled bank called the Tenth National. At the same time, however, they were worried about the $80 million in gold that the U.S. Treasury held, part of which could be thrown on the market at any time, causing them great financial loss.

To forestall that day, Gould befriended the man who had married President Ulysses Grant's middle-aged sister. To make sure this man used his influence correctly, Gould bought him $2 million in gold bonds on margin, so if the price of gold continued to rise, Grant's brother-in-law could reap sizable profits. When Major Dan Butterfield was named Assistant U.S. Treasurer at New York, he, too, suddenly had somewhere around $2 million in gold bonds in his account, purchased, of course, by Gould.

By September of that year, Gould and Fisk really did have a corner on the entire gold market, when the price of gold was at $141 in greenbacks for $100 in gold. When Gould got wind that the president was going to force the U.S. Treasury to unload its holdings of yellow metal, he quietly started selling out, as did all of his associates, while simultaneously acting and talking like a bull: The price of gold first went up to $150, then to $164 in greenbacks, for $100 of gold.

Finally the president ordered the U.S. Treasury to sell $5 million in gold immediately. In fifteen minutes, the price fell twenty-five points.

Gould and Fisk were already in their headquarters, guarded by police and their own men. Gould alone made $11 million. But, kindheartedly, he announced his regret over the Black Friday panic. And Assistant Treasurer Butterfield sanctimoniously pointed out that only speculators had lost money.

No one had ever dreamed that little Jason Gould, who was born in Roxbury, New York, the son of poor hill farmers, would become a great American financier. He first started working for a blacksmith, then became a clerk in a country store. He learned the rudiments of surveying and obtained enough education before his twentieth birthday to write the *History of Delaware County and Border Wars of New York.* Before he was twenty-one, he had $5,000 in capital, with which he joined hands with a New York politician and opened a large tannery in northern Pennsylvania. He abandoned the tannery, became a leather merchant, and finally found where he had a special genius—speculating in small railroads.

His notoriety became immense during his battle with Cornelius Vanderbilt over the Erie Railroad. While they were attempting to bring the price of Erie stock down, Fisk and Gould found a printing press in the cellars of the Erie offices and turned out phony stock certificates. Eventually, they did get control of the Erie, the stock of which they success-fully "watered."[2] The money he made on the Erie and other speculative ruthless adventures was Gould's starting capital for cornering the gold market. The public scandal was so great that Gould was finally ejected from his control of the Erie on March 10, 1872. At that time his fortune was estimated to exceed $25 million.

Furthermore, he went on to still greener pastures. He took over the Union Pacific Railroad, became its director, and remained in virtual control until 1878, while at the same time buying control of the Kansas Pacific. Then in 1879 he bought control of the Denver Pacific, Central Pacific, and Missouri Pacific. In another seemingly unscrupulous deal with the Union Pacific and Kansas Pacific, he made a stock deal that supposedly netted him $ 10 million. Gould was the epitome of the ruthless American businessman. He apparently had few friends, but some observers point out that he was a warm and kindly family man, enjoying the diversions of books and gardening. He died of tuberculosis at age fifty-seven with an estate of $70 million.

The Great Steel Maker

Andrew Carnegie (1835-1919)

INDUSTRIALIST AND SCIENTIFIC PHILANTHROPIST

"A messenger boy of the name of Andrew Carnegie, employed by the O'Reily Telegraph Company, yesterday found a draft for the amount of $500. Like an honest little fellow, he promptly made known the facts, and deposited the paper in good hands where it awaits identification" (news clipping from the *Pittsburgh Dispatch*, November 2, 1849).

Five hundred dollars was indeed a lot of money for the son of a Scottish weaver— it represented ten years' wages. Later in life, it would represent merely what Andrew would earn every ten minutes of every day. The saga of Andrew Carnegie has indeed inspired generations of schoolchildren. At age twelve, the young immigrant worked in a cotton mill for $1.20 a week. Then he moved into the telegraph department of the Pennsylvania Railroad, where he quickly became the private secretary of its head. He started investing, first in a small oil company, and then in the Woodruff Palace Sleeping Car Company. Soon the young man was building railroad bridges, iron rails, and the like. Carnegie also made a small fortune in oil and took several trips to Europe selling railroad securities. His operations in bond selling, oil dealing, bridge building, and the like were so dashing and successful that conservative Pittsburgh businessmen regarded him as somewhat of a Young Turk. By 1873, however, Carnegie thought that steel was the new American industry. He began his famous policy, which he described as "putting all my eggs in one basket and then watching the basket." He was then thirty-eight years old. His business life for the next three decades was to some extent a microcosm of the industrial history of the United States for the same period. During this time, he was a staunch advocate of tariffs for infant industries, but he considered them wicked "when used merely to swell the profits of an established business." Even before he retired, he advocated the removal of tariff duties on imported steel. (As well he might, since his firms could produce at lower cost than the British!)

Industrialist Andrew Carnegie rose to power in the steel industry during the period after the Civil War that has been characterized as one of uninhibited exploitation and cutthroat competition. Even Calvinist attitudes were insufficient to excuse what was happening. Carnegie found his philosophical underpinnings in the English writer Herbert Spencer, who applied the fundamental principles of Darwinian evolution to society. His thesis was that of social Darwinism—in the struggle for existence, survival went to the fittest, whether it be in business or economics. And the fittest had to become the wealthiest. When Carnegie read Spencer, he found an idol. The industrialist said that when he read Spencer's *First Principles* in 1862, "light came as in a flood and all was clear." Carnegie and other businessmen of the day used Spencer as an argument against government intervention and also against the rise of unions. However, during this period big business, in conjunction with the government, was active in attempting to throttle free competition.

In 1868, the steel maker wrote a memo to himself: "Thirty-three and an income of $50,000 per annum! Beyond this never earn—make no effort to increase fortune, but spend the surplus each year for benevolent purposes. Cast aside business forever, except for others." He did not follow his advice until he was sixty-six, but then he engaged in what he called *scientific philanthropy*. The major projects worth giving money to were universities, free libraries, hospitals, and parks, in that order, in addition to swimming baths and churches, which ranked low on his list.

Carnegie retired after the sale of his steel company to the new United States Steel Company in 1901. Of the $250 million he got, he left a $5 million pension and benefit fund for his trustworthy employees. He did not stop giving from that moment. Over $60 million of his money went into almost 3,000 free public libraries around the world. The size of Carnegie's gift depended on the town's population; it averaged $2 per person. (This formula left some small towns with an uneconomical library that had to be closed down; nobody ever thought of pooling the funds for regional libraries.)

Giving away money seemed to be as hard as making it. "Pity the poor millionaire, for the way of the philanthropist is hard," he wrote to a newspaper in 1913. After working for ten years at giving away $350 million, he realized that no one man could do such a big job; the Carnegie Corporation in New York started with an endowment of $125 million. It was the first modern philanthropic foundation administered by trustees who were skilled in their different areas. Carnegie chose only trustees who had been good businessmen.

He died in 1919 after fulfilling his personal pledge of giving away just about everything he had accumulated.

Nine
Peace and Renewed Progress

Once the Civil War was over, the nation returned with renewed vigor to its primary economic task—raising its standard of living. The railroads expanded far into the West, investment banking became big business, and the health standards and educational attainment of the population rose. The period from 1865 to 1890 has been considered the epoch of unbridled freedom for business. Fortunes were made. Wealth was accumulated. This was the era of large trusts and monopolies, the development of which prompted the passage of our first antitrust act in 1890. This was also an era of a tremendous increase in the communications capacity of the nation. The harnessing of electricity for communications by Samuel F. B. Morse was only a beginning. Thomas Edison and Alexander Bell continued Morse's pioneering work, giving the nation an intricate telephone network. In 1908, another great achievement had been heralded by the introduction of the first Model T. Mass production techniques had become available for a mass market created by continuing population growth and unprecedented immigration rates.

Increases in Living Standards

While per capita income had been increasing rather steadily through the 1840s and 1850s, the Civil War brought an abrupt pause to this upward march. In 1870, the average income in the North was slightly above its prewar level; in the South, it was dramatically below the prewar level. However, the standard of living after 1870 began to rise at an unusually, but only temporarily, high rate. This rate of advance was about the same for both the North and the South, but recall that the South was now at a much lower level relative to the North. The 1870s growth spurt for both regions was in part a catching up (or making up for lost ground) phenomenon, a counterpart to the pause of the 1860s. The growth rate remained high in the 1880s, but was lower than in the 1870s; finally, it slowed again and resumed its long-run normal trend by the turn of the century, about 1.6 percent per year. In addition, there were large amounts of immigration during that period, and population grew at a fairly rapid rate. Hence, total output expanded even more than per capita income. Its average rate of growth was around 4 percent a year.

The Growing American Citizenry and Territory

During this half century between the Civil War and World War I, there were expansions both in the number of people in the United States and in the extent of territory in which they lived. Population grew at an average rate of 2 percent a year, rising from 37 million at the end of the Civil War to over 100 million by the beginning of World War I. By the end of the period, however, the growth rate of the population was slower than at the beginning.

Why Population Grew

Population in this period grew for two reasons: (1) there was a large influx of immigrants, and (2) the birth rate exceeded the death rate. The second reason contributed far more to population growth than the first.

IMMIGRATION

Nevertheless, immigration was important, and many thousands of immigrants landed on our shores during this period. However, net immigration decreased during business depressions in the United States. This shouldn't be surprising since the major reason that people spend the energy and money and pay all the other costs involved in migrating to another country is increased real standards of living. When business recessions and depressions in the United States reduced the possibility of finding employment, there was less economic incentive for immigrants to come.

FERTILITY

It is perhaps less easy to explain why the fertility of the native population decreased toward the end of this period. But perhaps by addressing the economics of this matter, at least a partial explanation can be found. Urbanization increased during this period as more and more people moved off the farm and into the city. When this happened, children no longer were as much of a productive asset as they had been on the farm, where they could start working from very early ages. Rather than being an investment in productive capacity, child-bearing created for the city dweller an item that we will call a **consumption** good. That is, yielded mainly pleasure; it could not generate as much future net income for the producers of it, the parents. Hence, children were a less valuable asset in the city. Also, twentieth-century urban women had greater opportunities to work outside the household. Therefore, if they chose to stay home to raise children, they bore a cost—lost wages—that they did not bear on the farm. This was an additional incentive to limit the number of children per family in the city.

Economics at Work

Information Costs

Today, news of events around the world are available almost instantaneously. With satellite communication, television, and radio broadcasts it is very difficult to be unaware of the events around the globe. But this was not the case in earlier times. Information moved very slowly.

For example, the information costs associated with spouse search were particularly high in the rural community of Seattle during the mid 1860s. The roughly 300 or so men outnumbered the women by at least 10 to 1; making the odds of a man finding a wife in Seattle extremely low. Well, Asa Mercer (who later founded the University of Washington) devised a scheme to attract women to the new territory.

Mercer figured that since the Civil War exacted such a heavy toll on the male population that there were many eligible and willing widows looking for husbands. So he raised money from Seattle bachelors to finance his trip to the east coast. Upon arrival, he combed the area for prospective brides. He advertised widely for female music and English teachers and had as many as 500 women signed and ready to go. Then the story of the "Mercer-nary Adventures" broke. The *New York Herald* and other newspapers warned women that they would be signing up for a life of bondage and would ultimately end up in a Seattle brothel. As a result, only 100 women made the trip. However, the story does have a happy ending—within a year, almost all of the "Mercer Girls," were married.

Education and the Labor Force

Many activities raised the levels of skills of the working force. Among these were investments in education and other investments in human capital. Strictly speaking, these are investments because they create the possibility of increased production in the future. That is a primary effect of education, whether it be formal or informal. Formal education is, of course, going to school. But informal education is important also. This involves on-the-job training—gaining more experience in one's work and by observing what is happening around oneself.

Together, these investments greatly enhanced the productivity of the labor force. The American nation has always had high literacy rates. In 1870, almost 90 percent of all adult white Americans could read and write. By the beginning of World War I, this figure had risen to 96 percent. The black population, while having only a 20 percent literacy rate in 1870, increased it phenomenally to 70 percent by 1910. In 1860, the total resource cost devoted to education was 1.4 percent of the GNP; by 1900 this proportion had doubled. This figure includes not only the direct but also the indirect costs of education. The direct costs are fairly obvious—books, tuition, and the like. The indirect costs involve current income lost by going to school. Clearly, one of the greatest costs of going to school is the forgone income that could have been earned had a person remained in the labor force. This is the **opportunity cost** involved and these costs are forever present.

Investment in Health

Investing in education was not the only way to raise the productivity of the labor force and of the population at large. Investment in health was another way, a most important one, in the nineteenth century. Compared to today, health standards in those times were abysmal, although they were probably superior to what existed in other countries in the world. There were numerous epidemics: yellow fever, smallpox, typhoid, diphtheria, typhus, and cholera were common. There was also dysentery and malaria. Tuberculosis was rampant. Today we know the causes of these diseases, but at the end of the Civil War, medicine could hardly be called a science. During the half century following the Civil War, very few improvements in medical care were made per se; in fact, one was often better off by not going to a doctor. There were only two serious diseases that responded to medical treatment: malaria could be treated by applications of quinine, and smallpox prevented by a vaccination.

It was, rather, the discovery of the need to improve sewage disposal and treatment and to provide pure water that accounts in large part for the vast improvement in health standards at the time. The discoveries of Louis Pasteur and the subsequent pasteurization of milk contributed much. A falling death rate was sure to result, and indeed it did; in 1915, it was about 60 percent of its 1870 level. But more important economically, better health conditions allowed workers to be more productive, to be absent from work less, and to feel generally more like pursuing their individual endeavors.

Improving the Land

Although there were more people than ever before, and more living in cities than ever before, there also was much more land being worked. The U.S. acquired tremendous additional acreage in territories before the Civil War: The Republic of Texas joined the states in 1845; the U.S. acquired the Oregon Territory in 1846; the Mexican Secession gave the U.S. even more land in the West and Southwest two years later. These additional lands gave us 70 percent more territory. But land that is idle or in isolation is useless. Only when it is improved can it increase the productive capacity of the nation; so improving the land was a vital task, especially for a nation of individuals striving for increased standards of living. At the end of the Civil War, this 70 percent increase in the national domain was virtually uninhabited by whites. Less than 50 years later, however, there were no longer large areas in the United States that had no white population. This large availability of land allowed Americans to forestall any detrimental effects that crowding or falling output per additional worker (diminishing returns in production) might have had. The specter of a zero increase in output from an additional worker never haunted North America as it occasionally haunted Europe. We always had new land to ease the population pressure and lower the labor-to-land ratio. Far more important than land availability, however, to the rise of cities was the rise of productivity in agriculture. Whereas in colonial times nearly 90 percent of the population was engaged in agricultural activities, by 1860 this figure had fallen to 60 percent; by 1880, 50 percent; and by 1900, 38 percent. In spite of this percentage decline of the agricultural labor force, there were tremendous gains in total output. Acreage and productivity per worker increased, as did, in absolute numbers, the population engaged in this activity. So this period was still one of absolute growth, both of workers and of output, in the farming sector.

Little frontier was left the end of the nineteenth century. The amount of land in cultivation doubled after the Civil War. The expansion in agricultural output was not as rapid as in industry, but it grew faster than before the Civil War. Two different factors accounted for this expansion, the most obvious being the physical extension of cultivated land. But also important was increased productivity, the rise of output relative to the inputs of land, labor, and capital. Although productivity change in agriculture was less rapid than in manufacturing, it accounted for perhaps 40 percent of the increase in total farm output. And the pace of agricultural productivity advance in the last half of the century was several times higher than in the first half. This was the age of the mechanical reaper, the horse-drawn cultivator, and the improved harrow. The U.S. saw, therefore, a rapid rise in the agricultural implement industry. The fortunes of Cyrus McCormick can attest to that.

It must not be overlooked, of course, that many of the advances in agriculture were inseparably linked to transportation improvements and, in particular, the coming of the iron horse. It was only with the expansion of the railroad network that farming moved westward to the fertile new lands in Nebraska, Kansas, Texas, Oklahoma, the Dakotas, and the Far West.

The Golden Age of the Iron Horse

At the beginning of the Civil War, there were perhaps 30,000 miles of railroad track in all of the United States. By the end of the nineteenth century, most of today's existing railroad bed and track had been completely laid. There were over 200,000 miles of track, and most of it was standard-gauge width, quite unlike the unintegrated system that had existed in 1860. Moreover, whereas in 1860 there were hardly any bridges, in 1900 they dotted the landscape. Locomotives increased in power and grew in number; freight cars multiplied by 20 in only 40 years. And the capacity of each car increased 300 percent; hence, the rolling car capacity of the railroads had jumped by a multiple of 80 by the end of the century. Employment on the railroads also jumped, growing from 100,000 to one million individuals. Whereas in 1860, 1 percent of the labor force was engaged in railroad employment, three times that proportion were involved in it by the turn of the century. Passenger miles and ton freight miles increased immensely—500 percent and 6,000 percent, respectively. The railroad had become a freight carrier. Because other means of traveling had been found, the role of the passenger train was relatively diminishing. By 1910, the railroad reached its peak years of carrying people.

High Finance

The 1880s saw a wave of competitive construction in the railroad industry. Each system found itself in competition over certain routes with other systems. There were 11 lines going from New York to the Midwest!

The monetary debt of all the railroad systems combined began to exceed that of the entire United States government. In floating much of this debt, numerous deals—some of them shady—enriched speculators. These were the days of the Vanderbilts, the Fisks, and the Goulds. Some schemes led to local monopolies. Cornelius Vanderbilt, for example, was busy during and after the Civil War buying all the small railroad lines he could. He controlled the lines running from New York City to Albany. Then he started buying New York Central stock in 1865. Not content with the rate at which he was acquiring that company, he devised a scheme to cause the price of Central's stock to drop. Part of this scheme involved stopping his trains short of a bridge at Albany, thus forcing the Central's passengers to cross by themselves to make the connection (even in the rain). There were other underhanded deals and ultimately capitulation of the Central Railroad and the combination of the Central line with Vanderbilt's Hudson line, with Vanderbilt, of course, as president.

There were also scandals with the construction of the railroads to the West, the most famous involving Credit Mobilier, an ephemeral construction company. It was rumored that the Mobilier made direct profits for building the Union Pacific at between $33 and $50 million. This scandal involved congressmen as well as business people.

RATE WARS AND PRICE FIXING

Whenever possible, the railroad systems tried to get together to fix rates so that they would not compete and could therefore avoid price competition. All parties to an agreement could feel they would be better off. These associations (cartels) were usually only temporary. The incentive for cheating on such agreements is tremendous, particularly if one is not caught. If one railroad cheated on a rate-fixing agreement, it could obtain lots of business, thereby increasing its profits, since the other railroads would not lower their prices if they were still abiding by the agreement. There were continuous pools and internal regulating committees for railroads, but none of them seemed to work; none of them seemed to ensure a continuous system of rate fixing. This was a time, then, of secret rebates. This was also a time of **price discrimination**. Most railroads ended up charging more for short hauls than for long hauls because there was generally no competition in short-haul routes. It was only in the long-haul routes that more than one railroad would build competing lines.

Finally, in 1887, the Interstate Commerce Act created the Interstate Commerce Commission (ICC) and with it a set of rules to create "fair" business practices by railroads. In reality, however, many economists and historians believe that the railroads supported the ICC so that they could have government supervision of their rate fixing.

Forging a National Economy

For decades historians have hailed the expansion of the railroad as a major factor in the transformation of the American economy. Indeed, some have gone so far as to single out the railroad as the cause of increased and sustained economic growth in the United States in the nineteenth and twentieth centuries. And if that isn't enough, the railroad is held responsible for everybody's ability to "Go West, young man."

The improvements in transportation in the pre– and post–Civil War era were extremely important for forging a national economy. Several kinds of favorable influences that transportation had on the economy can be singled out. The importance of lower transportation costs allowed new lands to be cultivated and allowed the market to grow in size. Remember that specialization is determined by how large the market is. The larger the market, the more specialization, and generally the higher real incomes will be.

Moreover, total expenditures in the U.S. transportation network, and especially in railroads, were very large relative to the capital invested in other areas. The increased demand for labor, particularly in the beginning, was brought about by the very labor-intensive construction of both railroads and canals. On the other hand, because we imported rails from England free of duty, little manufacturing of them was done in America. This was to change later on.

Secondary Effects, Too

Transportation improvements also had secondary effects. For example, they caused the expansion of existing capacity to supply the larger market that was made available by canals and railroads. After the Civil War, the sheer magnitude of railroad investment and activity made it one of the most prominent features in our economy. The debt of the railroads exceeded that of the entire United States, and the total capital stock of the railroads was almost 15 percent of that of the entire economy by 1900. To at least some extent, the railroad set the tempo of American life during the half century after the Civil War.

Opening Up the West

The most prominent feature of railroad expansion after the War Between the States was the fairly rapid attempt at opening up the West to transcontinental passenger and freight service. Between 1865 and 1878, 30,000 miles were laid just for transcontinental lines. There was additionally some filling in of the networks during that period. A second boom came between 1878 and 1882, almost all of it devoted to construction west of the Mississippi River, especially in Texas.

This is not to say, of course, that railroad expansion grew steadily. There were drops of as much as 50 percent in railroad investment in a one- or two-year period. This, of course, had destabilizing effects on the entire economy.

Other Effects of the Railroad

The extensive network of railroads created a large demand for skilled technicians; this demand was met. This perhaps represented an additional impetus to industrialization because these skilled technicians were scattered throughout the United States and would be available during the period to go into other lines of work in industries where their skills could be used. By 1900, 3 percent of the total labor force was in railroads. This is almost equivalent to the percentage of farmers there are in the United States today.

The railroad also allowed more regional specialization within the United States itself. We can be fairly certain that the railroad played a pioneering role in the development of the Great Plains because development of that area depended on a low-cost transportation system to provide the necessary inputs to raise livestock and to ship products back to market. The railroads also created numerous towns, such as Des Moines, which would not have been important otherwise because they did not lie on natural transportation links such as large bodies of interconnected waterways. Most important, though, the railroad created a national market. This allowed certain types of activity to be concentrated in big cities where economies of scale could be realized. Economies of scale occurred when, say, a doubling of the capital and labor used by a firm results in more than a doubling of output. Only by large-scale production techniques can economies of scale generally be obtained. In other words, there has to be a large enough market for one to cater to in order to take advantage of this economic fact of life. The railroad allowed for this large scale market by interconnecting cities and states throughout the country.

Reexamining the Data

To be sure, the railroad was extremely important in the development of the United States' economy. Absolute facts and figures, however, do not tell the whole story. We have to look at relative facts and figures. That is, was the railroad important relative to the rest of the economy, or relative to the totals involved?

CONSUMPTION OF IRON

Take the railroad's consumption of iron, long considered one of the major impetuses to economic growth in the nineteenth century. Numerous historians have stated that the railroad was "by far the biggest user of iron in the 1850s." A cursory inspection of some of the data indicates that by the start of the Civil War, the iron horse used up one-half of the annual iron production in the United States for laying tracks. However, looking particularly at the demand for pig iron to make rails between the years 1840 and 1860, for example, we find that it consumed only about 5 percent of the total iron output in the United States. This was chiefly because by 1860, 60 percent of domestic rail production involved re-using previously worn-out rails—that is, rerolling them into new ones. Obviously there was an increase in the rerolling industry, but there was no increase in the demand for the product of blast furnaces.

If we take into account the other uses of iron in the railroad industry, such as for engines and things like that, this figure rises to an average of 17 percent of the total United States production during the twenty-year period just mentioned. How important was this figure? Well, if we compare it to other uses of iron, not very important. Some historians have stated that the initial leap in iron production between 1845 and 1849 was due to "nails, not rails" because the domestic production of iron in nails exceeded that of rails by a factor of two in 1849.

COAL

The railroads' use of coal was negligible before the Civil War. Charcoal was the major fuel in making the rails and in engines in the period before the Civil War. The amount of wood used to feed the hungry iron horses and to lay the ties for the tracks previous to the Civil War was about one-half of 1 percent of all lumber production. The demand for different goods by the railroad industry may have been important, but certainly not as much as we previously thought. This, of course, does not tell the full story, for we have to compare what happened with the railroads with what would have happened without them. If it can be shown that transportation, for example, would have been in a much worse state without railroads, then indeed there is a case to be made that life without the iron horse would have been quite a bit more constrained and expensive.

What Could Have Happened

It is unrealistic to assume that without railroads no transportation networks would have been built. After all, roads and waterways had been developing for some time before the railroad came into being. The canal system, for example, could have been extended to take advantage of the demand for improved transportation during the period between the Civil War and World War I. The idea of substituting canals for rails is not as farfetched as it might initially sound. For example, in 1890, it has been estimated that a system of canals that could have been built in the absence of the railroad would have brought all but seven percent of agricultural land within forty miles of navigable waterways.[1]

By some ingenious calculations, one can come up with the actual savings accounted for by having a railroad system rather than relying on an extension of the canal system. The difference between the two is called the **social savings.** If the social savings turn out to be large, then the railroads were important to increasing the standard of living in the United States. But if they turn out to be insignificant, then in fact an alternative transportation network of canals, rivers, and roads would have allowed a similar (though certainly not the same) development in the United States. One such study, by Fogel, came up with the social savings attributable to the railroads of less than 5 percent of gross national product in 1890.[2] In other words, had the railroads never existed and an alternative transportation network been used instead, annual gross domestic product would have been only about 5 percent less. Now this may seem small, but it could add up. So even if this estimate were to be believed completely, the railroads did have a small but important effect on the growth of the American economy, but not as important as many historians had thought previously.

There are lots of important caveats in a study of an entire transportation system. No matter how impressive and detailed the analysis, there will always be areas where research was not carried out. For example, in assessing the impact of railroads, we must remember that the speed and flexibility advantage was with the railroad. This is taken account of when assessing the social savings to railroads by looking at the higher costs of inventories of goods. Inventories would have to have been kept because replacements could not have been obtained as fast with the waterway system as they were with a railroad system.

However, two important aspects of railroad transportation were left out in this calculation: One, the ability of fresh fruit, vegetables, and meats to be brought to the cities during all seasons may seem trivial, but it probably accounted for many improvements in health and general well-being of city dwellers. This may have meant an increased demand for an urban living environment that would not have existed had railroads not been built and canals had been used instead. We have no idea how to quantify this effect, but it could be important. Two, passenger traffic was not included. After all, American passengers traveled almost 12 billion miles by rail in 1890. In fact, one study shows that when savings from passenger services are added to Fogel's figures the social savings climbs to roughly 7.5 percent in 1890.

Others have argued that Fogel's study does not take into consideration some of the indirect benefits or secondary effects of the railroad, such as the impact on the rate of capital formation, the stimulus to interregional specialization and trade, the effect on migration patterns, and so on. Taking the indirect benefits into account, one researcher arrived at a social savings rate several times larger than that estimated by Fogel.[3]

Moreover, if we look carefully at an alternative canal system, we note immediately that it would have required gargantuan amounts of water. In many cases, it is not obvious that enough water was available. Additionally, it certainly would have been a long time before California would have developed without the railroad.

Issue: Unrest on the Farm

The Farm Problem

The late nineteenth century was a period of dramatic change for the country. Because of emancipation, it was a period of severe adjustment for blacks and many whites as well. Because of impending industrialization, new situations and hazards caused rising concerns for decency, security, and fairness. For many reasons, farmers (and others) complained that the fruits of economic growth were passing them by. It was an era of agrarian discontent.

Structural Changes

Accompanying these many important changes in the economy, the rising standard of living, the increasing pace of life associated with the railroad, high finance, communications, and increased city dwelling were basic changes in the structure of the economy. We can view these distinct changes in the structure of the economy by looking at Table 9.1. There we see that the percentage of commodity output attributable to agricultural production fell from 53 percent in 1870 to 33 percent by the end of the century (although there was still an absolute increase in farm output). At the beginning of the period, agriculture accounted for 53 percent of total commodity output, whereas manufacturing only a third. These proportions reversed themselves by the turn of the century. The opposite was the case for manufacturing, whereas in the areas of mining and construction combined, there was no change.

During these decades, the U.S. economy had transformed and had become primarily a manufacturing instead of an agrarian economy. At the same time, the percentage distribution of the labor force was changing accordingly. Farming, fishing, and mining engaged more than half the working population in 1870, but barely a third by 1910. This trend was to continue even until today, when roughly 4 percent of our population is in these fields. What happened, of course, was that the labor force became more

Exhibit 9.1

The Changing Composition of Commodity Output

Year	Agriculture	Manufacturing	Mining and Construction
1869	53	33	14
1874	46	39	14
1879	49	37	14
1884	41	44	15
1889	37	48	15
1894	32	53	15
1899	33	53	14

Source: R. E. Gallman, "Commodity Output, 1839-1989," in *Trends in the American Economy in the Nineteenth Century,* National Bureau of Economic Research (Princeton, NJ: Princeton University Press, 1960), p. 26.

active in the manufacturing, trade, and construction sectors.

There was also a distinct movement to the West. This was understandable, since migration usually responds to economic opportunity, and that is where the opportunities were. People moved in an attempt to improve their economic standard of living, and Americans have always been highly mobile.

Money and Prices

Curiously enough, these changes came primarily during decades of falling prices. The period after the Civil War was generally one of a drop in the price level; that is, of deflation. However, falling prices or deflation did not mean depression or declining real incomes in the long run.

REDUCED SUPPLY OF GREENBACKS

There was, however, a distinct relationship between changes in the price level and changes in the stock of money during that period. Right after the Civil War, the federal government deliberately reduced the quantity of greenbacks in circulation in order to raise the value of a greenback to a dollar in gold. This exchange, "at par," finally happened in 1879. Meanwhile, there were some—primarily farmers—who wanted more, not fewer greenbacks. In particular, the greenback Labor Party associated a rising price level with a higher price of products and hence higher incomes and a higher standard of living.

ON A GOLD STANDARD

After the year 1878, we were on a *de facto* gold standard. That is, gold served as a medium of exchange and also as the backing for reserves in the banking system. Hence, the entire money stock was tied to the production of gold, which did not increase rapidly enough to keep up with the need of money for the nation's transactions. Consequently, the economy experienced deflation for three decades. It was only after gold discoveries in South Africa and the Yukon, plus development of the relatively inexpensive cyanide reduction process, which allowed the gold stock—and, hence, the money stock—to increase faster than the increased rate of output that the deflation was stopped. Lastly, notice that in the latter period under study (1898–1915), a rise in prices finally occurred.

THE AGRARIAN MOVEMENT

The plight of the farmer was vocally expressed through a number of novel political movements in rural America (mainly the Midwest) shortly after the Civil War. These movements flourished all through the 1870s and in the latter part of the 1880s. Their peak of effectiveness coincided with two periods of falling prices.

Agrarian discontent was also based on hatred of capitalist creditors, whom the western farmers thought were gouging them with usurious interest rates. Another complaint was discrimination in railroad rates that were not consistent with the differences in costs for different types of railroad transportation. There was a hatred for the common practice of charging more for short hauls than for long hauls.

The most influential force was the Populist Movement, but in addition to the Populists, there were several other groups—the Grangers, the Farmer Alliances, and the Greenback Movement.

To make higher profits for the farmer, some Grangers tried to eliminate the middleman. In addition, they attempted cooperative mass marketing schemes to eliminate the profits of distributors and encouraged state laws in the 1870s to regulate railroads. They also had important educational and social functions. By and large, the Grangers were organized most effectively in the farming states of the upper Mississippi Valley.

The Farmer's Alliances and the Greenback Movement focused primarily on the issue of falling prices and what to do about it. They wanted an increased circulation of paper money. The Alliances, which were eventually absorbed into the Populist Party, pressed for the free coinage of silver (as well as more gold, which was then in use).

As noted, one of the purposes of the agrarian movement was to stop falling prices. Farmers were convinced that the price of manufactured goods was rising relative to the price of agricultural goods. While it is true that farm prices were falling during this period, so were the prices of manufactured goods. In fact, it looks as if the average **terms of trade** for farmers—the average prices of farm products relative to other prices—stayed about the same, overall, between 1865 and 1900. During this period, the relative amounts of goods and services that the farmer could buy with a unit of his or her crop (their terms of trade) did not decline. By their actions and discussions, however, it is clear that many of them apparently believed otherwise.

THE CREDIT QUESTION

Farmers were convinced they were being ruthlessly exploited by large creditors from the East. They complained about the high interest rates they had to pay, particularly about the conditions under which they were able to obtain credit. It is true that prices fell over this period and hence debtors were hurt in the process—at least until people adjusted their expectations to these conditions of deflation. But before this adjustment, debtors paid off their loans in dollar amounts greater than they anticipated. As people became accustomed to the fall in prices, however, the price of credit, like all other prices, fell accordingly. In any event, since most mortgages held by farmers were of relatively short duration—three or four years—they could not have been hurt for very long (unless they were foreclosed or renewed their loans with the conditions prevailing). And at the same time, the largest debtor group in the nation was the railroads, not the farmers, so the unexpected falling price level affected the profits of the railroads and the manufacturers as much as or more than farmers.

It is quite true that credit was somewhat limited, particularly in the western and southern agricultural regions. We stated, however, in Chapter 8, that one of the reasons for the restriction in credit was the National Banking Act, since it prevented the growth of smaller banks in less-populated regions and allowed those that did exist to have a monopoly on money lending. In this instance, the farmers did have a legitimate gripe. But consider also that farmers often were not very good credit risks at that time. A tremendous number of mortgage companies failed during this period because of the poor credit risks they had taken with farmers.

RAILROAD RATES

The farmers were rightly concerned and annoyed about the discriminatory railroad rates. But it is not clear that a large percentage of farmers were really victimized by actual price discrimination against them. For example, rates west of the Mississippi were higher than those east of the Mississippi, but this was a function of the actual costs of providing railroad transportation in these two different regions. The real factor was that western railroads had lower loading ratios. That is, because of major seasonal fluctuations in the demand for their services, their cars were not loaded as much as were those in the east. Essentially, then, during certain times of the year there had to be empty freight cars shipped from the east to the west to take account of seasonal peaks. This increased cost for railroads operating in the West, and one would expect them to charge a higher price. In fact, the rate of return to western railroads was less than to eastern ones.

CREDIT AND COMMERCIALIZATION

The discontent among farmers was real enough, and there was just too much smoke for there to be no fire. However, the many issues farmers raised and causes they damned were not central to the real problems underlying agricultural conditions in America in the last half of the nineteenth century.

In earlier times, most farmers were relatively isolated from the market and were involved in commercial agriculture only on the periphery. Basic essential tools and equipment, which were not generally too costly, and various luxury items were obtained by sporadic selling of crops or livestock. But after the Civil War, agricultural productivity soared and so did the degree to which farmers were engaged in commercial agriculture—production for market. This brought forth a host of new problems. For instance, farmers were often forced into debt because, after the Civil War, one could not be a farmer without also being a capitalist.

Farmers had to buy equipment: reapers, planters, harrows, and the like. They also had to buy chemical fertilizers and large amounts of land and sometimes irrigation facilities. Besides depending on banks, farmers had to depend on grain elevators and railroads to market their crops.

Often this required an extension of credit, and when prices fell for their crops, foreclosures on their farms sometimes resulted. It was a time when farmers seemed forced to take risks that earlier generations of farmers had not encountered. It was a time when the stakes were higher than ever before. And, to make matters worse, it was a time when U.S. agriculture became heavily involved in the international economy. As well as approaching industrial dominance in the world, the U.S. was becoming the most modern and productive agriculture economy. The welfare of American farmers became increasingly dependent on conditions remote from them and little understood by them. For them, it was an impersonal world where a bumper wheat crop elsewhere could cause world (and U.S.) wheat prices to drop sharply. Whose fault was it? Many thought it was the person at the railroad, or at the grain elevator, or the creditor at the bank.

DEFINITIONS OF NEW TERMS

CONSUMPTION GOOD A good that yields utility in the current period, but not in future periods. Consumption goods are such things as food, movies, and trips. To be contrasted with an investment or capital good, which yields a stream of services or utility in the future.

OPPORTUNITY COST Opportunity cost is the alternative cost of doing something. Opportunity costs can be explicit, as in the case of a clearly marked price of a good or service, or implicit, as in the case of a value of a person's leisure time.

PRICE DISCRIMINATION Price discrimination is charging some people higher prices than other people when these higher prices do not reflect higher costs. Price discrimination is usually illegal, although often practiced. (Every time you go to a movie or the zoo and there are special student prices or prices for senior citizens, you are the beneficiary or victim of price discrimination.)

SOCIAL SAVINGS The reduction in costs to the whole society by using one specific economic enterprise over another one. In the case of railroads, we compute the social savings by comparing the costs of transportation without the railroads and the costs of transportation with the railroads.

TERMS OF TRADE Terms of trade are the terms on which a specific sector trades with another sector. In agriculture, for example, the terms of trade can be found by seeing what a unit of agricultural product will buy in terms of units of manufactured products.

ENDNOTES

[1] See Robert W. Fogel, *Railroads and American Economic Growth: Essays in Econometric History* (Baltimore, MD: Johns Hopkins Press, 1964).

[2] Ibid.

[3] See Jeffrey G. Williamson, *Late Nineteenth Century American Development: A General Equilibrium History* (Cambridge, Cambridge University Press, 1974) Chapter 9.

Ten
Increasing the Tempo of Economic Life

The half century after the Civil War was a period not only of rapid economic growth and of large increases in population and westward movement, but also of tremendous structural change—that is, change in the basic makeup of the entire U.S. economy. We were able to allude only briefly to some of these changes in the last chapter. It is time now to deal with them more thoroughly. The years between the Civil War and World War I was a period of the rise of cities, with all the accompanying gains and costs; a period of increasing industrial power and concentration; and finally, a period of massive changes in the agricultural sector. These trends continue even into the present, and we are still faced with finding solutions to the multitude of complex problems of modern society.

Urbanization

At the end of the Civil War decade, about one-fourth of the population lived in cities of 2,500 or more. Fifty years later, almost one-half the entire population was crowded into cities. In fact, by the end of World War I, there were more city dwellers than country folks. Of course, this does not mean that everybody lived in big cities. In fact, it was not until more recently that the population concentrated itself into what we consider the major cities in the nation. In 1870, for example, out of the 663 cities, almost 500 had a population of less than 10,000. This proportion was to fall somewhat, but not drastically; even by 1910, 1,665 of the 2,262 cities still had populations of less than 10,000. Before assessing the problems that the city dweller of the past faced, let us examine some of the reasons why cities exist in the first place.

THE ECONOMICS OF WHY CITIES EXIST

It is not accidental that many major cities are located near areas of significant mineral deposits or natural resources, or in areas that can be easily serviced by natural transportation networks. In other words, there are many natural reasons why cities are located where they are. Cities serve as focal points for commerce and in some cases extractive industry (mining). Also, concentration of industry within a fairly constrained area allows for decreased costs of production. This is because there are many interactions between firms; if the firms are spread out, they have to engage in extensive long-distance communication and transportation in order to trade. When they concentrate in one region, they save on many of these costs. Furthermore, a concentration of production will generally lead to what are called economies of scale. That is, firms that can obtain sufficient levels of production will find that their average costs fall. This may be due to factors often associated with the techniques of **mass production**, such as assembly-line means of production.

In addition, the concentration of people and resources in the city allows for more efficient provision of such public services as education, fire and police protection, pottable water, improved sewer systems, and the like.

A HIERARCHY OF CITIES

Prior to the Civil War, most cities were retail trade centers. It was only after the war that many of them became oriented toward manufacturing. As manufacturing grew from barely one-third of commodity output in 1860 to over one-half in 1900, we would expect certain concentrations to occur in very physically constrained areas, and indeed they did.

A regular hierarchy of cities grew up that remains with us even today. The most basic characteristics of this hierarchy are as follows:

City Size	Characteristics
2,500 to 10,000	Mainly trading centers; the reduction in costs are enough to get people to drive short distances in from the countryside; total demand not high enough for the provision of specialized services.
10,000 to 50,000	Still mainly trading centers, but provision of certain specialized services, such as stock brokers and the like.
50,000 to 250,000	Still commercial trading, plus increasing specialized services: stock brokers, insurance salesmen, more specialized doctors, and so on.
250,000 and more (Major Urban Centers)	Commercial trading, many specialized services, operas, orchestras, brain surgeons, gourmet food, and so on.

By 1890, we had indeed reached the era of big cities, New York, Chicago, Philadelphia, Boston—they all had their special characteristics and their special brands of vice and social disamenities: tuberculosis, slum housing, crimes, pollution, and corruption. At that time, the top ten cities were also the big manufacturing centers. They accounted for more than 40 percent of all manufacturing output and were the focal points of commerce, finance, and communications.

VALUE OF LAND

Despite their bad effects, cities certainly provided ample rewards to thousands of businesses that located in them. For example, in Chicago, from 1873 to 1910, the value of inner-city property rose by more than 700 percent. Land and other property was immensely valuable in the centers of crowded cities.

A STRUGGLE FOR LIFE

Urbanization may have allowed for more profitable business opportunities; it may have resulted in economies of scale; it may have resulted in increased specialization and higher real living standards for the nation at large; but it also meant, particularly at the beginning of the period we are talking about, increased mortality and morbidity among the urban populations. In 1860, it was far safer to live on the farm than to reside in the city: The death rate per 1,000 in the countryside was about 20, as compared to about 30 in the large city. What did people die of in the city? Mainly communicable diseases: diphtheria, tuberculosis, and the like. They drank foul water from wells that were polluted by improper and unsafe sewage systems, and hence they contracted typhoid and dysentery. Because they were unable to obtain as much fresh food as people who lived in rural areas, their diet was not as healthy.

This was all to change with passing decades. Rising real incomes enabled people to demand better health conditions. For example, they were willing and able to pay for better diets, which lowered morbidity rates. They also could afford more spacious housing. In addition, purification of water, improved sewage disposal, regular garbage collection, and swamp draining became more common. So in spite of the numerous unhealthful aspects of congested urban living, people had obtained distinct improvements in health in the city by the eve of World War I. There still remained numerous problems for the urban dweller, as there are today. Nevertheless, the benefits from living in the city apparently outweighed the costs, and progress was made.

For instance, the difficulties of movement within the cities eased as technological changes in intra-urban transport occurred, such as trolley lines. And, of course, one of the most obvious benefits from living in the city was higher income: Uncorrected for the higher skill level of the workers in the cities, real wages were twice those in the countryside. Also, and perhaps no less important, there were many more things to do in the city, just as there are today. Farm life must have been quite dreary in the good old days compared to the numerous possibilities for diversified lifestyles in New York, Chicago, New Orleans, and San Francisco.

Monopoly Capitalism

The structure of American business was changing throughout this period. There was a shift away from **proprietorships** and **partnerships** to a form of business organization called the **corporation.** The corporation wasn't really new, but it became most popular during this period for several reasons. A corporation is a legal entity owned by stockholders, who usually all have limited liability; that is, the most they can lose is the value of their stocks. They cannot be assessed any further liability even if the corporation goes bankrupt. Another appealing aspect of the corporation is that it is essentially eternal: The death of shareholders does not terminate the legal existence of the corporation, whereas it does for proprietorships and partnerships. A corporation has another advantage—its enhanced ability to obtain large amounts of capital. A corporation can sell shares in itself, and it can float large amounts of debt capital. This is generally more difficult for partnerships and proprietorships because of their uncertain longevity. Because this was a period of industrial expansion and because, as never before, it was an era of large-scale manufacturing, the corporation became a common feature of business enterprise.

Steel was certainly one of the most preeminent of the industries that required large amounts of capital. The Bessemer and open hearth processes for making steel allowed the rapid development of this industry. Moreover, these two processes are most efficient when used to produce large amounts of steel. It is not hard to imagine, then, that large companies were soon to spring up in this industry, the most famous being the one founded by Andrew Carnegie in 1872. Eventually his properties were consolidated with others by J. P. Morgan. Here we had the first billion-dollar company in the world—United States Steel.

The petroleum industry also saw rapid development. Many people know that John D. Rockefeller made his fortune providing such petroleum products as kerosene for heating and manufacturing. In the twentieth century, the automobile became a most conspicuous consumer of Rockefeller's oil. Henry Ford's application of assembly-line mass production techniques, using interchangeable parts to produce the Model T, gave a tremendous boost to this industry. By 1919, annual automobile sales were a billion-dollar affair.

All of this rapid industrialization was merely an extension of what had occurred in England and was similar to what was occurring in France and other European countries. This was the era of America's industrial revolution. This industrial revolution was paralleled by a scientific revolution and the beginning of a technological elite, or technocracy. Massachusetts Institute of Technology (MIT) was founded. Engineers were universally recognized as necessary and desirable in an industrial society. The age of Taylorism was upon us. Frederick W. Taylor, while working at Bethlehem Steel Company, discovered that worker efficiency could be improved by analyzing in detail the movements required to perform a job and then carrying on experiments to determine just the right size and weight of tools. Thus, time and motion studies became fads. It was realized that industry could profit through advances in scientific knowledge, and it did. It was also realized that higher profits could be made by creating monopolies and many attempts to erect monopolies occurred at the time. That is why we call this the age of monopoly capitalism.

The Growth of Business Consolidation

In 1890, there were 12 important trusts, or combinations, worth a total of $1 billion. By 1903, such combinations had a capital of $3 billion, and by 1904, $7.2 billion. This represented 40 percent of all American industry. One of the reasons business consolidated was to gain greater market control. Another was to reap the benefits from economies of scale. When one is able to cater to a national market—which was the case during this period—why not take advantage of falling average costs per unit by expanding production? And what easier way to expand production than to merge with similar companies?

There were basically two types of consolidations. One was the **vertical merger**, and the other **horizontal**. These descriptions have nothing to do with geometry, but merely with what aspect of the production process is acquired by merger.

VERTICAL INTEGRATION

When firms vertically integrate by merger, the various production processes are brought under one name; for example, a coal mine is consolidated with an electric utility plant. Mergers of this type were not so feared in those days, but the other kind was.

HORIZONTAL INTEGRATION

In horizontal integration, one company buys up similar companies, the most famous example being Rockefeller's Standard Oil, which acquired or forced many competitors into the Standard Oil Trust.

ANTITRUST LEGISLATION

Of course, people naturally feared monopolies and even the possibility that giant companies might take over the country. Therefore, Congress passed the Sherman Antitrust Act in 1890. However, the Sherman Antitrust Act unexpectedly contributed to a wave of consolidations, which peaked between 1897 and 1903. This is because one way around the illegality of conspiring in restraint of trade was to merge. Mergers at that time were not against the law, even if they resulted in reduced competitiveness in an industry. Eventually, in 1910 and 1911, Standard Oil and American Tobacco were prosecuted under the Sherman Antitrust Act, but until then this was generally a period of a government hands-off policy. As Jefferson once said, the best government is "that government which governs least." And many congressmen, senators, and presidents felt it best to leave business alone.

Issue: Did Workers Gain from Industrialization?

The Plight of Workers

During the first half of the nineteenth century, the pace of economic change accelerated. The Civil War was a costly interruption to a trend of industrial expansion that would lead the United States to a position of industrial dominance throughout the world. Considered in terms of the broad span of history, there is little doubt indeed that an industrial revolution was unfolding in America between the Civil War and World War I.

Emphasizing an alternative perspective, many social commentators and historians have noted that during this era of monopoly capitalism, the little person—the factory worker and others—suffered greatly. There is little question about the sordidness in the slums and factory lives of many workers in America. There is little question that many people lived an existence that by present standards was almost unthinkable.

Making Correct Comparisons

We cannot properly apply today's standards to the kind of life that existed before World War I. Instead, we should cautiously compare the circumstances of the past in its proper historical context and in terms of the hopes, expectations, and the conditions of yesterday. And, most importantly, we need to find out what really took place.

What was actually happening to workers during this period? Were they becoming worse off than they had been used to or than they could have expected to become? Was a large percentage of the population feeling the pinch of industrialization?

Blue-Collar Discontent

For many years, the available scattered evidence on wages confirmed some historians' claims that workers suffered losses in real wages during the era of unbridled monopoly capitalism. Because of monopoly elements in the economy, it was believed that the standard of living of workers fell from the time of the passage of the Sherman Antitrust Act until the days of World War I. However, the most recent and more complete estimates of real wages of manufacturing workers counter those beliefs. Real wages did fall in several short periods, but over the entire quarter century, from 1890 to 1914, they rose considerably, being about 30 percent higher at the end of the period than at the start.

It is also instructive to consider alternative income distributions. For instance, what would have happened if monopoly capitalists had been unable to extract any monopoly profits during this period? In the first decade of the twentieth century—a decade near the supposed zenith of monopoly in the economy—corporate profits totaled about $1.4 billion per year, on average. Not all corporations were monopolies

but, for the sake of exaggeration, we may assume they were. Of course, some of this profit was attributable to monopoly practices, but actually most of it was a normal return to capital, like interest on your bank savings—say 5 or 6 percent. If the president or the courts could have taken the amount in excess of the normal rate of return and redistributed it to everyone (except for the stockholders and company managers), individual incomes would have increased by about 1 or 2 percent, on average.

Monopoly certainly was more visible than ever before in the late nineteenth century. This was largely due to the tremendous growth in the size of firms and also to the growth of trusts and mergers of firms. But it is not actually clear that the economy was becoming more monopolistic. As transportation costs fell and communications improved, isolated regional monopolies came under increasing competitive pressure. For the average American consumer, the unfolding of the nineteenth century may have actually brought on less monopoly rather than more. In any case, we can be sure that in this era of industrialization, workers were earning more and that real incomes were rising.

Some Real Costs

The rise in real wages and the lack of leverage of corporate abnormal (monopoly) profit on average incomes does not indicate, however, that no problems were caused by industrialization. Certainly the rash of strikes between 1880 and 1914 and the appearance of considerable labor violence in the 1890s (not to mention the "get tough" attitude toward labor of many conservative states and local authorities) amply attest to the tensions of the times. Clearly this was directly related to the process of industrialization. But progress always has a price, and this was a period of significant growth and economic change. Against the benefits of rising material standards of living, we can now compare some of the costs that were brought about by the rapid industrialization in the nineteenth century.

LIVING ENVIRONMENT

Consider the living environment in which many industrial workers found themselves. Life in many factories was dismal, and there was little job security because "the boss" could discharge workers abruptly if they wished or business conditions warranted it. Moreover, life in the homes near the factories was often less pleasant than in the countryside. In addition, workers were subjected to more severe and costly business cycles. Recall that when the United States had mainly an agrarian economy, with many largely self-sufficient farms, the effects of bad business conditions on the vast majority of people were not as great as when the economy became industrialized. By the end of the nineteenth century, however, workers increasingly experienced periods of more severe recession and the unemployment rate during the recessions from the 1870s to the early 1900s was considerably higher than

Exhibit 10.1

Unemployment During Recessions and Depressions

Year	Percentage Unemployed
1876	12–14
1885	6–8
1894	18
1908	8

Source: S. Lebergott, *Manpower and Economic Growth* (New York: McGraw-Hill, 1964), pp. 187, 512, 522.

those during the recessions and depressions in prior periods. In fact, the unemployment rate in 1894 is exceeded only by the periods during the Great Depression. In Table 10.1 we see the percentage of the labor force unemployed in depression years (starting in 1876).

UNEMPLOYMENT AND INDUSTRIALIZATION

There has been a slight but noticeable upward trend in the average rates of unemployment from 1800 to the present. In the past, unemployment meant hardship for workers. Unemployment is an integral part of an industrialized capitalist society. Mass unemployment rarely exists in any society where everybody is basically self-employed or a slave or serf. To minimize the cost of economic progress, we can attempt, as we have by many government programs, to alleviate unemployment and its effects. We have not yet found the magic formula for stopping recessions, but that does not mean that we are worse off as a highly developed industrial society than we would be if we all went back to self-sufficient activities.

This conclusion would also apply to the situation on the eve of World War I. Many people had been hurt by the progress of the last half century, but even more had gained from it. If we take a very broad view of the changes of the period, it would be difficult for us to conclude that the common person was hurt by the industrial revolution. Life for the average worker was difficult at the turn of the century, but it was probably better than that of the previous generation of workers.

Definitions of New Terms

MASS PRODUCTION Mass production is a production technique involving many units of a product. Mass production techniques are generally associated with a conveyor belt and large-scale assembly factories. When the techniques of mass production are used, the fixed or sunk costs are distributed to an ever-increasing number of units, thus reducing the average per unit cost of production.

PROPRIETORSHIP A single-owner business.

PARTNERSHIP A partnership is a business entity involving two or more individuals joined together for business purposes but who have not incorporated. Their liability is generally limited to their personal assets.

CORPORATION A corporation is a legal entity owned by stockholders in the company. Normally the stockholders are only liable for the amount of money they have invested in that company.

VERTICAL MERGERS OR INTEGRATION Vertical mergers or integration involves the joining together of businesses that engage in the various stages of producing a final product. For example, the merging of a coal company with an electric utility would be a vertical merger.

HORIZONTAL INTEGRATION Horizontal integration involves the merging of businesses in the same activity, such as the merger of several gasoline companies or several shoe-manufacturing companies.

Eleven
The Great War

With the assassination of Austrian Archduke Franz Ferdinand in Sarajevo in 1914, war began in Europe. Soon the Great War spread to most of the rest of the world. The Central Powers, Germany, and Austria-Hungary were fighting against the Allies—France, England, and Russia. In 1914, America was in the throes of a recession. Unemployment had reached an uncomfortable one million the year before. From the very beginning, America attempted to stay out of the conflict. In fact, the Democrats used a slogan for President Wilson's reelection that would soon be forgotten: "He kept this country out of war." That was in 1916. In April 1917, the United States declared war on the Central Powers. War production and preparation for war had started earlier, however, and we had started sending war materials and supplies to the belligerents as early as 1914. It was not unlike an earlier time, in 1793, when, as a neutral country, we were able to trade with both parties to the conflict. After the first shock of war, our exports increased by leaps and bounds. The trade surplus for each of the years 1914 and 1916 was over $5.2 billion. Other countries made up for this deficit vis-à-vis the United States by liquidating investments, shipping us gold, and by borrowing from us. In some cases, we were never repaid, particularly for the loans made to Germany. Nonetheless, most observers have concluded that our preparation for the war and entry into it pulled us out of a serious recession. By 1916, most of our unemployment had vanished.

World War I was the first modern war—one fought with formidable weapons that required large amounts of capital, supplies, and manpower and that involved, at least indirectly, the entire industrial economy of each modern nation involved. War had become expensive. While the Civil War cost the Union $3.5 billion, the Great War cost the United States alone $33.4 billion. This was a period of increased government expenditures and increased government powers. Government spending after World War I was significantly higher than before. Federal revenues, for example, were only $750 million when we entered the war, but rose to almost $5 billion after it.

Labor and Production

Of course, the war had to be fought with soldiers. Although the United States did not use large amounts of its available labor force for the actual fighting, the total number of Americans who finally served during the conflict numbered almost five million—about 5 percent of the population. In addition, another three million were needed for war production. It is true that during this time unemployment was lowered, but most of the civilian population did not become materially better off. This is because a significant fraction of our labor, capital, and resources were expended for the war effort. Of course, the final victory for the Allied Forces is not to be downgraded, but it must be concluded that the actual standard of living fell during the war period. Industrial production did not increase very much after an initial spurt when hostilities broke out in Europe. Industry produced about 1 percent more from 1916 to 1917, but in 1918 and 1919, it produced less than it had several years earlier. Since we were using up part of our real output for the war effort, fewer consumer goods and services were available to the private sector, particularly since production did not significantly increase during the height of the hostilities.

Were We Unprepared?

It may seem that we were totally unprepared for the war effort because the president was relying on his ability to keep us out of the war in order to be reelected. However, this is not a completely accurate view. The Naval Consulting Board had an Industrial Preparedness Committee as early as 1915. This became a full-fledged Committee on Industrial Preparedness in 1916. This organization was financed solely by private contributions, although it was officially an arm of the federal government. By late 1916, there was a new organization called the Council of National Defense (CND). President Wilson said that the purpose of the CND was to organize "the whole industrial mechanism . . . in the most effective way." Even before we entered the war, the CND set up a Munitions Standards Board in February 1917. Eventually, the CND was to designate an entire system of food control, censorship of the press, and purchasing war supplies. Finally, a couple of months after we joined the Allies, a War Industries Board was established to take control over much of the economy.

Controls

War always creates an atmosphere conducive to expansion of government powers. The Great War was no exception. In fact, we might view World War I as a period that developed much of the administrative machinery that set the stage for many of the government control mechanisms instituted during Roosevelt's New Deal.

To be sure, the War Industries Board took its job seriously. It soon became the coordinator and allocator of commodities and allowed the fixing of prices and the setting of priorities in production. Bernard Baruch became head of this great bureaucratic organization in March 1918. Baruch was an obvious candidate, for he had been an earlier supporter of our entry into the war and he had already presented a scheme for industrial war mobilization to the president in 1915, well before most people thought we might enter the conflict. All of the leaders of the various departments in the control mechanism for war mobilization proved to be from big business. And, as can be expected, they looked out for their own. For example, in the granting of war contracts, there was no competitive bidding. The big business-dominated War Industries Board handed out contracts as seemed appropriate to it, often ignoring costs and efficiency in the process.

PRICE FIXING

Since wars have generally been associated with inflation, government controllers sought to establish price-fixing mechanisms to control inflation. Despite their attempts, however, inflation was inevitable because of the methods of war financing. Nonetheless, the stage was set and so a Price-Fixing Committee of the War Industries Board was formed. Naturally, the public was told that the committee would set maximum prices so the consumer would not be hurt.

Price fixing in the agricultural sector was presided over by none other than Herbert Hoover. Instead of direct control over food, his Food Administration used a vast network of licensing agreements. Every producer, warehouser, and distributer of food had to obtain a federal license from the Food Administration. The licenses were used to control prices, because they were only granted if the licensees set prices to allow "a reasonable margin of profit." The goal, it would seem, was not to lower prices, but rather to stabilize and ensure higher noncompetitive prices. Certainly that was the end result, and any competitor who tried to increase profits above prewar levels by price cutting was threatened with the loss of its license. And when direct price controls were applied, a maximum was not set, but rather a minimum. For example, the Food Control Act of 1917 set a minimum price of $2 a bushel on the 1918 wheat crop. This figure was later upped by $0.25 in the summer of 1918.

OTHER FORMS OF CONTROL

The government completely took over some industries, such as the railroads. At the beginning of the war, the railroads agreed to form a Railroads War Board and to cease competitive activities. However, the quest for higher profits superseded the railroad managers' patriotic promulgations. Price cutting became common, and more and more overt forms of competition appeared. Finally, President Wilson seized the railroads on December 28, 1917. Hence, railroads were monopolized and given direct government operation. Many important railroad personnel were appointed to leading positions in the Railroad Administration. Soon there were numerous rules for compulsory standardization of locomotive and equipment design and for the elimination of duplicate passenger and coal services. Additionally, no railroads were allowed to solicit business that they did not already have. All of this was done even before the Railroad Administration was legalized by the Federal Control Act of March 1918.

WHERE IT ALL LED

The entire system of controls was more or less dismantled after the cessation of hostilities. However, the stage had been set for collective action by which government and business joined together in a cooperative atmosphere. This was similar to, but on a vastly different scale than, the government involvement in early nineteenth-century transportation mediums. This cooperative atmosphere was to prevail again years later under Franklin Delano Roosevelt's administration.

Financing the War

Federal expenditures rose rapidly during the period 1916–1919. But federal expenditures do not arise out of thin air. Even the government faces a **budget constraint,** just as you or anyone else does. If expenditures are increased, they must somehow be financed. There are generally only three ways that the government can finance its expenditures: (1) taxation, (2) borrowing from the public, and (3) money creation.

TAXATION

Taxation is the most obvious manner in which the government pays for its expenditures, but in looking back it seems clear that none of our major wars have been completely financed by taxation. The Great War was no exception, although Congress continuously increased tax rates in an effort to offset its increased expenditures. Moreover, there was a change in the entire tax structure during the war, emphasizing more direct taxes and more progressive tax rates. For instance, in 1916, the maximum personal income tax rate was raised from 7 percent to 15 percent, and the maximum corporation rate was raised to 14.5 percent. In 1917, there were increases in estate taxes and again in personal and corporate income taxes. The maximum rate went up on the personal taxes 67 percent, and the normal corporation rate rose from 2 percent to 6 percent, with the maximum excess profits rate going up to 60 percent. This still was not enough, so the Revenue Act of 1918 (which was eventually passed in February 1919) increased the maximum personal rate to 77 percent, the normal corporation tax rate to 12 percent, and the maximum excess profits tax rate to 65 percent. Ultimately, taxes provided about one-third of the revenues needed for the war effort.

BORROWING FROM THE PRIVATE SECTOR

When the government runs a deficit—that is, spends more than it receives—it may borrow by selling government bonds to the public. The federal government took full advantage of this option during World War I. In addition to its regular bond sales, which occur all the time in today's dynamic economy, it instituted four Liberty Loan drives, and one postwar drive, joyously called a Victory Loan. A total of $19.1 billion was raised in this manner. But, in fact, the government's increased bond sales were, and still are, a postponement of the inevitable, a disguised form of increased taxes. After all, when the government sells a bond, it obtains money from people either as individuals, or owners of banks, or corporations. In return, it promises to pay interest for a certain number of years and then pay back the original price of the bond, called the *principal*. But how does the government pay the interest? Out of revenues. Where does it obtain revenues? From taxes. That means that when the government runs a deficit and makes up for it by selling bonds, it is increasing the future tax liabilities of the nation.

Of course, it is obvious that one cannot get something for nothing. If someone gives up part of his or her income to buy bonds so that the government can increase its expenditures, that person has to be paid a reward. The reward is the interest rate, which we can call a reward for waiting. So we have these options: Either pay taxes today to finance government expenditures, or pay higher taxes in the future to pay for those government expenditures. Lastly, the money used for government finance (bonds) is diverted from elsewhere, leaving less for private investors and consumers.

MONEY CREATION

The last method of government finance is money creation. It happened during the Revolutionary War when Continentals were printed. It happened during the Civil War when Confederate notes and greenbacks were issued. And it happened again during World War I but by this time a more formalized machinery for money creation had already been established.

The Federal Reserve System and Money Creation

You may recall that the National Banking System was established by legislation during the Civil War. However, it did not create a national system as originally intended. Moreover, its check clearance system was costly and inefficient. Because there were so many faults in the National Banking System, government officials felt the need to create a new one, so in 1913 the government passed the Federal Reserve Act. The Federal Reserve System was based on twelve district banks; every member commercial bank would belong to one of these. In each of these district banks, the member banks would be required to maintain a certain amount of reserves. That is, if the **reserve requirement** was, for example, 20 percent, a member bank that had a million dollars in checking account deposits and outstanding notes would have to keep $200,000 on reserve in its district's federal bank. The Federal Reserve banks were empowered to issue a new type of paper money called Federal Reserve notes. These were to be secured by **commercial paper** (the promissory notes of businesses) and gold. The district banks were also empowered to lend reserves to member banks who requested them. Note, however, that this function was considered a privilege and not a right of the commercial banks. Finally, a more efficient and less costly check-clearing system was instituted.

The Federal Reserve is governed by the Federal Reserve Board. Originally, this was merely an administrative agency with little control over the system's operations. Today, the board of governors of the Federal Reserve essentially take responsibility for the total supply of money in the economy. The various committees decide which monetary policies to pursue and how to effect them. But this was not the case during World War I. Then the system was relatively passive, and it felt obliged to give the United States Treasury its full support. This meant essentially that it was to pursue an easy money policy to allow a large amount of money—demand deposits and currency—to enter the economy. This helped the bond sales of the federal treasury.

One of the easiest ways for the Federal Reserve Board to create a situation of easy money is to increase the reserves of its member banks. When member banks have more reserves, they can loan out more money. One of the ways that member banks can obtain reserves is to borrow from the Federal Reserve Banks. During the war, the Federal Reserve Board lowered the interest rate charged and also freely granted loans to member banks at that lower interest rate. In this manner, the banks' reserves increased dramatically. This, in turn, led to a rapid increase in the money supply in circulation. For example, in 1917, money per capita was $225. In 1919, it had risen to $350 per person. Not surprisingly, the wholesale price index jumped by 20 percent and the consumer price index by 35 percent. We had already noted the outcome of massive increases in the amount of money in circulation; obviously, spending is easier when there is excess cash available, and so prices rise. This happened in Europe because of the gold and silver flows from the New World in the fifteenth and sixteenth centuries, it happened in the American Revolution, in the Confederacy and the Union during the Civil War, and again in World War I.

It is generally thought that government expenditures financed by taxation and borrowing from the private sector are not inflationary because in both cases, private purchasing power is reduced therein. If a person pays part of his or her income in taxes, other private expenditures are usually reduced. If an individual or a business firm decides to lend money to the government by buying a bond, then again, individual power, or ability to spend in the private sector, will be reduced. Such is not the case when expenditures are financed by money creation. People who eventually receive this extra cash do not want to reduce expenditures. Indeed, they want to increase them. Notice that inflation is also another form of taxation, but a very special kind. If the price level rises, everybody who holds dollar bills or has a non-interest earning checking account suffers. After all, if one has $1,000 in the bank and keeps it there for a year while the price of everything goes up 10 percent, that $1,000 has lost 10 percent of its value. It has depreciated by 10 percent. In effect, then, you have paid a 10 percent tax on holding these dollars. There is no way to avoid this tax unless one converts and trades only in goods, not dollars. But that would be extremely inconvenient. Consequently, governments often resort to this type of tax. It is easy to collect and very difficult to avoid. In addition, government officials can avoid the touchy questions of legislating new taxes and higher rates.

U.S. Involvement

The United States was an active participant in the war for only 19 months. The American casualty rate was not high compared to that of the Civil War or World War II, but it was significant: 75,000 dead and 225,000 injured; a total of 300,000 casualties. Certainly many Americans had been reminded of the realities of scarcity after World War I, although they really had not paid the kind of price that Germany, France, England, Russia, and other participants in Europe had paid.

Issue: Was World War I the Real Emancipation?

Abraham Lincoln signed the Emancipation Proclamation on September 22, 1862. It stated:

> That on the 1st day of January, A.D. 1863, all persons held as slaves within any State or designated part of a State of the people whereof shall then be in rebellion against the United States shall be then, thenceforward, and forever free; and the executive government of the United States, including the military and naval authority thereof, will recognize and maintain the freedom of such persons and will do no act or acts to repress such persons, or any of them, in any efforts they may make for their actual freedom.

We all know by now that just because legislation goes into effect, the world does not necessarily turn upside down (or rightside up). While legislation obviously can have an immediate impact, it generally takes time for the full effect to be felt. Although blacks were freed during the Civil War, their emancipation certainly was not obvious during the next five decades. Blacks generally remained in the South, where their political freedom and economic standing were held in check. Even in 1915, there were still lynchings: Fifty-four blacks were hanged that year.[1]

MOVING OUT OF THE SOUTH

There had been some migration of blacks from the South to the North ever since the Civil War. However, until the beginning of World War I it was only a trickle. Starting in 1916, there was a mass exodus of blacks to northern cities unprecedented in the history of the nation. And the entire geographical distribution of this minority group in the United States radically changed. Whereas in 1900 only 23 percent of blacks were living in urban areas, the trend toward urbanization picked up so rapidly that barely a half century later, 60 percent were urban. Almost all of the migration to the North during World War I was a movement to cities. In fact, the 1920 census revealed that almost three-fourths of northern blacks were found within the ten industrial centers of the nation, such as New York, Chicago, St. Louis, Pittsburgh, and Kansas City. If we look at different cities, we find that by the time of the Great Depression, more than 50 percent of the blacks in New York, Chicago, Philadelphia, Washington, Detroit, Memphis, St. Louis, Cleveland, and Pittsburgh had been born in some other state. Detroit, for example, had more blacks from Georgia than did Augusta or Macon. Chicago had as many Mississippi-born blacks as the entire black population in Vicksburg, Meridian, Greenville, and Natchez.

Why Did It All Happen?

Why did it take 50 years for blacks to start their massive migration to the

North? Was it merely fortuitous that the start of World War I signaled the start of black migration? Perhaps, but another explanation may be more plausible. It involves two aspects of the war: the increased demand for workers and the decreased immigration from Europe. Additionally, at this time, the boll weevil was ruining cotton cultivation, making it less profitable for rural blacks (and whites). In Table 11.1 we see the percent of reduction from full yield per acre of cotton due to the boll weevil. It started out as only 1.3 percent in 1911, but it grew to 13.4 percent in 1916 and increased dramatically until the middle of the Roaring Twenties.

The notion that reduced output led to a general decline in farm income is only true if the demand for cotton was significantly price elastic (that is very responsive to price changes). However, the evidence indicates that it was not. For example, cotton prices rose from 7 cents a pound in 1914 to 35 cents a pound in 1919. To be sure, there were farmers who saw their income decline because of the boll weevil but there were also many farmers who saw their income enhanced as a result of the higher cotton prices.[2]

Exhibit 11.1

Boll Weevil Destruction (1911–1925)

Year	% Reduction in Yield/ Acre of Cotton Due to Boll Weevil	Year	% Reduction in Yield/ Acre of Cotton Due to Boll Weevil
1911	1.3	1919	13.2
1912	3.3	1920	19.9
1913	6.7	1921	31.0
1914	5.9	1922	24.2
1915	9.9	1923	19.5
1916	13.4	1924	8.0
1917	9.3	1925	4.1
1918	5.8		

Source: U.S. Department of Agriculture, Statistical Bulletin No. 99, Table 52, p. 67.

While there were many social and political reasons why blacks would want to go to the North, as there were many such reasons for Germans and Swedes and Italians and Scots to want to come to America, the overriding reason was economic: They went North to achieve a higher material standard of living. In the period just before our entry into World War I, blacks were making 10 to 15 cents an hour in the South. Soon they were hearing stories about northern employers willing to pay 30 or even 40 cents an hour.

A decision to migrate, in purely economic terms, includes not only the potential gain in income but also any costs involved in migration.

Costs of Migration

The most obvious cost of migration is transportation. By World War I, the transportation costs had been drastically reduced because the railroad had essentially linked all parts of the nation together. Potential black migrants would look at the price of a railroad ticket as the most immediate cost they had to endure. After that would come the cost of searching for a job on arrival in another city. The job search cost could be high if, in fact, the migrant were out of work for a long time. During this period, however, migrants generally felt that job search costs would be minimal since they expected to find work immediately on arrival.

Another cost to consider was the cost of setting up a new household in a different city, and dismantling the one the migrant left behind. The costs here were not only economic but also psychic—losing old friends and trying to make new ones, leaving relatives, and so on. In the economic decision, then, the expected stream of differences in wages must be compared with the anticipated migration costs.[3]

Labor Raids

There was a very good reason for many blacks to believe that they could obtain instant work in the North at higher wages, for the South was filled with northern labor contractors who advanced or covered the cost of transferring North. Whites in the South were becoming increasingly upset at what they called labor raids to lure southern blacks to northern jobs. In fact, various state and local governments in the South attempted to prevent the raids by passing ordinances that allowed the fining and imprisonment of anybody convicted of "enticing" a laborer to leave the city for another place of employment. Other states placed heavy license taxes on emigration agents. The demand for labor was high enough in the North, however, that it still paid four licensed agents to put up $1,000 each in Birmingham in order to "entice" blacks to come North.

The Effects of Immigration Laws

Even though the North had been expanding its industrial economy for many years, our liberal immigration laws had made it unnecessary to go South to obtain workers. Immigration into the United States each year sometimes reached as many as 1.28 million foreigners. During the first 14 years of the twentieth century, over 12 million immigrants found their way to the United States. This all came to a screeching halt, however, as we became more involved in the war and more xenophobic. For example, literacy tests of foreign immigrants were enacted. In 1915, less than one-third of the 1914 number of immigrants arrived, and in 1916, only one-fourth. By 1918, a mere 110,618 foreigners landed in the United States, while 94,585 left. The flow of relatively cheap foreign workers had stopped. But by 1915, the North still needed more labor. This opened up employment opportunities for blacks and other low-skilled labor on an unprecedented scale. Northern industry was expanding to meet the demands of a war-torn older continent, and eventually we were to enter that struggle and increase the demands for war production even more.

New Meaning for the Black Franchise

It is generally considered that, by 1914, blacks were completely disfranchised in the South. Even the handful of black voters who remained were considered such a challenge that, in South Carolina, the General Assembly voted in January 1914 to repeal the Fifteenth Amendment to the United States Constitution! But in the North, blacks could vote and even hold office. Civil rights for blacks in the national political arena made a great leap forward during this period of massive migration. The large numbers of blacks who came into northern cities were potential voters. Politicians had to take greater cognizance of this increasingly important subsection of the population. By 1915, Oscar dePriest was the first black elected to Chicago's City Council. Blacks were registering and voting in the largest numbers since the turn of the century, and by 1921, the New Jersey House of Representatives had a black president, Assemblyman Walter G. Alexander. Later on, the Democratic Party in New York State made an attempt to win the black vote by taking a strong position against the Ku Klux Klan.

According to students of black history, the migration caused by our entry into World War I, the increased demand for more labor, and the shutting off of immigration from abroad are responsible for laying the groundwork for equal rights for black people.[4] Of course, blacks were still far removed from a status of equal rights and socioeconomic quality, and race riots occasionally marred the landscape of the United States, especially in the northern cities. But World War I ushered in a new momentum toward equality, because "in the very process of being transplanted, the Negro was becoming transformed."[5]

DEFINITIONS OF NEW TERMS

BUDGET CONSTRAINTS This is the constraint that an individual, a government, or event the world has on its spending capacity. One is limited in how much one can spend by one's budget constraint. So, too, is the government, except that it has the means of expanding its budget constraint by selling bonds and by creating money.

RESERVE REQUIREMENT The reserve requirement is the reserves that commercial banks that are members of the Federal Reserve System must keep on account in their district Federal Reserve Bank or in currency in their vaults. These reserves are expressed as a percentage of checking and savings account deposits outstanding.

COMMERCIAL PAPER Commercial paper is the debt issued by individual corporations or by business persons.

ENDNOTES

[1]So, too, did 13 whites die by the rope.

[2]See, Vedder, Gallaway, Graves, and Sexton, "Demonstrating Their Freedom: The Post-Emancipation Migration of Black Americans," *Research in Economic History,* Volume 10, January 1986.

[3]One reason blacks did not move North for 60 years after their emancipation is that they moved within the South to enhance their level of satisfaction. For a formal discussion see Graves, Sexton, and Vedder, "Slavery and Factor Price Equalization: A Note on Migration and Freedom," *Exploration in Economic History* 20 (April 1983): 156–162.

[4]It is important to note that although the particular statistics would differ, the general forces and trends of this time period were also applied to women. The substitution of female for male labor was very evident, just as was the substitution of black for white workers.

[5]Alain Locke, "The New Negro," *The Negro Caravan* (New York: Random House, 1969), p. 950.

Part Five

Economic Life in Modern America, 1920–1990

Biographies

The Industrial Unionist

John L. Lewis (1880-1969)

PRESIDENT, UNITED MINE WORKERS, 1920-1960

"I have never faltered or failed to present the cause or plead the case of the mine workers of this country. I have pleaded your case not in the wavering tones of a mendicant seeking alms, but in the thundering voice of the captain of a mighty host, demanding the rights to which free men are entitled."

These dramatic words from John L. Lewis were a combined program, epitaph, rallying call, and challenge to business management, consumers, and presidents alike. During his forty years as president of the United Mine Workers (UMW) and as the major spokesman for industrial unionism in an era of increasing consolidation between craft and industrial unions, Lewis ran the United Mine Workers with absolute control. He brought the union to prominence in the American Federation of Labor, formed the Congress of Industrial Organizations (CIO) and broke with the American Federation of Labor (AFL), then returned to the AFL and eventually forced the union to stand on its own for the twenty years before his death.

Industrial unionism received its greatest push during the early 1930s. The combined effects of the Depression and the increased numbers of unskilled and semiskilled workers in most American industries presented a serious challenge to the craft union doctrine of the AFL, founded by Samuel Gompers. It became evident to men such as Lewis that it was no longer valid to base union solidarity and bargaining positions on skills, irrespective of industry; he believed strongly that it was important instead to organize unions within specific industries, drawing the membership from as wide a basis within the industry as possible.

One of the major "advantages" of the tactic is the crippling effects of a strike within the industry. And through the late 1940s and into the early 1950s, Lewis led some of the most economically dangerous and emphatically effective strikes in American history.

Lewis was born to Welsh immigrant parents in Iowa in 1880. His father was a miner and a strong trade unionist. Along with some of his brothers, Lewis entered the mines at the age of fifteen, after leaving the only formal schooling he would receive. Six years later, he traveled in the western United States, working in various mines and learning about the mining industry. Lewis eventually became one of America's foremost experts on the coal mining industry, and almost all of his expertise was the result of his own reading and study. Upon returning to Iowa, he joined the UMW local and began extensive work in the Union leadership.

He came to the attention of Samuel Gompers, and in 1911 was named a field agent of the American Federation of Labor. While traveling widely throughout the United States, he rose in the UMW ranks, becoming president of the Union in 1920.

Lewis had his first of many confrontations with the federal government during World War I, while serving on the National Defense Council; in that position, he opposed government operation of the mines, a controversial question he was to take on again twenty-five years later.

The AFL convention in 1935 was torn by the economic troubles of the country and the internal disagreement between the trade and craft unions. In a dramatic walkout, Lewis joined with several other trade unionists to form the Congress of Industrial Organizations, leaving the AFL to the craft unionists. The momentum behind Lewis' move resulted in several important gains for his union and for labor at large.

In 1933, he had successfully fought for the passage of Section 7a of the National Industrial Recovery Act, which provided workers with almost complete freedom to choose representatives of their own choice for collective bargaining purposes. In addition to its effect on the total strength of the labor movement, the provision weakened the ability of the present union leadership to retain control.

He eventually organized four million workers into the CIO. The early years of the organization, of which the UMW was the core, were marked by violent strikes, one of which drew sharp criticism for both sides from Franklin Roosevelt. Up to that time, FDR had received Lewis' personal and organizational backing. "It ill behooves one who has supped at labor's table and who has been sheltered in labor's house to curse with equal fervor and fine impartiality both labor and its adversaries when they become locked in deadly embrace," declaimed Lewis. After that point Lewis and Roosevelt were on strained terms, culminating in Lewis' support for Wendell Wilkie for president in 1940.

Lewis resigned as president of the CIO in 1942 and pulled the UMW out of the organization. He returned to the AFL for a period of less than two years before taking the United Mine Workers down its own road. In 1955, the AFL and CIO merged without the participation of the man who had had a significant impact on the histories of both organizations.

Lewis' direction of the UMW was based on an "all the wagons in a circle" approach to confrontation with the government. "It is better to have half a million men working at good wages and high standards of living than to have a million working in poverty." (Lewis certainly knew that the law of demand applied to coal miners, too.)

His program to improve the wages and living conditions of his membership was based on his skillful ability to turn potential crises to his advantage. During the 1950s, increases in automation in mining were threatening to cut his membership; but automation was needed if coal was to remain competitive with oil and natural gas. He obtained a contract agreement that placed a royalty on mined coal. The royalty was channeled into the union's pension fund, eventually boosting its value above $170 million.

Probably Lewis' most trying years were those of the Truman administration, as he attempted to lead strikes in both the soft and hard coal industries in the face of court injunctions. Truman seized the mines and had them worked by federal troops, but Lewis eventually received the settlement he wanted. He ran up more than $2.1 million in strike fines, and probably damaged the competitive position of the industry.

One of his major achievements was the 1952 Federal Mine Safety Act, the first of its kind in the United States. His dramatic appearance at the site of a mining disaster in 1951 provided a strong push for the Act in Congress. Also during the 1950s he won extremely favorable settlements, including payment for underground travel time.

After his semiretirement in 1960, the UMW fell on hard times. Under the leadership of Tony Boyle, the union suffered through a membership slowdown, and then was subject to a series of government investigations into corruption and the murder of a candidate for Boyle's office.

Two weeks before he died, Lewis was called on by Ralph Nader and other concerned observers to rescue the union from Boyle's heavy-handed policies. But Lewis was too old, and there was a conflict of interest inherent in the situation; Boyle was a devoted disciple of Lewis and held his position partially through Lewis' influence in the union.

Lewis' tenure as a major influence in American labor was rivaled by few men in its length and probably by no man in its power. His commitment to his union's membership and its needs was single-minded. When he died, the miners closed the mines in memory of him, as they had done many times in response to his call to strike.

The Miracle Man of Wartime Merchant Shipbuilding

Henry J. Kaiser (1882-1967)

AN AUDACIOUS INDUSTRIALIST

A World War II Liberty Ship was big, very big. Nonetheless, Henry J. Kaiser was able to produce one in eight days flat! In his seven shipyards in Oregon and California he produced over 1,500 ships during the war. How did he do it? By introducing prefabrication and assembly-line techniques, along with a new and better welding process. This feat may have seemed a miracle, but should only have been expected from the man who had built up empires in paving and construction before the war. He had done that by submitting lower bids than much larger firms on all the government contracts he could apply for in the 1930s. He went on to help build Bonneville and Grand Coulee dams. Kaiser even had the audacity to bid on providing five million barrels of cement for Shasta Dam even though he did not have a cement company! He got the bid and founded Permanente Cement Company, which had the largest plant in the entire United States, located in Permanente, California. Between 1931 and 1945, he completed seventy major construction projects.

Kaiser was not a boy to stay in school in his native Sproutbrook, New York. He quit at the age of thirteen to become a cash boy, later becoming a salesman for the J. B. Wells Dry Goods Store in Utica. Then he went into the photographic supply business, and while still in his teens became a partner in the firm of Brownwell and Kaiser in Lake Placid, New York. Tiring of the photography business, he sold out in 1906 and moved to Spokane, Washington, where he went into the hardware business as a mere employee. Then the paving industry took his fancy, and he soon became a self-employed contractor, handling numerous highway and street projects in Washington, Idaho, and British Columbia. Then he moved his headquarters to Oakland, California. While still a road builder, he constructed 200 miles of highway in Cuba at a cost of over $18 million. One of the biggest innovations Kaiser introduced while in the road-building business was the substitution of diesel engines for gasoline motors in his tractors and steam shovels, thereby greatly reducing operating costs. When he went into the dam construction business, his prowess as an organizer and innovator did not abate: As head of the contractors building the Boulder Dam, he got it completed two years ahead of schedule. Construction of dams led to the building of tunnels, bridges, dry docks, jetties, air bases, troop facilities, and even to the excavation for the third locks in Panama.

Kaiser, perhaps more than any other industrialist of the time, was convinced that vertical integration was the only way to solve supply problems. For building his ships in California, Oregon, and Washington, he needed steel, so he put up an integrated steel plant in Fontana, California. The ships also needed engines, so he and his associates purchased an iron works in Sunnyvale, California, where engines were built for Kaiser and other contractors. He also built a magnesium plant (magnesium was used not only for shipbuilding; in one form it was used as the incendiary material known as "goop").

The list goes on, for Kaiser got himself involved in airplane building during the war, also. He designed his plant in Bristol, Pennsylvania, where he not only built parts, subassemblies, and surfaces for flying fortresses, but also put together experimental Army and Navy planes.

After the war Kaiser saw the possibility of profit in the automobile industry. He formed the Kaiser-Fraser Corporation, which was the first major new U.S. independent auto producer after the war. The future of independent auto producers seemed bright right after the war, but by the early 1950s it was a downhill road. In an attempt to strengthen his market position Kaiser bought up the assets of the bankrupt Willys Motors in 1953. In the end, though, Kaiser Motors failed, and its over $90 million in debts were assumed by Henry J. Kaiser's more profitable enterprises.

Kaiser never stopped expanding his empire. He went into aluminum right after the war, and within five years Kaiser Aluminum and Chemical Company had sales of $150 million. By 1956, this figure had risen to $330 million, with a net profit of over $40 million. Kaiser has left his mark on American economic and social life. There are Kaiser hospitals, and Kaiser housing developments such as on Oahu, Hawaii. There are numerous other less obvious imprints of this audacious industrialist's activities, many of which are based on one man's quest for continued industrial efficiency.

Twelve
The Roaring Twenties and the Depressed Thirties

The Twenties: Social and Moral Upheavals

The 1920s was distinctive in many ways. It was ushered in by the 1919 smash hit, *How Ya Gonna Keep 'Em Down on the Farm After They've Seen Paree?* And, in fact, the twenties was a period when the absolute number of farmers in America declined for the first time. Large portions of incomes, which rose steadily over the decade, were directed away from agricultural products and toward services and other commodities, especially such consumer durables as refrigerators, electric appliances, radios, and, above all, automobiles. Technological change continued briskly, not only effectively reducing the costs of production, but also vastly widening the array of goods available to consumers. This was the decade of the consumer durables revolution: Many new goods (such as those just listed) were produced, and more and more common items became more readily available.

When the pitch of wartime excitement subsided, renewed sentiments for isolationism appeared. In addition, there were significant political changes when women finally gained the right to vote. It was the decade of the "great experiment," when the strength of a moralistic minority temporarily won over the rights of individuals to sin by the drink of their choice. Prohibition and speakeasies were colorful examples of the social and moral upheavals of that unique decade. So, too, were the Capone mob, the President Harding quip that "the business of America is business," and the collapse of the coal unions as electric power competition undermined the market for coal.

The routine of going to work, paying bills, worrying about this or that occupied the vast majority, much as it always has. But the comforts of life were rising and the automobile in particular opened up vast new opportunities for increased leisure, recreation, mobility—in a word, freedom. By the early 1920s, over three million new automobiles were being purchased each year, and by 1929, there were twenty-six million cars on the road. Although some did not share in the gains, for many it was indeed a decade of great prosperity.

Over the decade, real incomes per capita marched upward at a record rate of 2 percent per year. The growth of productivity was unusually high throughout most sectors—in manufacturing, construction, agriculture, and elsewhere.

Agriculture Looks to Government

Although output per worker in agriculture increased 26 percent over the decade, largely due to the introduction of the gasoline tractor, which replaced nearly one-third of the horses used on farms, many farmers were discontent. Farmers' per capita income rose slightly in the 1920s, but by comparison to the bonanza years of World War I, they were distinctly worse off.

During the World War I years many foreign countries were demanding American agricultural products since they were using all their productive facilities to fight the war. After the war, Europeans reduced their demand for American agricultural exports as they increased their own productive capacities in farming. In addition, the United States placed high tariffs on all imported goods. Because exports are what any country uses to pay for its imports, the less one is able to export, the less one is able to import.

The broad extension of government powers prompted by World War I was sharply curtailed in the twenties. But in one key area, namely agriculture, the pressure of government control and intervention remained.

One of the key figures responsible for this was none other than Herbert Hoover, who headed the Food Administration during World War I. After the war, Hoover became Relief Administrator in Europe; on returning to the United States, he was appointed Secretary of Commerce by President Harding. Immediately on his appointment, he set out to "reconstruct America." During the recession of 1920–1921, Hoover repeatedly presented his views on how public works could be used to stabilize employment during depressions. Keeping close to the food problem, with which he had been so familiar during World War I, Hoover helped write an act passed in 1921 which expanded the funds allotted to the still-existing War Finance Corporation (WFC). This act permitted the WFC to lend directly to farmers' cooperatives.

Not satisfied, Hoover attempted to create a federal Farm Board that would support farm prices by creating a federal corporation for stabilization. This corporation was to purchase farm products and lend money to cooperatives. For a short time this worked, and farm prices were supported by government purchasing. But the Farm Board's budget was too limited and there were no attempts to regulate (curtail) supply. Consequently, when farmers began growing more in response to the price supports, excess supplies drove prices down. Nevertheless, Hoover and others learned from these experiences, and they set the stage for subsequent attempts at price supports and supply controls made in the 1930s.

The Great Stock Market Crash

Toward the middle of the Roaring Twenties, the stock market was booming, and stock prices were rising at astounding rates. Barbers, janitors, butlers, and ditch diggers all had money in the stock market and were making money on their money. Increasingly, people wanted to buy, and were allowed to buy, on margin. That is, they only had to put up a certain percentage of the total price; in some rare cases only 10 percent; their brokerage company would furnish the rest. Of course, they paid interest on this loan, but since their stocks were going up so fast, they still made lots of money.

By 1929, stock prices were already two and a half times what they had been a mere three or four years earlier. Trading was increasing every day. Something had to give, and it did. In October of 1929, investors started to get jittery. There were new reports that economic activity was falling. With possible threats of a recession, confidence tilted downward, and people began to sell. Of course, nobody ever conceived of what would follow.

On October 1, an average share's price fell $5 to $10. On October 3, the same thing occurred again. The next day was no better. Prices kept declining, although the number of shares traded was actually relatively small. Toward the end of the month, when disaster seemed near, business and political leaders tried to intervene in order to stop the precipitous decline. However, on Monday, October 28, 1929, there was a nationwide stampede to unload stocks. In the last hour of trading, over three million shares were traded. In just one day, the value of all stocks fell by $14 billion. The next day was even worse. Blue Monday was followed by Black Tuesday. Although stock prices rallied for the first few months in 1930, that was the last major rally that a nation of investors was to see for many years to come. By the summer of 1932, the value of stocks had fallen by 83 percent from their September 1929 prices! For every dollar invested, only seventeen cents remained.

THE REST OF THE ECONOMY

It was not long before the entire nation was well into a serious recession. Of course, no one imagined that this recession would become the greatest depression in the history of the United States. In fact, at the time, the great American economist, Irving Fisher, who was also a leader in the

Temperance movement, was busy giving speeches to Rotarians and similar groups. He proclaimed that the economic troubles of the United States were bound to be short-lived because Prohibition had made the American worker more productive!

Despite Prohibition, total real output fell continuously after 1929, a phenomenon that rarely occurs. Because the population continued to grow, real output per capita was falling even more rapidly. By 1933, actual output was at least 35 percent below the nation's productive capacity. In fact, the total output lost during this Great Depression was a little over $350 billion, measured in 1929 prices. If the Great Depression had not occurred, America could have built, for example, another 700,000 schools or another thirty-six million homes. Never in peacetime was so much output lost.

THE EMPLOYMENT SITUATION

Of course, the employment situation also grew increasingly bleak. By 1933 fully one-fourth of the entire labor force was out of work; that is, one out of every four adult members of society who wanted to work could not find a job. And unemployment stayed high for many, many years. The Great Depression was not a short-term event. From 1930 through 1940, an average of ten million people were out of work in a labor force that was less than one-half of ours today.

Moreover, the labor force may have been understated at that time, thus understating the actual amount of unemployment. There was a consistent "no jobs for married women" policy throughout the entire 1930s, and married women were denied jobs in favor of men. Additionally, many moved their families into rural areas or onto squatters' land. Instead of looking for a job in the city, they attempted to scrape out a bare existence in the countryside.

THE BANKING SYSTEM

By March 1933, the entire commercial banking system in the United States had virtually collapsed. This was the end of a third wave of banking panics which began in 1930. To shore up confidence in banks, one of newly elected President Franklin D. Roosevelt's first steps was to close every bank in the country and declare a temporary moratorium on debts. Between 1929 and 1932, more than 5,000 banks—one out of every five—had failed and their customer's deposits vanished. When Roosevelt's banking holiday ended, another 2,000 banks permanently did not open their doors for business. Both personal savings and income fell.

By 1932, people were dissaving—spending more than they earned— almost three-fourths of a billion dollars, whereas in 1929 they had saved over $4 billion. Not only did banks fail, but so did thousands on thousands of other financial intermediaries—loan companies, credit unions, and the like.

AND FARMERS, TOO

As emphasized earlier, real agricultural incomes did not rise very much during the 1920s, and farmers were considered one of the few groups that had missed out during these years of prosperity. Then the Depression hit, and farm incomes declined tremendously. By 1932, the net income of farm operators was barely 30 percent of what it had been in 1929.

This does not mean, however, that total farm output was lower. In fact, it was about 3 percent higher. What had happened was that farm prices had plummeted. Prices received by farmers in 1932 were a little over 40 percent of what they had received in 1929. Of course, the demand for food is relatively price inelastic. When farmers tried to counter their falling incomes during the early years of the Depression by increasing their output, they found they could sell their increasing supplies only by lowering prices even more. After all, it takes a tremendous reduction in the price of corn or wheat to get consumers to buy much more of each. That is always the case when one is dealing with a product whose demand is relatively price-insensitive.

Unsurprisingly, farmers became delinquent in paying their taxes and their debts. In 1929 alone, there were almost 20 forced farm sales per every 1,000 farms because of failure to pay taxes or debts. This figure had risen by 100 percent in 1932. Even this understates what actually happened because, as the Depression wore on, local tax officials became more and more tolerant of farmers who did not pay their taxes. And it usually did not do much good to force a farm sale. Who would buy the farm and at what price?

THE REST OF THE WORLD

Although it was little consolation, the United States was not much worse off than the rest of the world. By 1932, the world's total number of unemployed measured at least 30 million. The international monetary system was in chaos. The value of gross trade in the world was falling daily. The year 1931 was one of international crisis never again to be matched. It began in May after the failure of the Credit Anstalt, which was the most important bank in Austria. Its failure made many other banks uneasy, both Austrian and foreign. Foreign creditors rushed to

Austria to take out deposits. Then Hungary suffered the same problem. Next was Germany. The crisis finally hit the center of the international monetary world—London. No country seemed able to maintain the price that its currency was valued at in terms of gold. No country seemed strong; no currency did either. By the time President Roosevelt was inaugurated, the international economy was as much in a shambles as was America's. And Hitler was winning votes in Germany.

Why Did It Happen?

Why did what would otherwise have been a normal recession turn into the greatest depression in modern history? The debate still continues. We have already obliquely referred to some general notions that people had about the Depression. One notion was that Americans were living beyond their means, but there is very little evidence for that; the productive capacity of the nation was not particularly strained in 1929. Others believe that the failure of the agricultural sector to prosper led to the ultimate demise of the rest of the country, but we find little evidence that such a small part of a big economy could bring on a great depression. Perhaps it could cause a recession, but nothing of the magnitude of what happened. That leaves us with two major, and in some sense competing, theories of why it all happened.

The first theory is associated with John Maynard Keynes, founder of **Keynesian economics**. The second is associated with Milton Friedman, the leading proponent of **monetarism**.

The Keynesian Explanation

In 1936, when we were still in the Depression, a rather remarkable book appeared, *The General Theory of Employment, Interest and Money.* It was written by John Maynard Keynes, a respected and eminent economist who lived and worked in England. In his book, Keynes introduced the possibility that unemployment would exist for a long period of time. That is, he introduced the possibility (hitherto unthought of) that unemployment on a large scale would not correct itself by natural forces within the economy. He pointed out that what was necessary to keep full employment was effective aggregate demand. He also pointed out that one of the key factors driving the economy was investment. To provide for investment, there had to be saving. In other words, consumers would have to be willing to save part of their income in order for investors to have resources for investment. But, noted Keynes, there might be times when there is not enough effective investment demand to use up all of the private sector's savings. When this occurs, there would be unemployment, for saving as such is only useful when it is put back into the economy, and it is put back into the active economy only when investors use it to build houses or machines or buildings.

Proponents of the Keynesian theory of how income and employment are determined point out that during the 1920s, the public engaged in an abnormally high level of saving. According to the Keynesian theory, this was dangerous, because unless those savings were put back into the economy by investment, a drop in aggregate demand would result. Unemployment would occur. In fact, however, during the 1920s there was a very high rate of net investment. But such a situation would eventually mean a reduction in the rate of investment as the stock of private capital reached excessively high levels. When this occurred, the expected profitability of future investment would probably fall. Hence, businesses would feel less desire to increase investment. Unless consumers decreased saving accordingly, the desired level of saving would exceed the desired level of investment. Reduced demand on the part of the entire public would result, as would unemployment. A recession would begin and could develop into a depression, according to this theory. The government would have to step in to increase effective aggregate demand by appropriate monetary and fiscal policies.

Basically, then, according to Keynesian theory, the Great Depression occurred because of a collapse in the desire for new capital formation on the part of business people. That is, there was a collapse in investment demand. Investment fell behind saving, reducing output, and thereby causing unemployment. This theory is borne out by all the available statistics. Net investment fell precipitously in the years following the stock market crash. But why the stock market crash? Perhaps the reduction in net investment could have been triggered by something else; at least, that is what the other major theory contends.

Milton Friedman and Monetary Theory

While not denying the possibility that investment decisions by business people relative to saving decisions by individuals are an important determinant of how the economy moves, the proponents of monetarism, led by Milton Friedman, place considerably more emphasis on what happens to the amount of money in circulation. While our sketch of their theory is simplified, perhaps even oversimplified, we can point out its most obvious aspects and apply it to what happened during the Great Depression.

Monetarists believe that what happens in the short run in the economy can be determined by how the Federal Reserve System alters the amount of money in circulation. Money, remember, is comprised of currency and checking account balances. As noted in the last chapter, the Federal Reserve System was chartered before our entrance into World War I to establish a sound money supply. According to the monetarists, during the Great Depression, it did just the opposite. Now, why should the amount of money in circulation be important?

The monetarist theory states that people have a certain desire for money because it facilitates transactions. That is, to live in a world without money would be quite costly indeed, for we would have to resort to barter. Therefore, people keep money in their checking accounts and in their pocketbooks in order to facilitate transactions and to have a temporary store of purchasing power. If the number of transactions goes up, therefore, the amount of money desired by the public should increase. In other words, there should be some relationship between the level of income and the level of money desired by the public. And, indeed, according to the monetarists, this relationship not only exists, but is fairly stable. Therefore, if the Federal Reserve System increases the total number of dollars and transactions do not increase, some people will find that they have excess money. In order to get rid of their excess money, these people will attempt to spend it or will buy bonds. This will lead to, among other things, an increase in the amount of goods and services demanded. Hence, if full employment prevails, this will lead to a rise in prices. If we are not at full employment, it will lead to, at least in part, a rise in output and employment.

Now, taking the opposite tack, if the Federal Reserve System, sometimes called the monetary authority, decides to decrease the amount of money in circulation, then some individuals and businesses will find they have less money than they desire, which is, as we have noted, a function of how much income they make. Accordingly, they will spend less. But when lots of people spend less, the total demand in the economy for goods and services falls, and either prices or output will fall. In any case, money income will be decreased, and so will employment.

THE MONEY SUPPLY

Now, using this very simplified version of monetarist theory, we can assess what happened during the Depression. Although the Federal Reserve made lots of overt attempts to stimulate the economy, the money supply in circulation actually decreased by a third from the start of the recession to the depths of the Depression. However, this should come as no surprise with the large number of bank failures. In addition, banks that survived the crash held more reserves to ensure their safety. Simultaneously, the public was withdrawing deposits to avoid losses. Both of these actions led to a reduction in the money stock.

According to the monetarist theory, the reduction in the money stock could only mean one thing: a reduction in the total demand for goods and services and, hence, a reduction in output and employment. The monetarists maintain that what would have been just another recession turned into the Great Depression because of the contractionary efforts that the Federal Reserve engaged in during this period. Whether or not the Federal Reserve was aware of what was happening is irrelevant; the money supply decreased rather than increased. The monetary authorities dealt a crippling blow to an already weak economy and, hence, the depression deepened.

POSSIBLE REVERSE CAUSATION

At this point, we should mention the possibility of the reverse causal link between the money supply and income. We find that, as incomes fall, banks are less inclined to loan out money, and individuals will demand less money. Peter Temin argues that there was a reduction in consumption (a nonmonetary factor) caused by the stock market crash and the decline in the agricultural sector. This consequently lowered income and the demand for money. Hence, not all of the reduction in the money supply is necessarily to be blamed on the Federal Reserve. In fact, some observers maintain that the Federal Reserve has the power to pull on the string, but it cannot push. Banks at this time were very unwilling to loan out any of their increased reserves. But, of course, that just means that the Federal Reserve would have had to increase reserves even more to reverse the decline in the money supply during this period. Moreover, much, if not most, of the decline in the money supply was created by runs on banks (bank panics). These failures were caused to a very significant degree by drastic declines in the value of their capital assets, mainly bonds. The Federal Reserve certainly had the power to strengthen these asset holdings by bond purchases. This would have made banks solvent, reduced the sense of alarm, and stemmed the tide of bank failures. Sadly, however, the Federal Reserve often sold rather than bought bonds. This action was unfortunately characteristic of many countercyclical measures that were misused during the 1930s.

Issue: Was the New Deal Truly Expansionary Fiscal Policy?

The Great Watershed: The 1930s

There are lots of myths concerning what happened before the election of President Franklin D. Roosevelt and what happened after. In the main, many observers contend that Hoover was a complete laissez-faire president who was unwilling to attempt any government intervention to pull the economy out of a deepening recession. On the other hand, many contend that President Roosevelt took Keynesian economics to heart and attempted, by every means necessary, to stimulate the economy through federal programs designed to increase aggregate demand. Both of these common notions are misleading. We have already made reference to the interventionist attitude that Hoover had exhibited during World War I. That attitude was to continue during his time as Secretary of Commerce and, more importantly, during his first three years as president.

HOOVER, THE GOVERNMENT ADVOCATE

Hoover was both a mobilizer and an economic planner during World War I. During the 1920s, he was a persistent advocate of government-business partnership in stabilizing industry. In fact, Hoover campaigned for reelection in 1932 on a platform of past government intervention into the private business affairs of the nation. He said, "We might have done nothing. That would have been utter ruin. Instead, we met the situation with proposals to private business and to Congress of the most gigantic proportion of economic defense and counterattack ever evolved in the history of the Republic."

He was not exaggerating much, for as soon as the stock market crashed in 1929, he started putting his program into operation. He called a series of White House conferences with the leading financiers and industrialists of the day. He got them to pledge, for example, that they would not reduce wage rates and that they would expand their investments. His theory was that the way to prevent recession was to maintain the purchasing power of the working people. How better to do that than by not reducing their wages?

KEEPING WAGES UP

What Hoover ignored during this period was that if prices are falling and wages stay the same, then the real wages are rising. Just as with any other good or service, the demand for labor is negatively related to its price. If labor's price—the real wage rate—goes up, a lower quantity will be demanded. If there is unemployment, an explicit program to keep real wages up will lead not to more employment, but rather to less. And that is exactly what happened. It was only in 1932, after several years of extremely severe depression and extensive unemployment, that money wages began to fall.

Hoover had been quite active in trying to prevent that decline and, indeed, was outraged by the United States Steel Corporation's first attempt at lowering wages in the fall of 1931. Overall, real wages actually rose from 1929 to 1933. In an economy that is growing, this is normal. But on the other hand, in an economy that is declining, we would not expect this. It could only lead to a decrease in the number of workers demanded because just like the demand for everything else, the demand for workers falls as the price rises, other things being the same.

EXPANSION OF PUBLIC WORKS

In December of 1929, Hoover proposed to expand public works by some $600 million. In 1931, Hoover was instrumental in pushing through the Employment Stabilization Act, which established an Employment Stabilization Board. This Board expanded public works during the Depression and was allocated $150 million to do so. Hoover was not content to stop there. He instituted the start of the Boulder, Grand Coulee, and Central California dams and also signed a treaty with Canada in order to build the St. Lawrence Seaway. Hoover was the first president to actively engage in large amounts of public works.

Finally, in January of 1932, Hoover created the Reconstruction Finance Corporation (RFC). It was modeled after the old World War I Finance Corporation, which extended emergency loans to business. The U.S. Treasury furnished the RFC with half a billion dollars, and it was allowed to issue bonds up to another $1.5 billion.

Also, even prior to the Depression, Hoover had established a Federal Farm Board, which was ready to take action as soon as the Depression arrived. Its first big operation was to cartelize wheat farmers into cooperative marketing units in order to withhold wheat stocks, thereby causing a rise in prices. But this did not work well. Persuasion was not adequate to keep wheat farmers voluntarily from producing more wheat. Then the Grain Stabilization Cooperation was set up. It was supposed to purchase enough wheat to prevent the price of wheat from falling. However, opposing economic forces were too great.

A CHANGE OF HEART

Finally, in the last year of his administration, Hoover changed course. Many advisors had encouraged him to continue his efforts to increase the scope of government intervention in the marketplace and to increase the amount of cartelization among industry leaders. When he declined, he was labeled a laissez-faire president. Although that label is somewhat out of line with what actually happened during the first three years of Hoover's administration, Franklin Roosevelt was nonetheless able to capitalize on it and become president for the remainder of his life.

THE FIRST HUNDRED DAYS

Roosevelt's sweep into office allowed him to push through Congress a massive amount of legislation in the first 100 days of his administration. Space limitations prevent us from giving the details of every program that America's thirty-second president instituted. We can, however, look at the major ones.

It must be noted that Roosevelt did not enter the presidency with the idea that government deficit spending was a necessary stimulus to economic recovery. In fact, it was only later in his administration that he appears to have believed deficit spending was indeed the way to prosperity for an economy in a gravely depressed state. We find in many of the utterances of the president that he was convinced that a balanced federal budget should be maintained. Nonetheless, he wanted to start numerous programs to put the country back on the road to recovery.

USING HOOVER'S IDEAS

Many of Roosevelt's ideas were merely extensions of Hoover's. Roosevelt felt that it was necessary to increase workers' wages in order to increase purchasing power in the economy simultaneously and reduce "cutthroat" competition. Therefore, he was convinced that a new system of cooperation among workers, businesses, and the government was necessary. Hence, the National Industrial Recovery Act (NIRA) was passed, and the National Recovery Administration (NRA) was formed. Its basic purpose was to allow collusion among businesses to prevent price cutting. Those businesses who joined in the national recovery effort were allowed to post the Blue Eagle emblem to identify themselves.

For labor, Section 7a of the National Industrial Recovery Act allowed for collective bargaining by employees. This was a great impetus to the union movement, which had started many years before.

From the very beginning, a considerable portion of the population was against the National Recovery Administration and its obvious monopolizing tendencies. Finally, on May 27, 1935, the Supreme Court, in the Schechter case, declared that the NIRA was unconstitutional.

FARM PROGRAMS

Remember that the Federal Farm Board had already been set up with an appropriation of half a billion dollars to be used to stabilize the prices of three major commodities in the program: wheat, cotton, and wool. The Farm Board soon ran out of money, though, in attempting to keep the price of these commodities high. The major replacement for the Farm Board was brought about by the Agricultural Adjustment Act of 1933. It established within the Department of Agriculture the Agricultural Adjustment Administration (AAA). Its stated goal was to support farm prices and to control the production of farm products. These were further supported by the Bankhead Cotton Control Act, passed in 1934, as well as the Cuff-Smith Tobacco Control Act. Both of these Acts levied fines on farmers who produced in excess of their quotas. Many farmers who signed agreements to limit their production were given benefit payments from the government. From the very beginning, there were scandals over the programs of the AAA. One was called "The Murder of Six Million Little Pigs."

What happened was that a survey at that time showed young pigs to be extremely numerous, indicating that in the near future there would be such a large quantity of pork supplied that prices would have to plummet in order to sell it all. So the Farm Bureau, the National Corn Hog Committee, and the Farmers Union recommended that six million pigs be killed. They were, and the baby pork was bought by the Federal Surplus Relief Corporation. In another incident, people were enraged that the AAA had farmers plow under eleven million acres of cotton already growing.

At this time, the Commodity Credit Corporation was formed. It was allowed to make what are called **nonrecourse loans** to farmers with cotton used as collateral. In other words, the farmers would pay the Commodity Credit Corporation cotton in exchange for a stipulated price that was above the market price. Farmers never had to repay the loan, but if they decided to, they could get their cotton back. The Commodity Credit Corporation is still in operation.

EFFECTS OF PRICE SUPPORTS

Finally, the original AAA was declared unconstitutional in 1936. Undaunted, Roosevelt revised the legislation and

the AAA of 1938 was passed. It contained a soil conservation program, production allotments, Commodity Credit Corporation nonrecourse loans, payments to farmers who kept their production within quotas, and federal purchase of so-called surpluses. All of these programs had essentially been in effect earlier, but the AAA of 1938 made them slightly more flexible. These programs were destined to have perverse effects on the farming sector of the economy from their very inception. After all, if a farmer is paid a price support, then the benefits he receives are directly proportional to the amount of production he has. The bigger the farmer, the bigger the payment from the government. What happens is that the richest farmers have received the most money from the U.S. Treasury and the poorest have obtained the least. It is estimated that about 15 percent of all federal farm payments go to farmers with net worths exceeding $1 million. Additionally, consumers pay prices considerably in excess of what they would pay without a farm program.

Unions and the Wagner Act

Soon after the NIRA was declared unconstitutional by the Supreme Court, the Wagner Act was passed. Using a slightly different wording from that used for establishing Section 7a of the NIRA, Roosevelt argued that the inequality in bargaining power between individual workers and large businesses depressed "the purchasing power of wage earners in industry" and prevented "stabilization of competitive wage rates and working conditions." To remedy all this, the Wagner Act guaranteed the workers the right to form labor unions and engage in collective bargaining. This Act was declared constitutional by the Supreme Court in 1937, after which the strength of organized labor grew rapidly in the economy.

UNION MEMBERSHIP

Of course, it was not in the 1930s that unions were first started. The concept of unions goes back as far as the Middle Ages when journeymen's associations were formed.

CRAFT UNIONS

The American labor union movement started, however, with what are called local craft unions. These were groups of workers in individual trades, such as baking, shoemaking, and printing. Many of the earlier craft unions were curtailed by unfavorable court judgments. The percent of the labor force organized into union was still extremely small in 1930. At the beginning of the Depression, labor union membership fell drastically, from 12.2 percent to 7.4 percent of the labor force. However, within a few years after the passage of the NIRA and then the Wagner Act, membership jumped by more than 100 percent. By this time, many national unions had been formed.

INDUSTRIAL UNIONS

To take the place of the Knights of Labor, the American Federation of Labor was started in 1886 under the leadership of Samuel Gompers. By 1900, the AFL boasted a membership of over one million workers. These federations were basically composed of numerous craft unions. Industrial unions, on the other hand, seek to organize the workers in an entire industry regardless of the individual jobs these workers are doing.

In any event, during World War I, an increasingly favorable climate of opinion toward unions developed. By 1920, membership had reached five million. Then there was a great decline until the New Deal. After the Wagner Act was passed, several other great unions were organized, one being the United Mine Workers Union under the presidency of John L. Lewis. He became head of the Congress of Industrial Organizations, a group of industrial unions. The combined efforts of the AFL and the CIO increased the percentage of workers unionized by leaps and bounds from the Great Depression until the end of World War II.

Other Programs: Relief and Social Security

Numerous other programs were instituted during the New Deal. Many of them were aimed at providing employment for the impoverished. There were the CCC and the NYA and the CWA and the WPA. Most of these particular programs did not last, but they did provide jobs for a certain number of people during the Depression years, and similarly designed programs are being implemented today. One program that did last was Social Security.

SOCIAL SECURITY

The Social Security Act was signed by Roosevelt on August 14, 1935. It provided one of the most important social insurance programs in the history of the United States. The major aspects of it were unemployment and old age insurance plus survivors' benefits. It started out small, enabling the federal government to provide grants to states to help them meet their old age assistance programs. There were also grants for aid to dependent children and to the blind.

The Social Security Act levied a basic payroll tax on payrolls of all employers, which was initially 1 percent but which rose to 3 percent after 1937. While it is not clear how effective the Social Security provisions were during its early years, today we have ample evidence of how the Social Security system works. All workers who are covered start paying Social Security the minute they start making money, no matter how little. The basic rate in 1990 was 7.65 percent for the employer and the employee alike, applied to $51,300 of earned income.

However, employers do not actually pay their 7.65 percent. Since the employers' payments are part of their costs of hiring, they accordingly offer lower money wages to workers than if there were no Social Security payments. The employee indirectly pays the Social Security tax because the Social Security payment is ultimately a tax on labor income. Of course, it is redistributed to older, retired workers, but those who are paying view it simply as a payroll tax. After all, it does reduce their spendable income. It is not, strictly speaking, a guaranteed insurance program. Death benefits can be small or even zero unless the deceased leaves a long-lived widow or minor children. Furthermore, Social Security payments are voted on by Congress. One can never be certain that Congress in the future will be as generous as Congress has been in the past. Nevertheless, it remains very visible, and it is one of the major social insurance programs in existence today.

The New Deal and Aggregate Demand

Despite all of the fanfare about the first 100 days of Roosevelt's campaign for programs against the Depression, it is not really clear that they had much effect on aggregate demand. After all, besides considering what programs were instituted, we also have to look at how they were paid and at what other programs were dropped.

In Roosevelt's campaign, he criticized Hoover for large budget deficits that had been marked up after the Crash of 1929. In fact, Hoover's administration had the largest federal deficit in the history of the United States prior to Roosevelt's election. Once elected, Roosevelt told Congress that he did not want the country to be "wrecked on the rocks of loose fiscal policy." Apparently he took his warning seriously. Deficits during the Depression years were indeed small. In fact, in 1937 the total government budget, including federal, state, and local levels, had a surplus of $0.3 billion. During this time, taxes were repeatedly raised. The Revenue Act of 1932, passed during the depths of the Depression, brought the largest percentage increase of federal taxes in the history of the United States except for periods of war.

Fiscal policies, then, were in fact extremely weak, and even perverse. At the same time that the federal government was increasing expenditures, local and state governments were decreasing them.

If we measure the total of state, federal, and local fiscal policies, we find that they were truly expansive only in 1931 and 1936 as compared to what the government was doing prior to the Depression. These two years were expansive only because of large veterans' payments, passed by Congress in both years—over the vigorous opposition of both Hoover and Roosevelt. In both 1933 and 1937, and, to a lesser degree, in 1938, fiscal policy was quite a bit less expansionary than in 1939.

Roosevelt's administration has often been characterized as expansionary. In fact, however, it was not; the New Deal's primary effects were reform and the establishment of pronounced government controls over wider spheres of American economic life.

DEFINITIONS OF NEW TERMS

KEYNESIAN ECONOMICS Keynesian economics recommends controlling the levels of economic activity (employment and inflation) by changing aggregate demand through taxes and government spending.

MONETARISM Monetarists believe that unexpected changes in the money supply cause fluctuations in real output and employment in the short run.

NONRECOURSE LOANS Nonrecourse loans are loans that farmers obtain from the Commodity Credit Corporation in exchange for their crops as collateral. These loans need not be repaid, and in such cases the government keeps the crops.

CRAFT UNIONS Craft unions consist of workers who have one particular skill, such as printers, bankers, or shoemakers.

INDUSTRIAL UNIONS Industrial unions, such as the United Auto Workers, are organizations of workers in an entire industry regardless of their particular job classification.

Thirteen
Facing Another World War

The decade of the 1930s was dismal indeed. Workers and business people were concerned with little other than pulling themselves out of a deep, dark depression. The publication in Germany of Adolph Hitler's book *Mein Kampf* stirred little excitement in America. Even the outbreak of European hostilities in 1939 did not concern many Americans. Little did they know that they were soon to enter into the most devastating war in the history of the world. On the eve of World War II, in September 1939, 9.5 million men and women were out of work. This accounted for 17 percent of the entire labor force. At that time we were spending 1 percent of GDP on war production.

The Situation Worsens

By and large, the 1930s were a period of relative isolationism; it seemed all too clear to the average American and to many of our elected representatives in Congress, that our major problems were at home. Few Americans were sympathetic to a military preparedness program even after fighting broke out in Europe. Although Roosevelt succeeded in appointing a War Resource Board in August of 1939, it quietly closed its doors a mere five months later. And yet things continued to worsen in Europe. France fell in 1940; the so-called invulnerable Maginot Line did not even hold against the first effective German attack. In May 1940, the office of Emergency Management was appointed, to be succeeded a few days later by the Council of National Defense.

Finally, the Selective Service Act was passed in September 1940 and war production started to increase. And by 1943 American war production was as great as the combined war production of Italy, Japan, and Germany.

Managing War Production

Although still quite unsure of our course in 1941, an Office of Production Management was established that January. It was to provide for emergency plant facilities in case we entered the war. There was no doubt by the summer of 1941 that we were in trouble with respect to our defense capabilities. The Japanese sneak attack on Pearl Harbor on December 7, 1941, caught us totally by surprise and found us shockingly unprepared. Nobody had anticipated that the war would reach us so

Exhibit 13.1

The Proliferation of Government Agencies during World War II

Office of Emergency Management
  Committee of Fair Employment
    Practice
  Foreign Economic
  Administration
  National War Labor Board
  Office of Defense Transportation
  Office of Inter-American Affairs
  Office of War Information
  Office of Scientific Research and
    Development
  War Production Board
  War Shipping Administration

National Housing Agency
  Federal Home Loan Bank
    Administration
  Federal Housing Administration

Board of War Communications

Office of Censorship

Office of Price Administration

Office of War Mobilization and
Reconversion
  Surplus Property Board

Organization
  Retraining and Reemployment
    Administration

President's War Relief Control
Board

Selective Service System

Join Chiefs of Staff

Office of Strategic Services

Joint War Production
Committee—United States and
Canada

Permanent Joint Board of
Defense—United States and
Canada

Combined Chiefs of Staff—United
States, United Kingdom, and
Canada

Combined Shipping Adjustment
Board United States and Great
Britain

British–American Joint Patent
Interchange Committee

Munitions Assignments Board-
United States and Great Britain

Joint Mexican–United States
Defense Commission

Pacific War Council

United Nations Relief and
Rehabilitation Administration

United Nations Information

soon. The War Productions Board was immediately set up to oversee industrial output. Agencies multiplied rapidly; a number of them are listed in Table 13.1. Because this rapid multiplication of war agencies cried out for overall management, the Office of War Mobilization was created in May 1943, at the height of hostilities. But by then it was literally impossible to oversee all of the war activities in which the industrial sector of the economy was engaged. The next year this office had a new word tacked on—Reconversion—for by 1944, we were convinced that the war would end shortly and that we would have to face the arduous task of reconverting the economy back to peacetime endeavors.

LABOR PROCUREMENT

We had a problem of providing sufficient "manpower" not only to fight the war on several fronts but also to generate war production on the factories. A War Manpower Commission was established in April 1942. Its task was to provide an adequate supply of labor to all sectors of the military and the civilian economy. The draft, of course, solved the military labor problem. In 1944 and 1945, 11.5 million men and women served in the Armed Services. The employed civilian labor force first grew quite rapidly and then leveled off toward the peak of the war. What happened was that members of the economy who were formerly not in the labor force decided to join. These included women, retired people, and teenagers who had quit their schooling early. That is, the **labor force participation rates** of various groups in the economy increased. A participation rate is the percentage of the total number of people in any given subsector of the economy who are engaged in the labor force. The participation rate of women over age fourteen, for example, was about 25 percent at the end of the 1930s; by 1944, it had risen to 36.5 percent. Over all, the participation rate in the population over fourteen years old jumped from less than 55 percent before the war to about 62.4 percent in 1944. Many of these changes were permanent, particularly with respect to female participation rates.

Paying for the War

As pointed out time and again, the government must somehow finance its war expenditures. It has three ways to do so: by taxation, by borrowing from the private sector, or by money creation. All three were used in World War II as federal expenditures grew by leaps and bounds from 1939 to 1945. So, too, did the federal government's deficitthat is, the difference between federal expenditures and federal tax receipts. The deficit reached an astounding $53.9 billion in 1945. This was more than one-half of federal expenditures in that year!

TAXATION

Of course, the president did attempt to raise taxes. As early as January 1940, Roosevelt asked for additional taxes to pay for anticipated war expenditures. How did Congress respond? In June 1940, it merely lowered personal income tax exemptions and added slightly to the personal income tax surtax rate. In addition, it charged a little more to corporation, and there were some nominal increases in gift, excise, estate, and other assorted taxes. Nevertheless, tax receipts quickly fell behind expenditures. In October 1940, when it was obvious that the fighting was intensifying rather than subsiding, an excess profits tax was passed, with rates ranging from 25 percent to 50 percent. The corporate profit rate was raised to a maximum of 24 percent. About a year later, the maximum personal income tax rate went up to 77 percent and the corporate rate to 31 percent. The next year taxes were raised again, the personal tax to a maximum of 88 percent and the corporate to 40 percent. In addition, the maximum excess profits rate on corporation profits was now 90 percent. When the president asked Congress the following year, 1943, for even more taxes, they refused. However, a year after his request they were amenable to increasing the maximum marginal tax rate on individuals to 94 percent.

None of these measures was enough. Only 61 percent of the entire war effort was financed by taxation.

SELLING BONDS

Because of the growing government deficit, bonds had to be sold. Just as there were Liberty Loans in World War I, there were Liberty Loans in World War II. In fact, the U.S. Treasury conducted seven of them, plus one Victory Loan. All told, during this period loans from the private sector accounted for 28 percent of government expenditures. That left 11 percent to be made up by money creation.

MONEY CREATION

During these years, government expenditures increased more than the increases in taxes and bond sales taken together. Therefore the Federal Reserve System was coerced into helping the Treasury. Its primary objective was to ensure the Treasury adequate funds to meet all government expenditures. In March 1942, a special committee in the Federal Reserve System asserted its desire to prevent a rise in the interest rates of government bonds. So from that date until 1951, the Federal Reserve either "pegged" or supported the interest rate at a very low level: 2.5 percent on long-term bonds, and 3/8 of a percent on 90-day Treasury bills. To maintain such low rates of interest, the Federal Reserve had to stand ready to buy all the government bonds offered when interest rates started to rise above the support level. At that time anybody could exchange cash for government bonds. But every time the Federal Reserve bought a bond, it increased the base on which the money supply rested. It is not surprising, then, that the money supply grew 12.1 percent a year from 1939 to 1948 as a result of the Federal Reserve's bond purchases.

Price Controls

Whether from an excessive demand by the government for war production or from the increased amount of money that the Federal Reserve was putting in circulation, mounting pressure on prices soon resulted. Many knew this was going to happen, but nobody wanted it. Hence, the Price Control Act of January 1942 established the Office of Price Administration. By mid-1943, fully 95 percent of the nation's foodstuffs were rationed, and maximum prices and rents had been established. The Anti-Inflation Act of October 1942 then established the Office of Economic Stabilization. Its purpose was to limit wages and salaries and to curb prices and rents not yet controlled. At the height of price controls, these two offices, along with the Office of War Mobilization, created in 1943, were aided and abetted by almost 400,000 volunteer "price-watchers" scattered throughout the country. Through this enormous nationwide effort, wholesale prices rose only 14 percent from November 1941 to August 1945.

CONTROLS AND REPRESSED INFLATION

Price controls were not new to Americans of course. But the effects of controls were little understood. Instead of inflation, the shortage of goods relative to money came in another way. During World War II, we had what is known as **repressed inflation**. That is, the inflation did not actually show up in the price statistics because of rationing and price controls. Obviously, during World War II workers and business people had extra cash to spend. Hence, there was a situation of pent-up demand, and yet the amount of resources for consumer goods production was limited, since so much was needed for war production. Normally, when there is an excess demand for goods or services, prices rise. But price controls held prices down. Queuing and rationing became common practices.

BLACK MARKETS

In addition, in many situations black markets sprang up. A **black market** is an illegal market where goods and services are sold at higher than controlled prices. There were also numerous other ways that individuals obtained goods and services, such as favors for the supplier of a rationed good or service, or special arrangement for under-the-counter payments in addition to the stated price. There are many ways in which individuals can circumvent price controls. It is not clear how much of this actually happened during the war, but many accounts indicate that illegal or semi-legal wheeling and dealing was rampant. Price controls were finally lifted after the end of hostilities in 1945 and then prices really soared.

This lends further support to the contention that repressed inflation existed during World War II. When prices were allowed to rise, they did, indicating that they would have risen all along in the absence of controls. Note that it took a large amount of bureaucratic effort to police controls effectively during the war, even during this period of active patriotism. Although it was modestly successful for a short while, it is very unlikely that such measures would be effective in normal times or over longer periods.

The War Ends Without a Depression

Even before the ended, government officials and other concerned individuals worried about the possibility of a postwar recession. They remembered what had happened after World War I, and they also were well aware of the new Keynesian ideas that had become popular in those days. As presented by Keynes during the depths of the Depression, demand must remain high for unemployment to stay low. It appeared that when the war ended there would be a serious drop in demand, because government expenditures would fall drastically. This would lead to a multiple contraction in the level of income, thus leading to high levels of unemployment. Everybody wanted to prevent this but nobody quite knew how. What actually happened was just the opposite: Many individuals had high levels of **liquid assets**. That is, they had large amounts of government bonds and cash on hand when victory came. They wanted to spend them once the many restrictions on the production and sale of consumer durables such as automobiles, refrigerators, and washing machines were lifted. This happy opportunity to purchase new durable goods whose production had been greatly curtailed led to booms in these industries right after the war.

There was also unprecedented activity in the construction industry. Housing units were being speedily built. And lastly, government services contracted somewhat, but not back to their prewar levels. While the unemployment rate did jump from about 1.9 percent in 1945 to 3.9 percent in 1946, this latter figure was a more normal peacetime level of unemployment. In fact, it is what is generally called *normal* or *frictional* unemployment in a dynamic economy. It was not until several years later, in 1949, that we actually experienced what could be considered a recession. Just in case, though, the Congress passed the Employment Act of 1946, sometimes referred to as the Full Employment Act. It reads as follows:

> The Congress hereby declares that it is the continuing policy and responsibility of the federal government to use all practicable means consistent with its needs and obligations and other essential consider- ations of national policy, with assistance and cooperation of industry, agriculture, labor and state and local governments, to coordinate and utilize all its plans, functions, and resources for the purpose of creat- ing and maintaining, in a manner calculated to foster and promote free competitive enterprise and the general welfare, conditions under which there *will* be afforded useful employment opportunities, including self-employment, for those able, willing, and seeking to work and to promote maximum employment, production, and pur- chasing power.

In addition, the Council of Economic Advisors was set up to make a continuing study of the American economy and to assist the president in preparing a report on the state of the nation every year. That council still exists today, and the government is continuously engaged in smoothing out economic activity in the United States.

World War II as a total war was unprecedented in scale for the United States and the rest of the world. During that time, government expendi- tures grew by leaps and bounds.

Issue: Did World War II Pull the United States Out of the Depression?

Many people assume that World War II pulled the United States out of the Great Depression. As the story goes, our tremendous unemployment was eradicated by the stimulus of a war economy. And the low levels of per capita real income at the end of the 1930s also changed during wartime.

First let us consider what happened to unemployment. Unemployment was in excess of 17 percent when hos- tilities began in Europe. This figure was still almost 15 percent in 1940. It then dropped to an incredible 1.2 percent by

1944. Overall, then, it seems clear that the war effort nearly eliminated unem- ployment. But something else was hap- pening at the same time, namely, conscription. The Selective Service Act was passed in 1940, and soon thereafter large numbers of men and women joined or were drafted into the armed services. These represented a signifi- cant fraction of the labor force. Is it accurate, then, to say that the war economy erased the prewar 17 percent unemployment rate, when 17 percent of the labor force was in the armed forces at the height of the war? Clearly, a very significant and increasing fraction of the labor force was conscripted. Of course, this is one way to eliminate unemployment, but it is rather a drastic procedure for generating unemployment reductions. Generally, it is assumed that high production rates create increasing demand for more and more workers, thus eliminating any residue of unemployment. Moreover, this is what most students of World War II believe happened during that period. In fact, however, it appears that conscription had much to do with eliminating the unemployment of the Great Depression.

Nevertheless, the fact remains that the output of the economy expanded rapidly during wartime.

INCREASING OUTPUT

Increases in war demand during the early 1940s definitely stimulated aggregate demand. The output of the economy increased at a tremendous rate. Total real GDP grew by leaps and bounds from the beginning of the war to its end. But were individuals really becoming materially better off during this period? The total amount of government purchases of goods and services skyrocketed during the war. However, much of the increase in output actually went to war production, not to enrich the personal lives of Americans. That is, the private sector of the economy was not much better off at the end of the war than at the beginning. The Depression was over, but people were not as well off as often is imagined. Of course, if we consider the psychological benefit of fighting and winning the war, overall social welfare broadly defined may have indeed increased. The war provided a new collective purpose, and certainly more people had jobs and the self-respect derived from being employed. Clearly the poorer segments of society were living more comfortably.

WHAT IS INCOME?

Nevertheless, this brings us to the crucial questions: What does income really represent? Does it matter what we produce? Can an armored tank yield satisfaction to the general public? In fact, many argue that it is an intermediate good, not a final good—intermediate in the sense that it is used to produce what we call *national defense*. As Adam Smith once said, "consumption is the objective of production." However, since World War II modern politicians seem to be saying that tanks and airplanes are also objectives. Who is right? That depends on one's value judgments. Economics or history cannot answers such a question, but individual reflection will certainly lead most of us to our own conclusions.

DEFINITION OF NEW TERMS

LABOR FORCE PARTICIPATION RATE The participation rate is the proportion of the total population working, or the percentage of the total subpopulation working. We can find participation rates, then, for the entire economy and for various subclasses, such as men, women, married men, married women, etc.

REPRESSED INFLATION Repressed inflation is inflation that is not allowed to manifest itself in rising prices. The symptoms of repressed inflation are shortages, black markets, under-the-counter "deals," and discrimination against certain classes of consumers.

BLACK MARKET The black market is an illegal market where goods and services are exchanged at prices that exceed legally controlled maximums or where national goods are transferred illegally.

LIQUID ASSETS Liquid assets are assets that are easily exchangeable for cash without a change in their value. The most liquid asset is, of course, cash itself. The next most liquid asset might be a savings account, and then a U.S. government short-term bill.

Fourteen
Issues in the Postwar Decades

The end of World War II saw the formation of the United Nations and a renewed commitment to prevent future conflicts endangering the peace and happiness of the world. The awesome destructive power of the atomic bomb had been amply demonstrated at Hiroshima and Nagasaki. The possibility of worldwide destruction and the end of the human species now truly existed. But despite the United Nations and the persistent fear of destructive atomic warfare, the four decades that followed World War II were ones of alternating hot and cold hostile actions. Only half a decade was to transpire before American men, women, and machines were again engaged in a conflict the Korean War.[1] After the truce in Korea it was again barely one and a half decades before American forces were involved in another costly and, as it appears in retrospect, senseless engagement in Indochina. But all during this time the economy was growing; the per capita income was increasing. Underlying this long-run trend of increasing prosperity, however, were numerous problems of unemployment and inflation.

Postwar Inflation and Unemployment

The very strict price controls that were in effect during World War II were lifted almost immediately after the war. Consequently the pressure of repressed inflation that had built up for three or four years was now allowed to vent itself. The rate of inflation jumped sharply after World War II. Then it slowed for a while due to a relatively minor recession at the end of the 1940s. Once the Korean War broke out, however, prices shot up at a very rapid rate.

Curiously, this happened despite the fact that neither government spending nor the money supply were increasing at very rapid rates during this period. However, people still vividly recalled the effects of price controls and scarcity during World War II. They feared the same thing would happen during the Korean conflict, and this fear touched off an extraordinary buying spree, particularly for consumer durables and automobiles. The American public bought now in anticipation of shortages soon to come, but few shortages actually developed, since U.S. participation in the war was relatively minor: 5.7 million men and women were engaged during a period just over three-years. There were 157,500 casualties, and the total cost was estimated to be in the neighborhood of $60 billion. The country experimented with a moderate amount of price

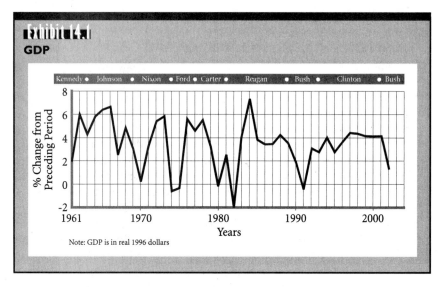

Exhibit 14.1

GDP

Kennedy • Johnson • Nixon • Ford • Carter • Reagan • Bush • Clinton • Bush

% Change from Preceding Period

Years

Note: GDP is in real 1996 dollars

controls during this war, but the effort was not very extensive, and the effects went largely unnoticed.

After the war, prices rose at very low annual rates—between 1 percent and 2 percent—until things heated up in Indochina. Starting in 1965, the rate of inflation advanced. Not only did this inflation continue, but it worsened as we entered the next decade. President Nixon imposed wage and price controls in 1971, and a modified form of controls were continued for a number of years afterward. Once again, however, they proved ineffective. Price controls will not usually work for long if the underlying forces of monetary and fiscal policies are expansionary. This is exactly what happened during World War II, during the Korean War, and again in the 1971–1974 period of government wage and price controls.

Exhibits 14.1, 14.2, and 14.3 show the GDP, CPI (inflation), and unemployment since 1961 under various administrations.

Ups and Downs

Increasingly, since 1946, we not only had times of inflation, but also times of inflation concurrent with high unemployment, now known as stagflation, a situation that was almost completely unknown in the history of the United States.

There was an immediate but short-lived jump in unemployment soon after World War II, as could be expected with large numbers of

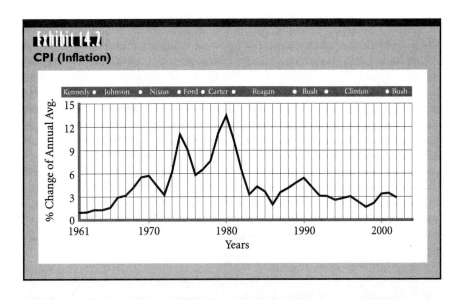

Exhibit 14.2

CPI (Inflation)

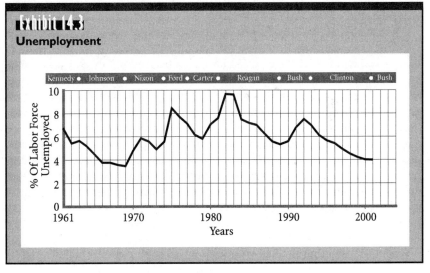

Exhibit 14.3

Unemployment

soldiers being mustered out. There was another period of exceptionally high unemployment at the end of the decade. We experienced yet another recession some ten years later, when the unemployment rate jumped in 1958 to almost 7 percent. Things improved for a few years, but in 1960–1961 another recession was encountered. However, this was followed by almost a full decade of prosperity.

THE KENNEDY TAX CUT

President Kennedy's economic advisors, under the leadership of Walter Heller, argued that a tax cut would give individuals more spendable income. When people spent this additional income, those who received it would also have more to spend, and this process would continue so that the tax cut would yield a more than proportionate increase in aggregate demand. Increased spending in turn would decrease unemployment, as unemployed workers were hired to produce the additional output demand. And later in the decade the unemployment rate did fall. The tax cut, however, did not actually occur until 1964, when Johnson was president, after Kennedy's assassination. The results of the 1964 Johnson–Kennedy tax cut seemed impressive. However, when the reverse tactic was used a few years later to quell an overheated economy, the same success did not arise.

THE TAX SURCHARGE

One year after the tax cut, the United States had become heavily involved in Vietnam. By 1965, federal expenditures had leaped ahead of federal tax revenues, and we encountered increasingly large deficits. At about the same time, the money supply was increasing at a rapid rate, except for a slight pause in 1966. Whereas it had increased at 3.3 percent per annum from 1961 to 1965, during the period 1967 to 1969 it increased at 7 percent. In any event, the Council of Economic Advisors told President Johnson that one way to stop the mounting inflation was to increase taxes. The Council presumed that a reverse Keynesian reasoning would hold: Take more income away from consumers and they will be able to spend less, thus causing a contraction in aggregate demand. Prices would stop rising as fast because people would not be demanding as many goods and services as before. The tax surcharge of 1968 was instituted on this basis. But it had little effect on prices, which continued to rise in the next decade.

A Change in Tactics

In 1969 and 1970, the government's monetary and fiscal policy was suddenly altered. The growth rate of the money supply was decreased, and federal government purchases fell. This led to a lower rate of growth in aggregate demand. But business people, who had no idea that this was anything more than a random occurrence, continued to raise prices because they based their predictions of what they could sell on what had happened in the past. However, at the same time consumers' incomes leveled off. Now they reacted to higher prices by buying less. Inventories started piling up, and layoffs occurred.

Meanwhile, workers still demanded ever-higher wages, for in the past several years they had been accepting wage increases that merely matched increases in the cost of living—inflation. Many union contracts were renegotiated during this period. The union leaders wanted not only to make up for the lost real income of the last three or four years, but also to anticipate future erosions of their paychecks by inflation. Hence, they made demands for higher wages. At first businesses granted them, fully anticipating that they could pass these higher labor costs on to the customer while still maintaining their previous sales records. Such was not the case, however, as both laborers and businesses were caught eventually by an unanticipated change in aggregate demand. Hence, we had a period of rising prices and rising unemployment.

Eventually, though, people started learning, so we saw a decrease in the rate at which inflation was growing until mid-1970. In fact, it appeared that the rate of inflation was abating when President Nixon instituted his New Economic Policy on August 15, 1971. The slowdown in price rises was soon to be reversed as the government's expansionary monetary and fiscal policies, instituted to pull us out of the recession, reinjected purchasing power into the economy and started us off on another inflationary spiral.

THE EIGHTIES AND BEYOND

In the early 1970s economists were very optimistic about their power to control the economy, but when President Reagan was inaugurated in 1981 he was confronted with several economic problems inherited from previous administrations: double-digit inflation, a decade of unusually low economic growth, a high average unemployment rate, large budget deficits, and high nominal interest rates. President Reagan confronted the toughest economic times since the 1930s. The economic downturn from 1979–1982 was the worst since the Depression; however, it was followed by the longest peacetime recovery ever.

The Reagan Administration sought renewed prosperity through a four-part program that included reducing the growth rate of the money supply, lowering the tax rates, reducing government expenditures, and deregulation. The Bush Administration tried to keep the previous Administrations policies intact while working with Congress on ways to reduce the huge federal budget deficits—with the read my lips "no new taxes" slogan. However, this approach was abandoned during the recession of 1990–1991 and may have led to an even larger budget deficit.

President Clinton inheritied a large deficit when he took office in 1993 but almost a decade of economic growth turned a large deficit into a surplus by 2001. However, with another recession in 2001 coupled with the events of September 11, the surplus had turned back into a deficit during the early years of George W. Bush's presidency.

GROWTH IN GOVERNMENT

While it is true that government spending has changed little since 1970, the composition of government spending has changed considerably. National defense spending has fallen from roughly 9 percent of GDP in 1968 to 3.5 percent in 2001. However, in the aftermath of September 11, and the addition of homeland security, we are already starting to see increases in defense spending.

Other areas had rapid spending growth as well. Educational expenditures, for example, tripled in the 1960s alone. By the mid-1970s and for the first time in the nation's history, roughly half of government spending was for social concerns such as education, health, and public housing. In the 1980s and 1990s, we saw a continued increase in income tranfer payments including Social Security, welfare, and unemployment compensation.

In 2001, 38 percent of federal government spending went to Social Security and income security programs. Another 21 percent was spent on health care and Medicare (for the elderly). The rest of federal expenditures include national defense (17 percent), interest on the national debt (11 percent), and miscellaneous items such as foreign aid, education, agriculture, transportation, and housing (13 percent).

American Economic Growth and Personal Welfare

CLEAN AIR AND WATER

Not long ago, fresh air was a free good. We could get all we wanted without depriving anyone else. In addition, every stream was a place to fish and swim in pristine conditions. Today, at times, in some cities, the air is literally not fit to breathe.

These are not entirely new problems; the smoke-fogs of London, for example, have been legendary for centuries, and only recently has London's air been purified by the banning of soft-coal fires. We have simply become more aware of ecological dangers (as population increases) and perhaps because our real incomes have also risen, we are willing to pay more for protecting our environment. Whether or not we are willing to pay the price for obtaining a much purer environment is another question. In any event, Congress has passed numerous pieces of legislation aimed at controlling the degree of pollution-causing activities of producers and consumers alike. The Clean Air Act of 1920 set maximum limits on how much pollution is allowed in urban areas; the polluting emissions of cars, factories, and so on. In addition, individual cities and states have passed their own environmental legislation. However, from the very beginning, for example, automobile manufacturers in Detroit pointed out that costly alteration in car motors would result in much higher costs to the consumer and would hurt the producers' competitive opportunities for economic survival.

Exhibit 14.4 shows that the air quality based on concentrations of the principal pollutants has improved nationally over the last 20 years (1980–1999). The most notable improvements are seen for lead, carbon monoxide, and sulfur dioxide with 94, 65, and 54 percent reductions, respectively.

Between 1970 and 1999, total emissions of the six principal air pollutants decreased 31 percent. This dramatic improvement occurred simultaneously with significant increases in economic growth and population. The improvements are a result of effective implementation of clear air laws and regulations, as well as improvements in the efficiency of industrial technologies.

Despite great progress in air quality improvements, approximately 62 million people nationwide still lived in counties with pollution levels above the national air quality standards in 1999.[2]

In 1990, President George Bush signed into law new amendments to the Clean Air Act. The new provisions tightened controls on specific toxic air pollutants such as sulfur dioxide and nitrogen oxide. In order to meet these new standards, some electric utility companies were encouraged to use "the market" to control pollution. That is, certain businesses would be allowed to sell their pollution rights to others as if it were any other commodity. In other words, if Company A had lower than the stipulated level of sulphur dioxide emissions it could sell its "right to pollute" to say, Company B or save the "right" for another year. By allowing firms to trade pollution rights, firms are able to behave more efficiently.

However, it is unreasonable to expect that we can clean up *all* the lakes and *all* the waterways in the United States. We have to realize when discussing ecological problems that every clean-up effort involves a cost. And the closer we try to come to purity, the higher the costs become.

REDUCE POLLUTION TO WHAT LEVEL?

We obviously have to make a choice, and the rule for maximum economic efficiency is to reduce pollution up to the point where the additional cost of pollution abatement is just equal to the additional benefit, then stop. Of course, this means that the level of pollution desired is not zero. (Finding out some of the hidden costs of pollution may be extremely difficult, however. When such hidden costs surface in the future, they may haunt us with a vengeance.)

Nation-wide standards for automobiles, smokestacks, and factories may be the best ways to control pollution, but they do cause inefficiencies in our economic system. After all, it is not the total physical quantity of pollution that is important, but rather how harmful it is in any given situation. Sulfur oxides are emitted in much smaller quantities than are numerous other pollutants. But they are much more injurious to human health. It would be absurd to set the same physical standard for sulfur oxide emissions as for, say, particulate emissions. What we have to examine is the actual economic costs of different types of pollution in different types of situations. The billowing, belching smokestacks of an electric utility coal-fed steam generators in high population density area certainly cause much more damage than the same amount of pollution would cause in the middle of the Mohave Desert.

If we are going to be economically efficient in our pollution-abating system, pollution must be reduced more in the heavier populated areas of our nation than in the less populated areas. National standards do not in fact take account of different degrees of population density and, hence, the different degrees of economic damage sustained per unit of physical pollution. That leads up to another seemingly serious problem in the United States—concentration and urbanization.

Income, Wealth, and Poverty

The United States is one of the richest nations in the world today. That does not mean, however, that everyone is rich and no one is poor. According to government figures, some 31 million Americans lived below the poverty line as recently as 2001.

The Official Definition of Poverty

In 1959, the President's Council of Economic Advisors originally set a poverty line of $3,000 income a year, regardless of family size. In 1965, it redefined poverty to take into account family size. In addition, the poverty line is updated annually to reflect changes in the cost of living by using the Consumer Price Index. For example, in 2000 the official poverty level for a family of four was roughly $20,000 a year.

Exhibit 14.1

Percent Change in Air Quality, 1983–2002

Pollutant	Change
CO (carbon monoxide)	−65%
Pb (lead)	−94
NO_2 (nitrogen oxide)	−21
O_3 (ozone) 1-hr	−22
8-hr	−14
PM_{10} (particulate matter)	−22*
SO_2 (sulfur dioxide)	−54

Year-to year air quality trends can also be affected by atmospheric conditions and the location of air quality monitors, which are usually located in urban areas. That is, air quality emissions are affected by urban emissions and tend to be different than nationwide emissions. Particulate matter (PM) is a general term used for particles in the air, some large enough to look like smoke or soot. Sources for PM include wood-burning stoves and fireplaces, motor vehicles, power generators, unpaved roads, and windblown dust. About 60 percent of the CO emissions come from autos. Lead levels dropped considerably when leaded gasoline was phased out. SO_2 and NO_2 contribute to acid rain. Ground-level ozone is the primary component of smog.

*between 1993–2002.

Is Poverty Absolute?

If the original poverty line of $3,000 a year were carried back to, say, 1935, we would find that one-third of all Americans were poor in that year. By 1955 one in five would have been classified as poor, and today roughly 5 percent would be poor. Clearly, if we were to keep $3,000 as the limit, even with adjustments for inflation, there would be very few poor in a few more years. That is, very few adults would receive any less than $3,000 (in adjusted dollars) a year. The poverty line, however, does not remain stable. Poverty is a relative concept. Today's official poverty income would have been considered opulence 200 years ago. Moreover, the poverty-line income in the United States is greater than the average income level in most other countries in the world.

Nevertheless, as long as the distribution of income in this country is not more or less equal, there will always be relative poverty, by definition. There will always be some individuals and families whose income is greater than that of others. Hence, in a realistic scene, relative poverty is impossible to eradicate. Yet this matter of the unequal distribution of income is linked closely with the problems of the poor and the drive to eliminate poverty in the United States.

The amount of poverty fell steadily in the 1960s, was steady in the 1970s, and rose during the recession in the early 1980s. The poverty rate then fell slightly during the rest of the 1980s and rose again during the recession of 1990–1991. As you would expect, when the economy is in a recession, unemployment rises and poverty tends to increase. Exhibit 14.5 provides some statistics on the U.S. poverty rate.

Income Distribution

First let's divide the population into fifths according to the total distribution of income and consider the fifth receiving the least income.

THE RECORD SINCE 1935

Exhibit 14.6 illustrates the changing distribution of measured income in the United States since 1935. As you can see in this table, the proportion of income received by the richest Americans (top 5 percent) declined sharply after 1935 but has been edging back up since the 1980s. The proportion received by the poorest Americans (the lowest 20 percent) has remained virtually unchanged since 1935. Most of the observed changes occurred between 1935 and 1950, probably reflecting the impact of the Great Depression and new government programs in the 1930s, as well as World War II. From 1950 to 1980, there was little change in the overall distribution of income. Two significant changes have occurred since the 1980s: The lowest one-fifth of families have seen their share of measured income fall from 5.3 to 4.3 percent of all income, and the top one-fifth of families have seen their share of measured income rise from 41.1 to 47.4 percent of all income.

GOVERNMENT ACTIVITIES

Some scholars have argued that the impact of increased government activity should be considered in evaluating the measured income distribution.[3] Government-imposed taxes burden different income groups in different ways. Also, government programs benefit some groups of income recipients more than others. For example, it has been argued that state-subsidized higher education has benefited the high- and middle-income groups more (because far more students from these income groups go to college) than the poor, as have such things as government subsidies to airports and airlines, operas, and art museums. Some programs, though, clearly aid the poor more than the rich. Food stamps, school lunch programs, housing subsidies, Medicaid, and several other programs provide recipients with **in-kind transfers**—that is, transfers given in a nonmonetary form. When these in-kind transfers are included, many economists conclude that they have served to reduce levels of inequality significantly from the levels suggested by aggregate income statistics.

On balance, the evidence suggests that inequality of money income in the United States declined from 1935 to 1950, then remained rather stable until 1980. Since then, the distribution of income has become less equal. However, if we consider age distribution, institutional factors, and in-kind transfer programs, it is safe to say that the income distribution is considerably more equal than it appears in Exhibit 14.6.

The Demand for Labor and Income Differences

One way to analyze the problem of poverty is to discover why there are such extreme differences in income among households in the United States. Today the bottom fifth of all workers receiving only 4.3 percent of the money income in the United States, whereas the top fifth gets close to 50 percent.

The price of labor—wages—is determined like the price of most things in the economy, assuming, of course, that there are no restrictions in the labor market. The price of labor is determined by the interaction of the supply of and the demand for labor. Basically, the demand for labor is a function of how productive each worker is. A worker's

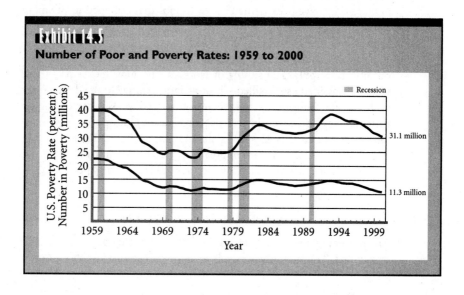

Exhibit 14.5

Number of Poor and Poverty Rates: 1959 to 2000

Exhibit 14-6

Before-Tax Income Shares

Year	Lowest Fifth	Second Fifth	Third Fifth	Fourth Fifth	Highest Fifth	Highest 5%
1935	4.1%	9.2%	14.1%	20.9%	51.7%	26.5%
1950	4.5	12.0	17.4	23.4	42.7	17.3
1960	4.8	12.2	17.8	24.0	41.3	15.9
1970	5.4	12.2	17.6	23.8	40.9	15.6
1980	5.3	11.6	17.6	24.4	41.1	14.6
1990	4.6	10.8	16.6	23.8	44.3	17.4
2001	4.2	9.7	15.4	22.9	47.7	21.0

productivity is affected by (among other things) intelligence, schooling, experience, and training.

One reason some people are poor is that they are not as productive as other individuals. They may lack innate characteristics that would enable or dispose them to be more productive; they may have been denied adequate schooling or training. Other individuals are poor because they have been denied access to jobs that are open to others in the society. In other words, racial or sexual job discrimination can prevent a worker from being paid according to his or her productivity.

As we know, the price of anything is determined not only by demand but also by supply. The supply of workers who have few skills—those who are classified as unskilled—is quite large relative to the demand for such workers. This means that the price unskilled workers can charge for their services is relatively low. Hence, one reason many poor people earn low wages is that they lack the skills that are in high demand. That is, they have only skills that are in great supply. The equilibrium wage rate for these unskilled workers is low, so they are classified as poor.

The Elimination of Poverty

The preceding analysis suggests several ways in which poverty might be eliminated. The first, obviously, is to improve the productivity of poor people. This is being done by job training programs, and improved educational opportunities for minority groups.

These are the direct ways of influencing the future productivity and earning power of relatively poor people in American society. To the extent that these programs are successful, they enable retrained workers to make higher incomes. But what happens in the interim? What about the poor who cannot be retrained? What about women who have children and no income-earning husband? Many are helped, at least partially, by existing **welfare programs.**

Welfare programs are one means of providing purchasing power to the poor to buy essentials. Most welfare payments are made through programs that are partly or largely federally funded. Welfare payments are not given out to just anyone, however. In fact, many poor people do not receive welfare. They cannot pass what are called **means tests.** These tests are used by welfare agencies to compare a budget plan with the potential resources of those who apply for aid. Furthermore, in the past, many poor could not obtain public assistance because they failed to meet state or local minimum residency requirements. However, these requirements have been voided by the U.S. Supreme Court as unconstitutional. Then, too, many poor do not know they are eligible. Others do not apply for benefits because they feel shame at taking what they view as charity.

A Negative Tax

Although most Americans agree that poverty should be eliminated, today's complex, often ineffective, welfare systems not only often fails to help those in need, it often benefits many who are not in need. And it sometimes appears that certain programs have helped give rise to a class of welfare recipients who are content to remain unemployed.

Inescapably, any plan will cause some reduction in the incentive to work. This is the cost society must bear for any type of income redistribution, a goal the society considers worthwhile. Yet there is much room for improvement in public assistance programs, and alternatives to the current situation must be found.

One alternative to the present welfare system is a **negative income tax.** The negative income tax is not a tax but a government payment to low-income citizens. It uses the personal income tax system to set up a series of payments to citizens and tax receipts by the U.S. Treasury according to a schedule based on family size and actual income earned. The plan would not require setting up a new system. It could be an extension of the fully computerized system that already exists.

THE CASE FOR A NEGATIVE INCOME TAX

Many economists favor a negative income tax. They point out that it would not require the massive bureaucracy that now exists for administering public assistance, food stamp, and other programs. Hence, many of the resources now spent for this huge bureaucracy could be spent on other priorities, or used to provide the negative tax (the government payment to needy families). Such a tax system might also restore dignity to the poor. Most welfare recipients must now fill out endless forms and generally submit to the inquiries of an occasionally insensitive welfare bureaucracy.

THE CASE AGAINST A NEGATIVE INCOME TAX

On the other hand, many economists oppose a negative income tax, pointing out that it might cost "too much." In particular, if for political reasons such current welfare programs as food stamps and subsidized housing cannot be dismantled, then the negative income tax would just be one more facet of the welfare system. These critics content that it would not really simplify the existing bureaucracy.

They also content that any effective negative income tax would have a strong **work disincentive effect.** That is, the payoff for returning to work would be so small with an effective negative income tax program that many who could work would nevertheless decide not to do so.

The Rising Cost of Healthcare

The United States spends more money on healthcare per person and as a percentage of national income than any other industrialized nation. Healthcare expenditures (which includes spending on physician, hospital, nursing home, home care, dental, vision, and other services) in the United States in 1999 exceeded $1.2 trillion. Medical expenditures comprise approximately 13 percent of the total value of the output of goods and services produced in the economy, GDP, or roughly $1 out of every $7.50 spent on goods and services.

Exhibit 14.7, shows how healthcare expenditures as a percentage of GDP have varied since 1960. Notice that spending on healthcare has increased significantly over the last several decades, averaging over 13 percent of GDP throughout the 1990s compared to only 5.1 percent in 1960.

Healthcare is often regarded as if it were a basic "human right." However, it is important to recognize that, as with the consumption of other goods and services, the utilization of medical care involves trade-offs. Scarce resources allocated toward the production of health services cannot be used in the production of other goods and services.

Investment in healthcare, however, does bear similarities to investment in human or physical capital. By promoting health and removing disabilities, medical care may (1) improve the productivity of workers on the job *and* reduce missed workdays; and (2) extend the average number of years of participation by people in the labor force.

The sources and uses of healthcare expenditures in the United States during 1998 are illustrated in Exhibit 14.8. Only 15.4 percent of the nation's healthcare expenditures are financed by consumers out-of-pocket. Private insurance funds 33.1 percent of the cost of healthcare. Public healthcare expenditures (both federal and state) comprise 45.3 percent of total U.S. healthcare expenditures and provide access to medical care to more than 74 million people.

THE DEMAND FOR HEALTHCARE

Both the demand for and supply of healthcare have increased over the last several decades. The increase in demand for medical care has been particularly significant due to changes in income, insurance coverage, and population. Consequently, the price of medical care has risen at the same time the utilization of services has increased.

INSURANCE

The health services market differs from many others in that, due to insurance, the consumer often pays only a fraction of the direct cost of care. Third-party payers, such as insurance companies or health maintenance organizations, play significant roles in this industry. In fact, the structure of the healthcare payment system can have important incentive effects and alter the behavior of both patients and providers.

In Exhibit 14.9 (on page 240) we see that approximately 84.5 percent of the U.S. population is covered by some kind of medical insurance policy. Most of that coverage (62.8 percent) is sponsored through employers. Despite the fact that the United States spends more on healthcare per capita than any other nation in the world, approximately 43 million people remain uninsured. However the healthcare system does provide a safety net.

SHORTAGES

In Canada, where a national healthcare program controls prices and strictly rations care, conditions of excess demand for surgery prevail. An estimated 172,766 Canadians were on waiting lists for surgical and medical services in 1996 (including 1,603 people on the waiting list for cardiac care). In 1999, on average the median waiting time between visiting a primary physician and finally receiving treatment from a specialist was 14 weeks. This has led some Canadians to travel to the United States and pay for treatment themselves, rather than wait for insurance-covered care. Medical referral brokers help match frustrated Canadians with surgical providers in the United States (where fees can vary drastically). In addition, research by Statistics Canada shows that for every one doctor permanently migrating from the United States to Canada, 18 Canadian doctors are migrating permanently to the United States. (The migration to the United States, across all occupations, is found grossly disproportionate among those earning $150,000 or more—the most highly skilled.)

Issue: Will Increasing the Income of All Lead to Greater Happiness?

According to Professors Blanchflower and Oswald, the levels of happiness have been falling over the last few decades in the United States and relatively flat in Great Britain despite increases in income. If this data is correct, what can explain the fall in happiness in the midst of rising incomes?

Individuals with higher incomes do appear do report higher levels of satisfaction, holding other factors constant. But other factors are important. For

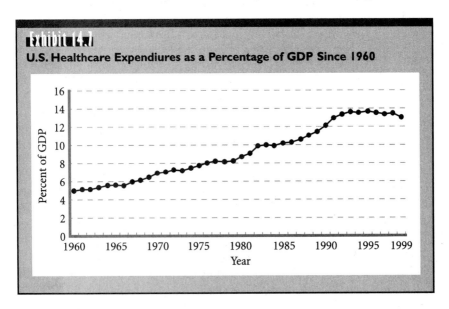

U.S. Healthcare Expendiures as a Percentage of GDP Since 1960

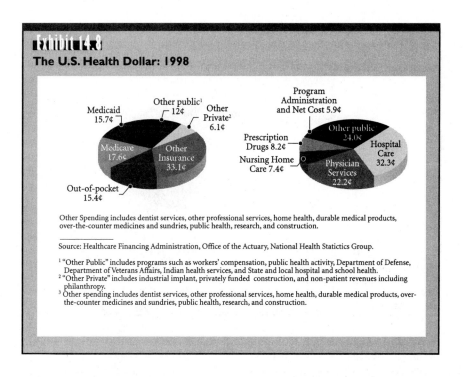

Exhibit 14.3
The U.S. Health Dollar: 1998

Medicaid 15.7¢

Other public[1] 12¢

Other Private[2] 6.1¢

Medicare 17.6¢

Other Insurance 33.1¢

Out-of-pocket 15.4¢

Program Administration and Net Cost 5.9¢

Prescription Drugs 8.2¢

Nursing Home Care 7.4¢

Other public[3] 24.0¢

Hospital Care 32.3¢

Physician Services 22.2¢

Other Spending includes dentist services, other professional services, home health, durable medical products, over-the-counter medicines and sundries, public health, research, and construction.

Source: Healthcare Financing Administration, Office of the Actuary, National Health Statictics Group.

[1] "Other Public" includes programs such as workers' compensation, public health activity, Department of Defense, Department of Veterans Affairs, Indian health services, and State and local hospital and school health.
[2] "Other Private" includes industrial implant, privately funded construction, and non-patient revenues including philanthropy.
[3] Other spending includes dentist services, other professional services, home health, durable medical products, over-the-counter medicines and sundries, public health, research, and construction.

example, Professors Blanchflower and Oswald find that unemployment and divorce can lead to lower levels of satisfaction, while a lasting marriage can lead to higher levels of satisfaction—worth roughly $100,000 a year compared to being widowed or single. They also reported that well-being is greatest among women, married people, and the highly educated. Not surprisingly, happiness and life satisfaction is very low among the unemployed.

Professors Blanchflower and Oswald also measured degrees of happiness for different groups in society. While whites had higher overall ratings for happiness, the gap between blacks and whites has narrowed over the last thirty years. Men report lower levels of happiness than women but the differences appear to be small. And lastly, happiness appears to peak at age 40.

Professor Richard Easterlin also finds that at any given moment in time, individuals with higher incomes, on average are happier but that raising the incomes of all will not increase the happiness of all. Why? According to Easterlin's work, happiness is a relative concept; it varies directly with one's own income and inversely with the incomes of others. That is, if your income rose significantly relative to everyone else, you would probably feel better off. However, if your income stayed the same while everyone else's rose, you would probably feel worse off, holding other things constant.

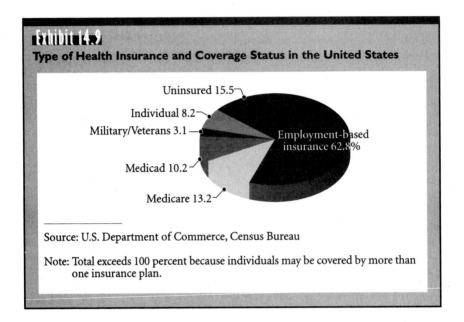

Exhibit 14.9

Type of Health Insurance and Coverage Status in the United States

Uninsured 15.5

Individual 8.2

Military/Veterans 3.1

Medicad 10.2

Medicare 13.2

Employment-based insurance 62.8%

Source: U.S. Department of Commerce, Census Bureau

Note: Total exceeds 100 percent because individuals may be covered by more than one insurance plan.

That is, material welfare probably depends not only on the amount people consume in a given period but also on the relationship of their consumption to their expectations as to what they want to consume. If my neighbor buys a new car, puts in a swimming pool, or hires a landscaper, I may have an increased desire to have the same consumer goods and services. "Keeping up with the Jones's" is a reality that confronts many of us. Karl Marx put it well when he said,

> A house may be large or small; as long as the surrounding houses are equally small it satisfies all social demand for a dwelling. But if a palace rises besides the little house, the little house shrinks into a hut.[4]

With rising incomes over time, our expectations also rise. That is, a rise in real per capita income or output may not mean an increase in happiness if expected consumption rises as fast or faster than actual consumption expenditures. As incomes rise, a given amount of income may mean less than before. For example, a person in 1900 may have derived more happiness than the same person in 2000 with the same real income per capita. And this unhappiness may be a result of rising expectations. For example, in in the early 1900s, our mythical person may have had a new radio, a house, and a Model T. Today, the same person would expect to have two color TVs, two or three radios, cell phones, DVDs, MP3s, and a couple of automobiles.

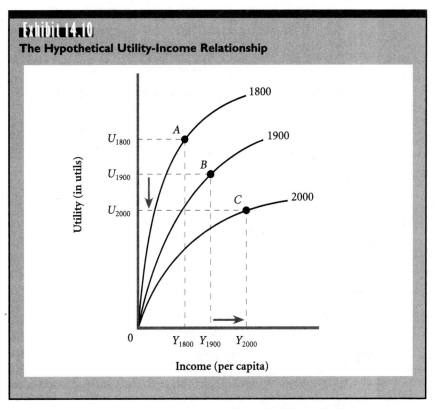

Exhibit 14.10
The Hypothetical Utility-Income Relationship

Studies have shown that, at any moment in time, the higher the income of a person, the happier he or she tends to be —that is, there is a movement along the utility curve. (Utility is a term economists use to "loosely" measure satisfaction.) On the other hand, similar studies show that over time, the level of happiness has not tended to increase in spite of rising incomes—a downward shift in the total utility curve. This phenomenon is graphically illustrated in Exhibit 14.10 which looks at the relationship between utility, or happiness, and income, or GDP per capita. Looking at the hypothetical curve for 1900, note that the person's utility rose as income rose. But over time, as a result of higher expectations and "bads" like air and water pollution, crime, and traffic congestio , the utility curve might shift down. The result could hypothetically be a situation in which higher per capita income might lead to lower utility.

Of course, this does not mean that today's consumers would be better off with the level of income and the consumption of the 1800s or 1900s. Today's expectations would surely make that level of income and consumption less desirable.

DEFINITIONS OF NEW TERMS

COST-PUSH INFLATION The theory of cost-push inflation states that costs are pushed up either by strong unions or by monopolistic businessmen, thus causing prices to rise.

IN-KIND TRANSFERS transfers given in goods and services rather than cash

WELFARE PROGRAMS government programs that help the needy

MEANS TEST welfare recipients must have low income and few assets.

NEGATIVE INCOME TAX a tax system that collects tax revenue from high-income households and gives transfers to low-income households.

WORK DISINCENTIVE EFFECT the payoff for returning to work is very small or negative.

ENDNOTES

[1] This is euphemistically called the Korean Conflict, in which American forces were merely engaged in a United Nations "peace-keeping mission."

[2] http://www.epa.gov/oar/aqtrnd99/brochure/brochure.pdf

[3] Edgar Browning, "The Trend Towards Equality in the Distribution of Income," *Southern Economic Journal,* July 1976, pp. 912–923; Frank Levy, *Dollars and Dreams* (New York: Norton, 1987), p. 195.

[4] Karl Marx, as quoted in S. M. Lipset, *Political Man: The Social Bases of Politics* (Garden City, NY: Doubleday, 1960) p. 63.

Index

A

Adams, John 49
Africa 52
Agrarian Movement 164
  railroad rates 164
Agricultural Adjustment Act 210
Alexander, Walter G. 189
Allies 179
American Federation of Labor 193-194, 212
American Revolution 80
Andrews, Charles M. 64, 87
Antebellum South 116
  commercial crops 117
  education 118
  growth rate 116
  income 118
  per capita income 116
Antigua 47
Antwerp 29, 54, 60
Articles of Confederation 95-96
  weaknesses 99
assembly-line 172
assumptions 5
atomic bomb 225
Australia 14
Austria 204
Austria-Hungary 179
automobile 172
  sales 173
Azores 52

B

Baltimore, Lord 65
Bankhead Cotton Control Act 210
Barbary pirates 85
barter 3, 34
Baruch, Bernard 181
Bell, Alexander 151
Bessemer 172
Bessemer converter 102
Bethlehem Steel Company 173
Biddle, Nicholas 91, 105
Black Death 29, 36, 41
Black Friday 147
black market 219
Black Slavery 67
  Caribbean 68
  first introduced 67
  major markets 67
  population 67-68
Black Tuesday 201
blacks 186
  franchise 189
  geographical distribution 186
  labor raids 188
  lynchings 186
  migration 186, 188-189
Bolivia 56
Boston Tea Party 76
Brazil 14, 19
British East India Company 76
Browning, Edgar 244
budget constraint 182
Bush, President George 229, 231
Bush, President George W. 230
Butterfield, Major Dan 147-148

C

Cabot, John 53

Cadiz 54

Calvin 48

Calvinism 33
  Protestant ethic 33
  Puritan ethic 33

Cambridge University 26
  Kings College 26

Canada 12, 14

Canary Islands 52

Cape of Good Hope 52

capital equipment 103

capital market 99

capital stock 16-17

Capone mob 199

Caribbean 55-57

Carlos, Ann M. 75

Carnegie Corporation 150

Carnegie, Andrew 149-150, 172

Catholic Church 55

Central Powers 179

checks 3

China 51

Church 28, 32-33

Civil War 7, 131
  Confederacy 132
    hyperinflation 133
    inflationary finance 133
    trade policy 132
  economic growth 139
  outbreak 131
  productive capacities 132
  recovery 137
  Union 134
    business atmosphere 136

capital investment 136
  finance 135
  government expenditures 137
  industry 136
  military 134
 urbanization 132

Clay, Henry 105

Clean Air Act 231

Clinton, DeWitt 110
  Clinton's Ditch 110

Clinton, President William J. 230

Cologne 29

Columbus, Christopher 52, 57-58

commercial paper 184

Commodity Credit Corporation 211

common property 36

comparative advantage 18, 68

Congress of Industrial
  Organizations 193, 212

Constitution 99
  money and credit 99
  Regulation and Commerce 100
  Taxation 99, 112

Constitutional Convention 49, 99
  1787 99

Consumer Price Index 232

consumption good 152

Continental Congress 95

Continentals 96

corporation 172

Cortez 56, 58

cotton 119, 187
  boll weevil 187
  New England textile industry 119

prices 187
  Southwest 119
cotton gin 93, 115
Council of Economic Advisors 221, 228, 232
Council of National Defense 215
CPI 226
Crawford, Stephen 130
Credit Anstalt 203
credit cards 3
Crusades 32, 34, 42
Cuba 55, 58
Cuff-Smith Tobacco Control Act 210
currency 3

D

da Gama, Vasco 52
Damascus 51
Daniels, Bruce D. 88
Declaration of Independence 49, 95
deficits 229
deflation 97
  effects 97
Demand for Labor 235
demonstration effect 32
dePriest, Oscar 189
devaluation 95
Dias, Bartholomew 52
diminishing returns 40
division of labor 33, 53
Dominican Republic 55
dumping 96

Dutch East India company 53

E

East Indies 52
Easterlin, Richard 241
economic analysis. 3
economic freedom 20-24
economic growth 11
economies of scale 120
Edison, Thomas 151
education 13, 19-20, 24, 153
  literacy rates 153
EFW index 21
Egypt 25
Emancipation Proclamation 137, 186
Embargo Act 101
empirical observations 4
Employment Stabilization Act 209
Employment Stabilization Board 209
Enclosure Movement 36
encomienda 55-56, 61
England 29, 31, 36, 41, 47, 53-54, 58-59, 64, 66, 71, 95, 101-102, 106, 173, 179
English Poor Laws 36
entrepôt 54
entrepreneur 16
enumerated articles 83
Ethiopia 12, 19
European Union 12
exports per capita 48

F

Far East 52

Farm Bureau 211

farm problem 162
  commercial agriculture 166
  credit question 165
  emancipation 162
  National Banking Act 165
  railroad rates 165

Farmer Alliances 164

farmers 8

Farmers Union 211

Federal Control Act of March
  1918 182

federal Farm Board 200, 209-210

Federal Reserve 207, 219

Federal Reserve Act 184

Federal Reserve Board 184

Federal Reserve System 92, 206

Federal Surplus Relief
  Corporation 211

Ferdinand, Archduke Franz 179

feudal system 26-27

feudalism 32

First Bank of the United States
  104

First Principles 150

fiscal policy 228

Fisher, Irving 201

Fisk, Jim 147-148

Florence 51

Fogel, Robert W. 129, 161, 167

Food Administration 181, 200

Food Control Act of 1917 181

Ford, Henry 172

foreign exchange market 3

France 26, 41, 49, 58-60, 95, 101,
  106, 173, 179, 215
  revolution 100

Franklin D. Roosevelt 182

Franklin, Benjamin 48, 72

free trade 18

frictional unemployment 220

Friedman, Milton 205

Full Employment Act 221

G

gains from exchange 53

Gallaway 190

Gallman, R. E. 163

GDP 11-12, 17, 226, 230

General Magazine, 49

Geneva 29

Genoa 51

Germanic tribes 27

Germany 26, 54, 179, 204, 215

Gilbert, Sir Humphrey 63

Girard, Stephen 104

gold 35, 147

gold standard 164

Goldin, Claudia 130

Gompers, Samuel 193-194

Gould, Jay 147-148

Grain Stabilization Cooperation
  209

Grangers 164

Graves, Philip 144, 190

Great Britain 49

Great Depression 176, 202

agricultural incomes 203
banking system 202
Crash of 1929 213
duration 202
employment 202
farm output 203
Keynesian Explanation 204
Monetary Theory 205
unemployed, world 203

Greece 25

Greeks 26

Greenback Movement 164

greenbacks 163

gross domestic product (GDP) 109

growth rates 11, 18

guilds 29
craft 30
merchant 31

Gutenberg 26

Gwartney, James 20

H

Haiti 19, 55

Hamilton Thesis 58

Hamilton, Alexander 104, 112, 142
30th Federalist paper 104
infant industry 142
Secretary of the Treasury 104

Hamilton, Earl J. 59

Hanseatic League 31

Harding, President Warren G. 199-200

Harper, Lawrence 85, 88

head rights 66

Health 154

healthcare 238
demand 239
expenditures 238
insurance 239
Investment 239
per capita 239
public healthcare expenditures 239
shortages 239
sources 239
trade-offs 239
uses 239

Heller, Walter 228

Henretta, James 88

Henry the Navigator 52

Henry, Patrick 72

Hiroshima 225

History of the Expedition Under the Command of Captains Lewis and Clark, A 91

Hitler, Adolph 204, 215

Holland 54, 95

Homestead Act 141

Hong Kong 14

Hoover, Herbert 181, 200, 208-209
laissez-faire president 209

horizontal merger 173

Hudson Bay Company 74-75

human capital 13, 17, 19-20, 24

Hume, Ivor Noel 64

Hundred Years War 41

Hungary 54, 204

Huns 27

hyperinflation 133

I

immigration laws 188
   literacy tests 189
in-kind transfers 235
income 7
income differences 235
income distribution 234
   government activity 234
income per capita 14
indentured servants 7, 67
India 12, 19, 51-52
Indigo 47, 70
Indochina 225
Industrial Revolution 39, 173
Industrialization 174
   comparisons 174
   workers 174
inflation 34-35, 39, 225
inflationary finance 133
innovation 15, 24
institutional arrangements 25
interdisciplinary approaches 6
International Monetary Fund 12
Interstate Commerce Act 157
Interstate Commerce
   Commission (ICC) 157
invention 15-16
investment in human capital 118
isolationism 199
Italians 26
Italy 54, 215

J

Jackson, President Andrew 91,
   105
Jamaica 58
Jamestown 63-65, 78
Japan 12, 14, 19, 215
Jefferson, Thomas 92, 174
Johnson, President Lyndon B.
   228
Johnson–Kennedy tax cut 228
Jones, Alice Hanson 77, 80-81

K

Kaiser, Henry J. 195
Kennedy, President John F. 228
   assassination 228
kerosene 121, 172
Keynes, John Maynard 204, 220
Keynesian 228
Keynesian economics 204, 208
Keynesian ideas 220
Keynesian theory 205
King Cotton 115
   plantation system 116
   production 115
   unskilled labor 116
Korean Conflict 244
Korean War 225-226
   casualties 225
   U.S. participation 225
Ku Klux Klan 189

L

labor 13
labor force participation rates 217

Labor Party 163
land 155
  availability 155
Land Grants 66, 111, 141
  Erie Canal 111
  Pennsylvania Canal System
    111
  railroads 111, 141
Lawson, Robert 20
Lebergott, S. 176
Levy, Frank 244
Lewis, John L. 193, 212
Liberty Loans 183, 218
Lincoln, President Abraham 142,
  186
Linden, Peter H. 88
Lipset, S. M. 244
liquid assets 220
literacy 19
Lively, Robert A. 113
Locke, Alain 190
London 54
London Company 63
Louisiana Purchase 105
Lowell, Francis Cabot 102
Lucas, Eliza 47, 70
  Indigo 70
Lucas, Lieutenant-Colonel George
  47

M

Madeira 52
Maginot Line 215
Main, Jackson Turner 81, 88

Malthus, Rev. Thomas Robert 37
  Essay on the Principle of
    Population, as it Affects the
    Future Improvement of
    Society, An 38
  Industrial Revolution 42
  Malthus 38, 40, 42
  Malthusian cycle 42
  Malthusian doctrine 40
  Malthusian model 38
Malthusian Trap 72
manor 26-27
  farm estate 27
manors 41
Manufacturing Restrictions 84
Marx, Karl 242, 244
mass production 170
Massachusetts Institute of
  Technology 173
material welfare 242
McCormick's reaper 143
means tests 237
Medicare 230
Medieval Period 25
Mediterranean 51-52
medium of exchange 3, 34-35
Mein Kampf 215
mercantilism 64
mercantilist policies 64
Mercer Girls 153
Mercer, Asa 153
merchant class 36
Metzer, Jacob 130
Mexico 56, 58
Middle Ages 25-26

Migration 67

Milan 51

Milanese craftsmen 26

Mint Act of 1792 104

Modest Inquiry into the Nature and Necessity of a Paper Currency, A 48

Molasses Act 87

monetarism 204

monetarists 206

monetary policy 228

money 34
creation 183
supply 96, 206

monopoly 30

monopsony 125

Moors 26

Morgan, J. P. 172

Morse, Samuel F. B. 151

Munitions Standards Board 180

N

Nader, Ralph 195

Nagasaki 225

National Banking Act 140
reserve system 141

National Banking System 184

National Corn Hog Committee 211

national defense 222, 230

National Industrial Recovery Act 194, 210

National Recovery Administration 210

Native Americans 57

buffalo 57
Plains Indians 57

natural resources 13-14

natural sciences 4

Naval Consulting Board 180
Committee on Industrial Preparedness 180
Council of National Defense (CND) 180
Industrial Preparedness Committee 180

Navigation Acts 76, 83-84, 86, 96

negative income tax 237
case against 238
case for 238

Nepal 12

Netherlands 54

New Deal 180, 212

New Economic Policy 229

New England 64, 69, 71, 80-82, 84, 86-88

New York City 8

New York Stock Exchange 3

Newfoundland 53

Nicholas, Stephen 75

Nixon, President Richard M. 226, 229

Non-Importation Act 101

nonrecourse loans 211

North, Douglas C. 120, 130

O

on-the-job training 13, 24

P

Panic of 1819 105

Panic of 1837 108

paper currency 49

Paris 54

partnerships 172

Pasteur, Louis 154

payroll tax 213

Peace of Ghent 102

Pearl Harbor 215

Penn, William 65

per capita income 151, 200

Persia 51

Peru 56

Pilgrims 66

Pitt, William 76

Plymouth Company 63-65

Poland 54

pollutants 231
  abatement costs 231
  air quality 233
  pollution rights 231

pollution 8

Poor Richard's Almanac, 48

Population 152
  fertility 152
  immigration 152

Populist Movement 164

Portugal 52-53

poverty 7, 232
  amount 234
  definition 232
  elimination 236
  poverty rate 234
  relative concept 233

premarket economy 25

Price Control Act 219

price
  controls 225
  inelastic 70
  level 96

primogeniture 67

principal 183

Proclamation of 1763 76

productivity 12-13, 18, 20, 23-24

Prohibition 199, 202

property rights 18, 20

proprietorships 172

Puerto Rico 55, 58

Q

quantity theory of money and
  prices 96

R

R&D 17-18, 24

railroad 156
  construction 156
  debt 156
  development of the United
    States' economy 159
    coal 160
    iron 159
  effects 159
  employment 156
  expansion 158
  miles of track 156

Railroad Administration 182

Railroads War Board 181

Raleigh, Sir Walter 63

Ransom, Roger 113

Reagan, President Ronald W. 229
  administration 229

real wage rate 39

Reconstruction Finance Corporation 209

regional specialization in production 53

Renaissance 26

repressed inflation 219

reserve requirement 184

Revenue Act of 1932 214

Reverse Causation 207

Ricardo, David 38

rice 47, 70

right to vote 199
  women 199

Roanoke Island 63
  lost colony 63

Rockefeller, John D. 172

Romans 26

Rome 25

Roosevelt, President Franklin D. 180, 194, 202, 204, 208, 213, 215
  First Hundred Days 210
  price supports 211

Rouen 29

rule of 70 11

Russia 179

S

saving rate 16

Scheiber, Harry 111

scientific philanthropy 150

Second Bank of the United States 91, 104-105
  closure 106
  wildcat banking 106

Selective Service Act 215

self-sufficiency 28

September 11 230

serf 27, 33, 41

Seven Years War 76

Seville 54

Sexton, Robert L. 130, 144, 190

Shays' Rebellion 97, 99

Shays, Daniel 97

Sherman Antitrust Act 174-175
  American Tobacco 174
  Standard Oil 174

Sheves, Langdon 105

simplification 5

Slater, Samuel 101

slavery 122
  Brazil 122
  capital investment 127
  Caribbean 122
  Dying Out? 127
  emancipation, Northern 123
  imports 115
  imports illegal 123
  marginal revenue product 126
  monopsonistic exploitation 125
  owners 124
  plantation 124
  prices 127
  profitability 128
  rise 122
  tobacco 122
  trade 122
  treatment 126

slaves 7, 47

Smith, Adam 39, 222

social savings 161

social sciences 4

Social Security 213, 230

Social Security Act 213

Sokoloff, Kenneth L. 130

South Africa 164

South Carolina 47

Spain 47, 52, 55, 58-60, 95-96

Spanish Crown 54-55

Spencer, Herbert 149

Stamp Act Congress 76-77

Stamp Act of 1765 76

Starving Time 64

Steckel, Richard 129

Strasbourge 29

Sugar Act of 1764 76, 87

T

Tammany Hall 147

Tawney, R. H. 48

tax surcharge of 1968 228

Taylor, Frederick W. 173

technical diffusion 74

technological advances 13, 15

technological change 74

technology 16-18

temperance movement 202

terms of trade 165

The South 69
   exports 69
   indigo 71
   naval stores 71
   plantation system 69
   population 69
   tobacco 69

Third-party payers 239

Times Almanac, 2000 19

Tindell, George Brown 87

Townshend Acts 76

traditional system 25

transactions or business costs 69

Treaty of Paris 95-96

U

U.S. Bank notes 105

unemployment 225-226, 229-230

unemployment insurance 8

Union Pacific Railroad 148

Unions 211
   craft 212
   membership 212

United Mine Workers Union 193, 212

United Nations 225

United States 12, 14-15, 19

United States Steel Company 150

United States Steel Corporation 209

United States Treasury 184

University of Paris 26

urbanization 54, 60, 169

V

Vanderbilt, Cornelius 148, 156
   rates 157

Vedder 190

Vedder, Richard K. 130

Venice 28, 51, 53

Verdun 29

vertical merger 173

Victory Loan 183

Vietnam 228
Virginia Company 65

W

Wagner Act 211-212
Walton, Gary M. 77, 88
war agencies 216
War Finance Corporation 200
War Industries Board 180-181
    Price-Fixing Committee 181
War Manpower Commission 217
    draft 217
War of 1812 101-102
War Productions Board 216
War Resource Board 215
Washington, George President 86,
    92, 97
wealth 7
welfare 3, 230
welfare programs 237
West Indies 71
whale oil 121
    energy crisis 121
white indenture 66
White, John 63
Whitney, Eli 92, 115
Williamson, Jeffrey G. 88, 167
Wilson, President Woodrow 179-
    180, 182
Wolcott, Treasury Secretary
    Oliver 93
Woolen Act 84
work disincentive effect 238
World Bank 17
World War I 179

Americans served 180
borrowing 183
controls 180
federal expenditures 182
Industrial production 180
standard of living 180
taxation 182
U.S. Involvement 185
World War II 215, 220, 225-226
    and the Great Depression 221
        aggregate demand 222
        income 222
        unemployment 221
    bonds 218
    civilian labor force 217
    deficit 217
    end 220
    finance 217
    Liberty Loans 218
    military labor 217
    money creation 218
    taxes 218
    Victory Loan 218

Y

Yukon 164

Z

Zevin, R. 113